Circle Stock Theater

CIRCLE STOCK THEATER

Touring American Small Towns, 1900–1960

by LANDIS K. MAGNUSON

with a foreword by BROOKS MCNAMARA

McFarland & Company, Inc., Publishers
Jefferson, North Carolina, and London

Frontispiece: Character performers Mason Wilkes and Marian Raymond appearing in *The Only Road*, Chick Boyes Players, 1930 (courtesy of the Museum of Repertoire Americana).

British Library Cataloguing-in-Publication data are available

Library of Congress Cataloguing-in-Publication Data

Magnuson, Landis K., 1954–
     Circle stock theater : touring American small towns,
  1900–1960 / by Landis K. Magnuson : with a foreword by
  Brooks McNamara.
        p.   cm.
     Includes bibliographical references and index.
     ISBN 0-7864-0101-X (lib. bdg. : 50# alk. paper) ∞
     1. Circle stock theater–United States–History–20th century.
  I. Title.
  PN2266.3.M35   1995
  792'.0973'0904–dc20   95-23422
                                                                             CIP

Manufactured in the United States of America

McFarland & Company, Inc., Publishers
   Box 611, Jefferson, North Carolina 28640

To Kathy
For her limitless patience
For her unfailing willingness to listen
For continued dreams of the future

To Eva Marie and John Kelly
For showing the future through the eyes of the child

Foreword

THE STUDY OF POPULAR entertainment is relatively new to theater history, going back to about the late 1960s. In no small part because of the increasing interest in the area, historians have begun to abandon many of their traditional prejudices against popular art. More and more, the emphasis among historians has come to be on the relationship of theater to public memory and to the field of cultural studies. Historians are looking with increasing respect to what Garff Wilson has defined as theater that "aims to satisfy the taste of a polyglot audience by providing novel and varied entertainment which is easily understood."

Within the study of popular entertainment, much of the work has focused on urban entertainment forms. But of course popular entertainment also flourished in small towns and rural areas—perhaps less frequently and less spectacularly than in the cities, but no less powerfully. In *Step Right Up*, my history of the medicine show, I recalled the stories my grandmother told me about shows that had visited her hometown, a speck on the map of Illinois called Brimfield, in the 1880s and 1890s. "Because they were the only traveling shows to appear in Brimfield for months and sometimes even years at a time," I wrote, "she recalled their visits as very special events in the life of the town. To her, even half of a century later, the medicine shows were still charged with much the same air of mystery and excitement that they had possessed during her girlhood."

Beginning at the turn of the century, circle stock would add to that mystery and excitement by making a far greater range of shows available to the residents of the many Brimfields scattered across the Middle West. Landis Magnuson has recognized and captured the spirit—and the cultural significance—of this forgotten small-town institution. His *Circle Stock Theatre: Touring American Small Towns, 1900–1960* adds a new dimension to the work already completed on such rural forms as the tent show—and an important new piece to the fascinating puzzle that is American popular entertainment.

—BROOKS MCNAMARA (*New York University*)

Contents

Preface

THIS STUDY–WHICH UNDERTAKES the first detailed examination of the practice of circle stock touring by American theater companies–depends almost exclusively on primary source material. Because circle touring existed as a form of popular theater found mostly in rural areas, it goes unmentioned in the standard studies of American theater, which tend to focus on theatrical activity in our major cities. Even exhaustive trade publications such as *Billboard* and *Variety* largely fail to report the business of circle stock. So too, Midwestern theater personalities rarely took the time to relate their circle stock experiences in biographical form.

This study relies principally, therefore, on the reminiscences of the veterans of circle stock, recorded in personal interviews, letters, and audio tapes. These engaging veterans paint a wonderfully rich portrait of this important branch of small-time show business, and I must express my deep appreciation to them for their unstinting cooperation in supplying me with information, anecdotes, and artifacts. From an author's point of view, they remain "troupers" of the first order. Although *repertoire* remains the preferred title given to the industry by these veteran performers, it was pronounced as if written *repertory* and in everyday parlance *rep* dominated. Therefore to address a varied audience I choose to use the colloquial terms of *rep* and *tent rep*. This remains exclusively an editorial decision in which veteran troupers and historians alike should recall the practical, working nature of circle stock.

Because letters and audio tapes received during the research process are not readily available for examination, I have attempted not to clutter the text with otiose bibliographic references. Hence, in documenting unpublished material in my possession, it seemed of little value to distinguish among personal letters to the author, personal audio tapes sent to the author, and personal interviews with the author. In such cases the reader is simply referred to the end of the text where the names of the respondents and their contributions are listed in the appropriate manner. In a

1

very few instances, these veteran actors wished to make anonymous comments. The reader of this study will therefore find a handful of unattributed citations; I can only respect the wishes of these troupers and ask that my lapses in proper literary documentation be excused. In quoting the written or recorded material provided by the veterans of circle stock, I have silently corrected obvious typos and errors without, I hope, altering the intent of the author or speaker.

My other major sources have been two modest newsletters—*Bill Bruno's Bulletin* and its successor, *Bob Feagin's Bulletin*—which served as trade publications for a significant part of the history of the circle stock industry. Both of these newsletters—copies of which are now rare—deal narrowly with the business of Midwestern touring rep theater. As such, they provide information not available anywhere else. Even more important, the editorial positions taken by their respective editors stand as barometric readings of the major issues and controversies that the industry faced.

Apart from these editorials, much of the text of these bulletins contains copy supplied directly from the field by the rep companies themselves, similar to the practices of larger trade publications such as *Billboard* or the *New York Clipper*. I have been mindful throughout that the information contained in such notices may be biased or exaggerated; indeed, even at the time of publication, the veracity and balance of reports in such publications was regularly questioned. While every effort has been made to evaluate such sources critically, the information they contain nevertheless remains vital to any consideration of circle stock, since this type of popular entertainment went largely unreported elsewhere. Even the unwarranted boasts of troupers sometimes take on value as evidence of their hopes and dreams and even their occasional recourse to competitive subterfuge.

I have also made extensive use of the business ledgers of the Chick Boyes Players, a prominent Nebraska-based troupe performing during the heyday of the rep era. These ledgers provide a rare glimpse into the day-to-day business dealings of a major touring rep company, which spent a good portion of each year following the circle stock format. The three Boyes ledgers—cited liberally throughout this study—are the only detailed circle stock business records known to exist at this time.

While researching this topic, I benefited greatly from rare information sources made available to me in a pair of small, yet exceptionally valuable museums devoted wholly or in part to this era of small-time show business. Thanks are extended to the officers and volunteer staff of the Otoe County Museum of Memories in Syracuse, Nebraska, especially Norma Jean Dittmer and Marlene Orton, for allowing extensive photocopying and photographing of the wealth of Chick Boyes memorabilia housed at the museum. Likewise at the Museum of Repertoire Americana located on the showgrounds of the Midwest Old Settlers and Threshers Association in Mount Pleasant, Iowa, special thanks are reserved for a number of individuals—some veterans of the profession, others dedicated volunteers. First of all, gratitude must be extended to Caroline Schaffner for sharing her extensive knowledge of rep theater and for valuable guidance concerning available sources of information and rep veterans to contact. Similar thanks go to Jimmie Davis for, in addition to numerous acts of kindness, sharing his extensive knowledge of the whereabouts of veteran troupers. Thanks must be offered to Billie Turley for every favor extended me while conducting research at the Museum of Repertoire Americana and also to Lennis Moore, Administrator of the Midwest Old Settlers and Threshers Association. Finally heartfelt acknowledgment goes to Joe Mauck for his willingness always to aid this researcher with skillfulness and courtesy.

Appreciation is advanced to members of the academic theater community who lent support to this endeavor: to Michael Kramme for making available copies of *Bill Bruno's Bulletin*; to Jerry Martin for first introducing me to the topic of circle stock and also sharing personal research materials; to Bill Slout for his encouragement and also for providing period play scripts to aid this effort; and to Brooks McNamara for his continued interest and insight. Special gratitude is held for my mentor, Robert Graves. His incisive comments and gracious perseverance are deeply appreciated.

At Saint Anselm College, my gratitude goes to Curt Nichols for his expert guidance in converting computer files. My thanks is also maintained for Bruce Chakrin, Wendy Mignault, and Jim Cirillo of the Saint Anselm Media Center for help with photographic plans and processing. Sincere appreciation is extended to Saint Anselm College for the Summer 1990 Faculty Research Grant and the Summer 1993 Faculty Development Grant, which aided the completion of this project.

On a personal level I wish to remember the numerous veteran troupers who graciously shared with me their experiences and insights. Since this research started nearly a decade ago, many quoted within are no longer with us. May their words stand as memorial. Above all, I am grateful to my wife, Kathy, for her assistance and understanding. We found a way to get the job done.

1

A Wagon Wheel with Spokes

P RIOR TO THE TURN OF THE twentieth century and for decades thereafter, the American public satisfied its need for entertainment with a dazzling variety of shows and diversions. Favorite entertainments included the circus, vaudeville, minstrel shows, burlesque, rep and stock theater, silent motion pictures, the "talkies," Chautauqua assemblies, medicine shows, showboats, and even Wild West shows. Some of these forms of entertainment experienced a relatively short life span; others survived longer, until tastes changed or technological innovation left them behind.

This era's particularly rich and varied entertainments, including both theatrical and para-theatrical forms, flourished in part because of the rapid expansion of the nation's railroad system following the Civil War. The ability of performers to travel the vast countryside with increased comfort and convenience fostered their penetration into previously isolated areas. This penetration fueled, in turn, the construction of small-town theaters (frequently christened "opera houses") by both civic and private groups, and as these new structures mushroomed over the length and breadth of this country, major touring companies from the East ventured farther and farther into rural America.

But large touring companies faced many problems when performing in the hinterlands. Difficulties of scheduling and routing regularly developed, especially when attempting to hold down the expenses incurred making lengthy jumps between performance sites. Even so, these large companies–almost exclusively presenting one-night performances–regularly avoided smaller towns and communities because such centers of population could not warrant a performance. Thus an entertainment void developed in many rural areas, a void gladly filled by small traveling rep troupes.

Tradition defines these companies as dramatic troupes with sufficient repertory to present no less than a week of productions or "bills." Frequently referred to as "ten-twenty-thirty" companies because of the standard prices of admission during their early years, rep troupes presented popular-priced comedies and melodramas during the last quarter of the nineteenth century and into the following century, catering to a public seeking not enlightenment but entertainment. Although "ten-twenty-thirty" companies also performed in major metropolitan areas—frequently in small, neighborhood theaters—the rep companies with which this study deals thrived in the hinterlands, largely in the Midwest.

Rep companies at first employed two well-documented methods of scheduling and touring: stock and week-long rep. In stock—normally referred to as "permanent" or "indefinite" stock—a company took up extended residence in a theater and presented one or possibly even two different bills a week. The company remained in this theater for as long as it could attract audiences, rehearsing the upcoming bill during the day and performing the current bill in the evening, until their popularity waned or until the lure of good weather called them back to the challenges of "the road." In the second traditional scheduling method—week-long rep (sometimes referred to as "house rep")—a company's stay in each theater lasted for a period of up to seven days. Week-long rep companies normally presented six to seven bills (depending upon whether Sunday or matinees were played) in one house and then moved on to another community. Each scheduling method, however, presented some difficulties. Permanent stock required a large population base to sustain the presentation of one bill (or at most two bills) for an entire week. Week-long rep necessitated lengthy weekly "jumps," when the company moved to a new theater. During the first decade of this century, however, a new organizational system for rep companies developed.

This widely used but virtually unreported method of touring, practiced by many of the rep companies, went by various names: "rotary" stock, "circuit" stock, but most frequently "circle" stock.[1] Although often considered only a product of the 1930s, circle stock can be traced back to the earliest years of the twentieth century when it originated on the East Coast. Following its creation, the use of circle stock spread to all parts of this nation, even extending into Canada and beyond. Yet the heart of circle stock activity always remained in the Midwest. Through nearly 60 years of existence (from 1901 to the late 1950s), circle stock maintained a basic structure and methodology, although it continually adapted to the needs of management and performers.

Circle stock companies essentially remained rep companies, but unlike other similar organizations, circle stock troupes toured communities following a strict order of rotation. Whereas traditional rep organizations toured to wherever they thought audiences could be assembled, circle companies toured to only a limited number of smaller communities usually surrounding a slightly larger one. The basic formula involved a circuit of six towns (seven if the company played on Sunday), very unlike the one-night-stand chains quickly developing at about the same time. One town–possibly one of the circle itself–served as the "base" or "headquarters" for the troupe. Here company members established living quarters–in hotel rooms, in rental apartments, or occasionally in entire houses, complete with hired help who performed light housekeeping.

Having established a base, circle stock companies toured to outlying communities arranged roughly in a circle around their headquarters. Sid Kingdon, who managed several circle stock companies during the Depression, provides a convenient description of the form: "A circle to me is like a wheel, a wagon wheel with spokes. The hub is the center of the wheel–that's where we would live. The spokes go out to the different towns." The system established in circle stock provided each outlying community the opportunity to see a performance by the company on the same day of the week on each weekly rotation of the circle. Because the one-way distance from the base to each venue normally ranged from only 20–40 miles and rarely over 50, the company could return each night to its headquarters following the performance. With such a "one-week circle" established, the company performed the same bill six or seven times in a week, each night in a different town, while rehearsing a new show for the following week's rotation.

Thus circle stock joined stock and week-long rep to furnish managers with an additional method for scheduling performances. In the opinion of many, however, circle stock provided significant improvements over these traditional touring methods. In its basic arrangement, circle stock required only one bill a week but could be played in less populated, more rural areas than either stock or week-long rep. In addition, circle stock could require lower transportation expenses than week-long rep, which normally demanded long trips when changing performance cities and possibly even attendant travel days when no performance could be given.

In its initial years of development, circle stock coexisted with stock and week-long rep. Over the years many companies employed two or even all three of these methods, alternating as conditions warranted. But during the 1920s in various parts of this country, circle stock emerged as a choice of preference for many troupes. The advantages of circle stock–foremost among them lower overhead costs–helped it grow in popularity through its first 25–30 years of existence. But at the same time that circle stock emerged as an attractive option for managers, a profound change in the whole pattern of rep playing began, the catalyst: the relentless march of technology, which would eventually cause rep's demise.

Increasingly, the small rep companies (previously welcomed in the

Sid Kingdon performing a character vaudeville specialty, circa 1934 (courtesy of the Museum of Repertoire Americana).

opera houses of minor towns) found that the skyrocketing popularity of silent films, beginning in the first decade of this century caused many opera-house managers to lease their theaters to the motion picture interests rather than the rep companies. Theater scholar William Slout summarizes the effect of the advent of silent films on the rep troupes:

> Repertoire companies were gradually being squeezed out of many opera houses, making it necessary for them to look beyond the small town theaters to places more remote, where one-night companies never appeared, where audiences could not compare entertainment values between ten-twenty-thirty prices and those of a dollar and over, where obscurity was a protection against tightened copyright enforcement, and where operations could be continued throughout the summer months. [*Theatre in a Tent,* 34]

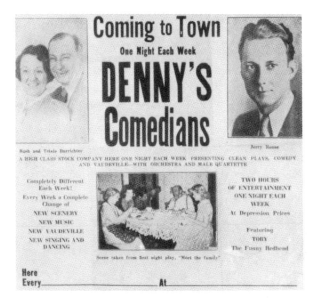

Detail from herald for Denny's Comedians which promises "TWO HOURS OF ENTERTAINMENT ONE NIGHT EACH WEEK at Depression Prices" (courtesy of the Museum of Repertoire Americana).

One response to the decline of opera house rep companies which also affected the emerging circle stock troupes was the rise of the rep companies playing under canvas. By the turn of the century, touring ensembles carrying their own tent had already become a recognized form of performance, and during the following quarter century tent rep grew to become, especially in the Midwest and the South, one of the most vital popular entertainments of the era.

It is important to note that tent rep and circle stock were largely parallel developments that grew further interrelated with each passing year. Early on, the companies that used tents did so when it was too hot to perform in permanent theaters or halls, while circle stock troupes traditionally performed in the cooler months. Inevitably managers saw that the two forms complemented each other, and many companies engaged in rep under canvas during the summer used circle stock during the winter. Thus, the rising popularity of both tent rep and circle stock produced a reversal in the tradition of the rep companies. When the small rep troupe's domain had been exclusively the opera houses, companies prospered while performing during the fall and winter, but playing in the midyear months (due to the oppressive heat in the theaters) had always remained very difficult. With the rapidly increasing popularity of the canvas shows–in spite of the considerable investment in equipment it represented–the situation

Tilton's Comedians, circa 1951, possibly performing *The Return of John Slater* (courtesy of the Museum of Repertoire Americana).

reversed: the winter season became less important for itself than as a bridge to keep the company together for more lucrative touring to follow. With such a shift in rep practice, circle stock furthered its reputation as a desirable system of scheduling and management because it provided one of the few ways the smaller companies could continue to perform in the winter.

Following the stock market crash of 1929 and the ensuing economic decline, circle stock no longer remained a choice of preference but became a choice of necessity. With the public having little extra to spend on entertainment, hard times also fell upon the touring rep companies, and because of its cost-cutting measures, circle stock became a means of keeping afloat for many small troupes. Barbara Brooks Emory, a performer whose circle experience dates from the mid–1930s, explains the economic necessity of circle touring in this fashion:

> Circle Stocks were born of the Depression and survival; the survival of actors to continue their craft and to eat. Few actors had ability in any profession except acting. As a matter of fact they didn't *want* to do anything except act. And they fought valiantly to continue in their profession.

When asked why companies turned to circle stock during the Depression, Maude Gentry, a performer who also began her circle experience in the bleak days of the 1930s, replied:

The Chick Boyes Players in an opera house venue, likely touring in circle stock format; Chick is seated at the far left (courtesy of the Otoe County [Nebraska] Museum of Memories).

> Simple answer—to eat. It was Depression time and we were not trained for much else. There were not as many prohibiting laws as now—no social security, no unemployment [insurance]. Get six people or so together, with a few scripts, a car and a circle usually paid our expenses. We loved what we were doing, so that is all we needed.

A typical day for a small circle troupe during the Depression and thereafter shows this dual concern for performing and making a livelihood. Performers usually rose by 10:00 to a morning essentially their own. Some company members might drive to that day's performance town to collect advertising fees from merchant sponsors or to search for new sponsors. The composition of the ensemble most likely included five to seven persons, many of them husband-and-wife teams, headed by a management/acting team, also likely to be married.

In the early afternoon (around 2:00) the company left for the performance site. Transportation was regularly in a large passenger car, owned by the manager, pulling a small trailer holding props, wardrobe, and canvas drops (referred to as "rag" scenery). Upon arrival at the venue, the "set up" occurred, with the men in charge of the stage, while the women prepared the dressing rooms. With the stage and backstage in order, a rehearsal of the next week's show frequently took place. Following rehearsal, the company visited a local café for a meal. Returning to the theater or hall, a quick rehearsal of the specialty acts for the evening might take place prior to making-up in the usually cramped backstage areas.

Traditionally at 8:00 P.M. the curtain went up on a fast-paced show, complete with vaudeville specialties between the acts and possibly a candy sale by the performers themselves. With the performance over by 10:00, the company struck the set, loaded the trailer, and drove back to the base town, arriving usually by 12:00 midnight. "Night lunch"–a light meal or sandwich–followed, but the performer's day was not yet over. Line study for the next show, in addition to building and altering one's wardrobe (especially important for the women of the company) often still took place. The day might end by 2:00 A.M., only to have another begin again all too soon, a routine followed six to seven days a week.

Yet, an account of a typical day would not be complete without the inclusion of some type of inclement weather. Because circle stock operated primarily during the winter months, bad weather remained a constant concern of the troupes. Countless tales exist of gallant efforts by the players battling against snow, ice, and wind to ensure that performances went on as scheduled. But an equal number of accounts record that harsh winter conditions often won out over such gallant efforts, requiring the cancellation of performances.

However, before investigating the characteristics, techniques, and procedures of circle touring, an appreciation of those individuals engaged in the early development of circle stock is of primary importance, to which we now turn.

2

Early Practitioners and Circuits

FEW HISTORIANS HAVE CONSIDERED the initial development of circle stock, and of this group, virtually all have based their conclusions on a 1936 feature story in *Bill Bruno's Bulletin* entitled, "Trousdale Brothers Were Originators of Circle Stock."[1] In this article, the experienced rep performer turned editor Bruno asserts that the "question of who was first to launch a circle stock company has never been given an argument, it being conceded that the Trousdale brothers were first to send a company over a given route of towns weekly" (17 Dec., 27). Theater historian Jere Mickel based his brief consideration of circle stock on this article, adding that "I have never run across any argument against one of the Trousdale brothers having the original idea" (24). In short, scholars who discuss circle stock at all follow this assumption. But while the Trousdales were certainly among the leaders who introduced the circle method in the Midwest, newly uncovered evidence demonstrates that they did not first practice the technique.

Character photograph of Bill Bruno, rep performer and founding editor of *Bill Bruno's Bulletin* (courtesy of the Museum of Repertoire Americana).

13

VERNON STOCK CO.

PRESENTS

"Flies in the Web"

AN ORIGINAL COMEDY

BY

John Brougham.

BETWEEN THE ACTS

Refined Vaudeville.

OVERTURE AT 8:30.

CLINTON HALL,

EAST HAMPTON,

WED. EVE'G, JULY 10.

Seats on sale at Gregory & Co's store.

This company will visit East Hampton
Wednesdays, July 24, Aug. 7, Aug. 21, Sept.
4, Sept. 18, Oct. 2.

Advertisement for the Vernon Stock
Company during the troupe's initial
season of circle stock, from the *East
Hampton Star*, 28 June 1901 (courtesy
of the New York State Public Library).

Benjamin B. Vernon

The use of circle stock likely dates
from late March 1901, carried out
by Benjamin Vernon, a member of
Richard Mansfield's acting company the previous three seasons
(*Long Islander,* 22 Mar., 3).[2] This two-
week circle was composed of, in order, the following 12 communities
on New York's Long Island: Glen
Cove, Oyster Bay, Huntington,
Northport, Port Jefferson, Riverhead, Greenport, Sag Harbor, East
Hampton, Southampton, Patchogue,
and Bay Shore (*East Hampton Star,*
15 Mar. 1901, 4). Vernon's modest
goal was "to play the circuit as often
as the business will permit" (*East
Hampton Star,* 15 Mar. 1901, 5).

Following the company's first
circle offering–*A Scrap of Paper*–the
editor of the Sag Harbor *Corrector*
predicted an enthusiastic response
to Vernon's efforts:

He has a strong company of ten clever
artists, and has met with gratifying success. We think he has struck the right
idea, and believe that the people of the Island will liberally support high
class entertainments. [6 Apr. 1901, 3]

And while, by all accounts, support for Vernon's troupe generally remained strong throughout this first year, following a particularly low turn-
out for the company's production of *Don Caesar de Bazan,* the editor of the
Corrector admonished his readers for not maintaining undivided support of
the company:

We do not think the Vernon Company are receiving the extent of public
patronage they are entitled to in Sag Harbor. They are by far the best dramatic company that has visited Long Island and made the effort to establish a regular summer circuit. Their performances are clean and good and
their selections popular and up-to-date. In artistic merit they are far above
ordinary itinerant show men.

The editor finished with what certainly must be viewed as a poignant comparison: "On Wednesday night *Uncle Tom's Cabin* in a tent drew a crowd" (27 July 1901, 3).

Yet, despite reports of essentially good business on the circuit, by late September of this initial year newspaper accounts record Vernon filing for bankruptcy with "liabilities of $1,118, and no assets" (*Corrector,* 28 Sept. 1901, 3). Perhaps the beginning of Vernon's financial woes stems from an incident that took place in Sag Harbor in mid–August of this initial year of touring. The *Corrector* records the event under the title "The Play Stops":

> The Vernon Company disappointed a good sized audience in Masonic Hall on Wednesday evening. When the time for ringing up the curtain arrived Mr. Vernon came out and with an apology stated that the performance could not go on, as some of his company had positively refused to take their parts. He dismissed the audience and entrance money was refunded at the box.
>
> The trouble was in the nature of a strike. One of the company informed us that they could not get any money from Mr. Vernon although they were playing to good houses. They demanded six dollars each before going on with the play. This was refused and the entertainment stopped.
>
> Mr. Vernon on the other hand says that he is under no money obligations to his actors; that he owes them nothing, and that they have had all he agreed to give them. Rather than stop the performance he offered them $4 each on the night in question. He would go no further.

The account further states, "The next morning Mr. Ivan C. Byram made a financial arrangement with the players to fill out their appointments in the Hamptons. Mr. Vernon continues in charge of the company but has no financial management" (17 Aug. 1901, 3).

In spite of major setbacks during 1901, Vernon returned to Long Island in a circle stock format the following year. With the company's return to its circuit, the *Corrector* argued: "Nothing its equal ever visited Sag Harbor before, and all who attended were pleased and expressed their approval by hearty applause." Concerning the incident in Sag Harbor when the show did not go on, the *Corrector* further records:

> Mr. Vernon then made a vow, should he get on his feet again, to appear before the people of Sag Harbor once again at any cost, with a better presentation than ever. Wednesday evening he kept his word. [24 May 1902, 3]

Whereas virtually nothing is found in print explaining Vernon's financial collapse, one somewhat fanciful anecdotal account is offered concerning his apparent recovery:

> One week [in New Orleans] the actor was impersonating the part of an old Indian chief. He visited the running races, and upon looking at the entries saw "Big Indian" quoted at 70 to 1. "I am playing 'Big Indian' at the theatre, guess I [will] play him at the races, so here goes $20," said Vernon. But strange to all, especially the bookmaker who paid Vernon $1,420, "Big Indian" won, and won easy. [*Corrector,* 26 Apr. 1902, 3]

A unique presentation of the second season entitled *On Long Island* is attributed to the authorship of Vernon, Charles Hart, and Jules Kusel. This comedy, made up of incidents of Vernon's company touring Long Island, met with favorable response over the circuit (*East Hampton Star,* 25 July 1902, 5). Since local newspapers frequently filled their columns with amusing anecdotes concerning the Vernon company, one can easily imagine the incidents that came together to form *On Long Island.* For example,

> The one particular rule of the Vernon Stock company is promptness; and it is always noticed that the play begins promptly on the time advertised, and during the performance there are no tiresome waits. This rule is also adhered to by the Long Island railroad and Mr. Vernon found it rather to his disadvantage last week in Easthampton. The company arrived at the station, the train came in and all went aboard except Mr. Vernon, who sat figuring in the depot. Some one called, and Mr. Vernon seeing the train pull out rushed wildly after, calling "Wait," "Hold on a second," but promptness was the rule, and away went train and company, leaving Mr. Vernon to his figures, which must be rather satisfactory, as they apparently quieted his temper. He joined the company later in the day at Southampton. [*Long Islander,* 28 June 1901, 2]

Following the 1902 summer circle season and a tour through New Jersey and eastern Pennsylvania, Vernon's company returned to Long Island in the fall but appeared in a three-night-stand format, presenting *Lost in London, Montana,* and *Dr. Jekyll and Mr. Hyde* (*Corrector,* 27 Sept., 3). Vernon's Long Island activities during the summer of 1903 revolved around the presentation of featured vaudeville programs and shorter plays, roughly maintaining the circle stock format of previous years.

Although reports projected a return to circle stock during the summer of 1904, sightings of Vernon's theatrical activity that season are infrequent. Virtually nothing is heard of Vernon until 1911, when Al Trahern (then the reigning monarch of circle stock) booked Vernon's Varieties into the Sayville Opera House, which he controlled. One can certainly believe this organization was led by Benjamin Vernon himself (*Suffolk County News,* 7 July, 6). Following this, Vernon drifted from the Long Island theater scene and ceased to play a part in the development of circle stock.

Another early promoter of theatrical activity on Long Island is one Carleton E. Brewster, cited as the manager/originator of the "Long Island Circuit." Reports as early as 1903 cite a circuit composed of Bay Shore, Patchogue, Sayville, Southampton, Greenport, Riverhead, and Huntington (*Long Islander,* 5 June, 2). An ad placed in New York's *Dramatic Mirror* boasted in 1905 of five towns offering "good business for real attractions" (29 Apr., 9).[3] However, all indications are that Brewster's circuit, with headquarters in Bay Shore, never utilized a circle stock format.

Albert L. Trahern

The efforts of men like Benjamin Vernon and Carleton Brewster notwithstanding, extensive early employment of circle stock is traced to the work of Al Trahern on Long Island, beginning late in the first decade of this century and continuing into the Depression era. But while the majority of his career involved circle stock, Trahern did not maintain continuous use of it during his nearly 25 years of touring on Long Island. Because historians have previously neglected to acknowledge Trahern's significant contributions, it is important to document his pioneering efforts here.

A native of the state of Kansas, Trahern began his association with the

Special
Fourth Tour
Vernon's Big Co.
PRESENTING
WORDETTE & KUSSELL,
IN A NEW ACT
COOK & HAYEYS,
MISSES
BLODGET & HARVEY,
THE FAMOUS JUGGLERS
KEELER & SILFKO,
CHARLES BLAKE,
and a new comedy
" What Do You Think,"
Overture at 8:30-
Clinton Hall, East Hampton,
Monday Evening, July 6th.
Tickets now selling at Edwards' Drug Store.

Promotion for Vernon's featured vaudeville programs during the summer of 1903, from the *East Hampton Star*, 3 July 1903 (courtesy of the New York State Public Library).

theater at the age of 17 in the position of a property boy, in the first of a series of backstage jobs that amounted to his unofficial apprenticeship in the theater. Because of such varied experiences, later in life he claimed proficiency in all aspects of the theatrical profession except scene painting. His first important indoctrination into theater management came near the beginning of this century, under the guidance of the noted producer William A. Brady.[4] For over five years, Trahern served as a stage manager and actor under Brady, a period of training thought responsible for much of his success in the theater (*Mirror,* 3 Sept. 1913, 14). Records also reveal Trahern married the noted Jessie Mae Hall in 1902 while she performed in Brady's production of *Lover's Lane* and Al served as stage manager.

The entertainment industry was not the only profession in which Trahern received training. Trahern's background included work (as young as ten years of age) as a "printer's devil" on various commercial newspapers

Al Trahern, circa 1906 (courtesy of the Billy Rose Theatre Collection, New York Public Library at Lincoln Center).

and also the publishing of his own small newsletter—experience that helped develop in him a keen eye for clever advertising. Trahern's use of striking visual images in newspaper ads for both his wife and himself could dominate the printed page in an era of straightforward advertising based almost exclusively on the unadorned word. Trahern also received wide recognition as the writer of popular novelty songs.[5] Writing the majority of these songs for his wife, Jessie Mae, Trahern's efforts—upwards of 200 compositions—received extensive use in vaudeville, burlesque, and musical reviews. Songs such as "I Won't Play Unless You Coax Me" ("a typical 'kid' song"), "Lights of Home" ("a home ballad"), and "I Never Get Enough to Eat" ("a comic coon song") are only a sampling of compositions attributed to Trahern, along with phrases used to advertise them. The "kid" song "I Wish I'd Been Born a Boy," "Under Southern Skies," and "Sweet Clover" are perhaps the most heralded of Trahern's creations.[6] In the area of theatrical management, Trahern's earliest efforts on record involve the direction of his wife's performance career.

Unquestionably, the talents of the diminutive Jessie Mae lay in her singing voice and comedic abilities. Combining these strengths with her short stature (claimed to be a mere four feet, eight inches in high heels), she frequently billed herself as "The Dainty Doll Comedienne" or "The Biggest Little Star." Hall, educated in the St. Louis area, specialized in a variety of comic soubrette roles, ranging from the ten-year-old girl in Augustus Thomas's *Editha's Burglar* to the fiesty young gal in the romantic comedy-drama *Pretty Miss Nobody*, which required the dramatic transformation in character she frequently sought in roles:

> In the first three acts she assumes the role of a crude, uncouth mountain lass of California, unused to the ways of society as it is known in the East or abroad.

In the last act she re-appears after an absence in Paris of eight years, a polished, educated, suave French society woman. The direct change from one phase of life to the other one is the most striking scene in any play. [*Suffolk County News,* 11 Sept. 1908, 7]

It remained her singing voice, however, that brought Jessie Mae widespread acclaim, particularly for her playful renditions of husband Al's juvenile songs. Labeled "phenomenal," Hall's soprano voice maintained a range of "three octaves, her top note being E above high C" (*Mirror,* 31 Mar. 1906, 25).

Early in her career she appeared in vaudeville, but as her stature as a performer grew, she headlined in starring roles of musical comedy productions in stock and also toured widely.

Jessie Mae Hall, photograph by Johnson (courtesy of the Billy Rose Theatre Collection, New York Public Library at Lincoln Center).

With talents combined, this husband-and-wife team brought together attributes that neatly complemented each other. Out of this personal and professional union developed the first extensive use of circle stock, starting in late April 1907.[7]

Under the informative title "How Al Trahern Came to Long Island," promotional material found in an early circle stock program ("Guaranteed Circulation: 20,000 Weekly") provides one perspective (surely written by Trahern himself) of the beginnings:

> During the winter of 1906, Al Trahern was starring Jessie Mae Hall in the well known drama, *A Southern Vendetta.* A long tour across the continent from the Pacific Coast closed Miss Hall's profitable season early in the Spring in New York City. Always a hustler, Manager Trahern was unwilling to remain idle until the Fall, when the regular theatrical season starts. He began to look about for some location where a stock company could be conducted during the summer months. Whichever way he turned, he found that stock companies were always in operation, until Long Island came before his attention. Upon investigation, Manager Trahern found that theatrically, Long Island was an afflicted land, its villages shunned by travelling

companies, and the theatrical companies shunned by the villagers, who had too often paid their good money to alleged attractions unworthy of patronage.

Al Trahern brought a company of fifteen high salaried actors, headed by the dainty doll comedienne, Jessie Mae Hall, and accompanied by a first class orchestra, and prepared to stay. The rest everybody knows. Good plays, capable players, new scenery and good music, combined with the fact that the Trahern players have always commanded the respect of the Long Island people, has made the name of Trahern a household word on Long Island. [collection of the author]

One of the earliest reports found in a national publication concerning Trahern's use of circle stock simply relates that Jessie Mae Hall and her supporting company "will spend the Summer on a circuit of six Long Island towns, arranged in such a way that the same town will be played the same night each week" (*Mirror,* 6 Apr. 1907, 2). Because the summer was considered the "off season," this article further states that during this period "several new plays will be put on, with the view of finding a suitable vehicle" for use the following fall. Reports characterized this initial season as a highly successful one for Trahern and his wife, along with some 25 members of the company, which included eight to ten musicians for a concert band and orchestra. In the form of a retrospective review of this first season, the *New York Clipper* praised Trahern's mounting of "the latest stock releases" while "keeping pace with the permanent city stock companies." The article further records, "Many prominent actors appear with this company, and there being no matinees, the Broadway actors regard this engagement as their Summer vacation" (1 May 1915, 23).[8]

During the first year of his experimentation with circle stock Trahern adjusted the circuit, attempting to find the most profitable arrangement of communities. Trahern's original selection of towns, however, proved largely successful. Throughout the season five communities appear consistently in route listings found in the *Dramatic Mirror,* namely: Bay Shore, Patchogue, Sag Harbor, Sayville, and Southampton. Three other communities—Center Moriches, East Hampton, and Oyster Bay—alternated as sites, as Trahern tested the communities to determine which one to make regular appearances in. By the conclusion of the first season, Trahern appears to have settled on the group of five communities named above, along with East Hampton from the second group—all of which lay in the southern half of Long Island, stretching over one-half of the island's 120 miles in length. Sayville served as headquarters, where an abandoned church converted into a warehouse provided space for the building and storing of scenery. Only three of these six communities possessed enough inhabitants to be incorporated at the time of the 1910 Federal Census of New York State. These communities—Patchogue, Sayville, and Southampton—averaged around 3,000 in population during Trahern's first touring season.[9]

Cover of "I Won't Play Unless You Coax Me" sheet music, featuring the image of Jessie Mae Hall (courtesy of the New York Public Library at Lincoln Center, Music Division).

Today the mention of Long Island conjures up various images. The western half of the island is seen largely as a sprawling metropolitan area, consisting of commuter communities for individuals who pour into New York City on weekdays via mass transit, or the Long Island Expressway for the more adventuresome. The eastern half of the island generates less of an urban image, still maintaining a more rural look, with both large estates and a thriving agricultural industry. But turn-of-the-century Long Island was considerably different and the social and economic conditions on the island at that time caused communities to be relatively isolated. Individuals in these small towns and villages found little reason to make a regular habit of venturing to nearby New York City, whether for necessary goods and services or for entertainment.

The editors of *Between Ocean and Empire* provide a portrait of Long Island following the turn of this century which depicts a growing contrast between its western and eastern sections:

> Despite the heavy influx of excursioners and estate owners, turn-of-the-century Long Island retained much of its rural character. Agriculture and fishing flourished, small-town life predominated, and local inhabitants viewed themselves very differently from their urban neighbors.... Yet, amid the placid landscape change was evident as well. Daily commuters already travelled to New York by railroad and steamboat, and a proposed tunnel under the East River promised to increase the flow. Although farming remained the single most important economic activity, its position on western Long Island had begun to decline. Instead, real estate development accelerated.... Suffolk County [to the east] experienced the same forces, but the pace was slower and the intrusion of modern urban life less persistent. [MacKay, Rossano, and Traynor, 160]

Furthermore, Robert MacKay, director of the Society for the Preservation of Long Island Antiquities, notes that the communities Trahern's company performed in during its beginning seasons of circle touring "represent quite a contrast" among themselves, part of an area undergoing significant change:

> Sag Harbor and Greenport which had been whaling ports until the middle of the 19th century, were respectively a manufacturing town (watch cases) and a fishing and ship building port in the early decades of this century. Huntington, an agricultural service town, was seeing a large influx of summer homes which had taken up most of its water front by 1906. Southampton and Bayshore had also become fashionable watering places by 1906. Sayville, "the clam capital of America," and to a lesser extent Patchogue, a south shore service town, were also feeling the impact of the resort boom. Riverhead was the county seat and a market town. All of which makes you wonder who the Trahern Company was playing to? The town's people? The summer folk? Or a combination thereof?

Undoubtedly Trahern played to combined houses of locals and tourists, all the time mindful of maintaining high artistic and moral standards. We are certainly made aware of the latter when the contents are revealed of an agreement entered into by Trahern and a theater visited regularly the first season. This contract, said to reflect the "staid character, cautious habit, and precautionary tendency" of rural Long Island, stipulated

> there shall be no profane or vulgar language, indecent allusions, ballet dancing, women performers in tights, or any indecent exposure of the person

[and that] the company is to be orderly on the street and about the theatre, and try not to influence the young people of the town so that they will desire to go on the stage; and the actors are not to be flirting with the village girls.... [*Mirror,* 7 Sept. 1907, 7]

Trahern's first season of circle stock ended following 22 weeks on the circuit, "breaking all records for the island in business and duration of season" (*Mirror,* 28 Sept. 1907, 7). Additionally, Trahern boasted of being "$10,000 to the good" at the conclusion of the tour—certainly an accomplishment for a young manager in his early thirties (*Corrector,* 21 Sept. 1907, 5).[10]

As the beginning of Trahern's second season of circle touring approached, the success of the previous season shone in the glowing terms used to describe his growing enterprise. The press hailed Trahern as the "exploiter of the wilds of Long Island," along with being the "first to successfully develop ... [the island's] resources in a monetary and theatrical sense" (*Mirror,* 7 Mar. 1908, 7). Yet even before experiencing such heady press, Trahern had decided to expand his operation in 1908 to a circuit of 12 towns covering both the south and north shores of the island.[11] According to plans revealed in the *Dramatic Mirror,*

Trahern will have two companies on the island, so as to play each town in the circuit once a week. The people will travel in large automobiles, and even the scenery will be transported from place to place in automobile trucks. The advance agent ... will travel ahead in a light runabout. [31 Aug. 1907, 7]

However, with the public clamoring for the return of a Trahern ensemble, word came that the company intending to tour the original southern route would open over one and a half months earlier than originally planned, a change resulting from "a general protest ... made by the up to date Long Islanders, to whom Winter was made unendurable by the absence of Trahern's popular organization" (*Mirror,* 7 Mar. 1908, 7). As a consequence, a company touring the southern circuit opened at Sag Harbor during late April, complete with a band of 15 pieces "to wake the natives."[12] Touring of the northern reaches of Long Island began in June, certainly to the appreciative response of Port Jefferson natives:

North Siders, ever since last summer, have listened with envy to the praises bestowed upon the Trahern Stock Company, which confined its performances to the South Side. This season, however, we are to have the pleasure of including this excellent organization among our amusements, and our period of enjoyment is to begin at once.

This theater company, however, alternated weekly performances with the Trahern Vaudeville Company, so that we will have two dramatic and two vaudeville performances each month. The vaudeville company will be composed of the best artists carefully selected from the high class vaudeville theatres in New York City. The bill will be changed on each appearance of the company. [*Port Jefferson Echo,* 13 June 1908, 1][13]

Shortly into the rotating performances of these two companies, the *Port Jefferson Echo* reverberated with support and satisfaction: "No use talking, Port Jefferson is strictly in it this summer in the matter of good shows. They all come from the same source, Trahern, but it appears that nothing but the best comes from that source, bright, sparkling, clean, wholesome" (27 June 1908, 1). Despite the enthusiastic response to productions throughout the northern communities of the circle, Trahern's expanded circuit failed to continue past the early fall of 1908.

Whereas local newspaper coverage relished detailing Trahern's productions, at times bordering on the excessive, reports appearing in the national trade publications generally highlighted only personalities and unusual incidents while touring. However, the *Dramatic Mirror,* reporting "Al Trahern Obtains High Class Plays," provides a distinct exception. Through the agency of Mrs. H. C. De Mille, a respected play broker and talent agent of the time, Trahern obtained rights to such contemporary hits as *The Charity Ball, The Wife, Sweet Clover, At Cozy Corners, Old Orchard, The Little Princess,* and *The Missourians.* Trahern also secured *Lord Chumley* and *Men and Women,* written jointly by Henry C. De Mille and David Belasco, along with *The Danger Signal,* a solo effort by H. C. De Mille (21 Mar. 1908, 5). This account asserts that "plays of the calibre of these have seldom if ever been offered in the Long Island towns" hosting Trahern's company.

Indeed, Trahern pocketed considerable positive press in these early years for the expense and effort involved in securing the latest theatrical offerings; yet the presentation of *The Devil* in 1908, featuring a Satan in modern dress, did little to further Trahern's developing reputation. Advance publicity claimed, "There is nothing of the vulgar or undesired in the piece, although the drama is based upon broad lines." And while the production received kudos for the special scenery and costumes, the play (and by association Trahern) was openly condemned. The *East Hampton Star* emphatically argued:

> As to the play itself there is very little to be said in its favor. There was certainly nothing elevating about it, and when one considers the great possibilities of the drama in uplifting and enobling people, there seems to be no excuse for the existence of the play called *The Devil.* [2 Oct., 5]

In similar fashion, the *Suffolk County News* attested:

> While most people were glad to have an opportunity to see the widely-talked-of foreign play, which is now the theatrical sensation of the country,

> the general verdict was that it is not the kind of play Long Island audiences care for. It's unwholesome—leaves a bad taste in one's mouth. [25 Sept., 8]

Such negative press notwithstanding, by the fall of 1908 Trahern controlled "every theatre of importance on the Island, outside of Brooklyn and Long Island City" (*Mirror*, 29 Aug., 6). Such an accomplishment caused area newspapers to refer to Trahern as "the Frohman of Long Island," after the prominent New York and London theater manager Charles Frohman. Trahern's newly acquired title does not seem an inappropriate one, for with the number of theaters either being leased or exclusively booked by him at the time, Trahern stood as the "sole provider of amusement for thousands of Long Islanders, and many more thousands of Summer visitors"—all accomplished within one year of "his initial descent upon the unexploited territory" *Mirror,* 29 Aug. 1908, 6).[14]

After abeling the system of circle stock as "unique in the history of stock dramatic organizations," a lengthy exploration in the *Dramatic Mirror* asserts three factors contributing to the success enjoyed by Trahern during his first two summer seasons of circle stock. Foremost among these factors was Jessie Mae Hall herself. Having appeared in no fewer than 50 roles in the two seasons, Hall "astonished all by her remarkable versatility" in "portraying child characters, soubrette and emotional leads with equal success" (29 Aug. 1908, 6). Other reasons cited for Trahern's success included his talented street band and orchestra units, and impressive scenery prepared for each production by scenic artist Alex de Beers. These elaborate technical elements reportedly required a special baggage car to transport the scenery and properties over the circuit by rail, rather than the "automobile trucks" for which Trahern had previously planned. Yet it remains unclear as to the transportation system utilized, for later in 1908 Sag Harbor's *Corrector* reported, "[Trahern] has ordered two autocars, one seating thirty-two persons, for the use of his players and members of the orchestra and band, and the other to be used as a freight truck for the carrying of scenery, trunks, etc." (3 Oct., 5).

As the controlling agent of many theaters, Trahern regularly received commendation for ambitious decorative and structural improvements made in the venues under his control, including the enlargement of stages, the remodeling of auditoriums, and the installation of new lighting and fire protection systems. Upon obtaining control of the Sayville Opera House, Trahern immediately announced plans for the "re-building of the gallery into the more desirable horse shoe form" (*Suffolk County News,* 17 July 1908, 1). Although holding a virtual monopoly on theatrical entertainment on Long Island, Trahern vowed to use such power only in the best interests of the public. As one Long Island weekly commented, "The people are fortunate in having a man of Mr. Trahern's good reputation controlling the

Unique goat cart advertising for the Trahern Stock Company while circle touring on Long Island (courtesy of the Suffolk County [New York] Historical Society).

local playhouses, as hereafter he will allow no show to go on the stage that is at all questionable." Mindful of his pledge of allowing only "meritable companies" on the circuit, Trahern booked the Quincy Adams Sawyer Stock Company, Gorton's Minstrels, and other "reliable offerings" in the fall of 1908 to perform in the absence of his own company (*Mirror,* 21 Nov., 3).

Over the next few years, the composition of the circuit did not remain rigid but slowly evolved to include the most profitable communities and theaters. By the summer of 1909 the circuit comprised

> the Lyceum Theatre, Patchogue, every Monday; Auditorium Theatre, Greenport, every Tuesday; Auditorium Theatre, Riverhead, every Wednesday; Opera House, Huntington, every Thursday; Opera House, Bay Shore, every Friday; and the Opera House, Sayville, every Saturday. [*Clipper,* 5 June, 440]

That fall Trahern scheduled the Schiller Amusement Company to present vaudeville on a weekly basis over the circuit, following the close of the summer circle season.[15]

By 1910 the *Dramatic Mirror* declared Trahern and his circuit "an established factor in the booking of all road attractions thereabouts" (19 Feb., 22). Clearly Trahern's dominance over entertainment events on the island was firmly established, an enviable position largely obtained through hard

Early advertising technique by Trahern captured outside a performance site in Patchogue, New York (courtesy of Hans Henke of Patchogue, New York).

earned acceptance and acclaim on the local scene. Early on, the editor of the Sag Harbor *Corrector* had thrown his support to the fledgling enterprise:

> Columns of praise have heretofore been printed about dramatic entertainments, given by home talent, justly due the amateurs who have taken so much interest in the histrionic art, but it is seldom that the traveling shows visiting Sag Harbor are up to the average, and consequently the villagers will not turn out and patronize foreign troupes.
>
> The Trahern Stock Company is a pleasing exception to the long list of failures, and with dainty Jessie Mae Hall, playing a leading part, as a child comedian and songster, [it] bids fair to draw a succession of capacity houses. [27 Apr. 1907, 6]

Additional evidence of local approval and recognition soon followed. In 1908 Trahern was elected to full membership in "Ye Village Club," the businessmen's association of Sayville—the first theatrical manager so honored. In reporting the event the *Suffolk County News* noted that Trahern recently had been elected a member of both the Greenport Board of Trade and the Suffolk County Board of Trade, concluding:

> It is another evidence of the rapid strides the theatrical profession is making and of the high regard in which it is now held by representative

business men all over the country. Such men as Mr. Trahern are the factors
that go toward the uplifting of what was once regarded as an undesirable
and shameful business. [9 Oct., 7]

A setback to Trahern's good fortunes occurred on 15 March 1910,
when the Huntington Opera House burned to the ground. The cause of the
fire in this theater leased by Trahern remains unknown, but the damage
included "several hundred dollars worth of properties, a complete installment of up-to-date opera chairs, furniture and several sets of scenery, besides a large wardrobe of stock costumes" (*Mirror,* 26 Mar., 10). Yet the loss
of potential income surely outweighed any material damage, for Trahern's
company drew large audiences when it played this theater, which seated
approximately 1,200 persons.[16] In place of the destroyed Huntington Opera
House—likely the most lucrative stop on the circuit at that time—Trahern
secured for the upcoming 1910 circle season a theater in Glen Cove, a community situated roughly ten miles to the west of Huntington. Following this
setback, Trahern's personal and professional fortunes returned to a steady
climb as he continued to garner applause for his presentation of noted contemporary plays. Among the enthusiastic reviews one finds:

> Manager Al Trahern has proven beyond a doubt that he is sincere in his
> efforts to give the followers of his company the best plays obtainable and
> he has presented several plays this season with royalties so large that the
> average manager would hesitate to pay, and the fact *The Three of Us* will be
> the one hundred and eighth play to be produced by his clever company on
> Long Island is proof positive that his efforts have not been in vain. [*Suffolk
> County News,* 15 July 1910, 3]

In early summer 1911, following an extended record-breaking stock
run at the Orpheum Theatre in Nashville, the Trahern Stock Company returned to the Long Island circuit, thus maintaining two distinct patterns of
performance scheduling within a 12-month period. During the summer
months Trahern used the circle format while appearing on Long Island, but
for the largest part of the year he set up in permanent stock where he performed in one theater for an indefinite period of time.[17] Extended stock
runs normally were quite lucrative. Nevertheless, the decision to leave his
successful extended engagement in Tennessee and return to the North

> grew out of several circumstances, viz., the approaching hot weather, the fact
> that the busiest part of the year is at hand at the summer resorts on Long
> Island ... and the fact that the members of the company are extremely anx-
> ious to spend the hot months in the comparative coolness of the resorts.
> The company will be taken intact to Long Island where the members will
> spend June, July and August presenting the recent New York successes.
> Early in September the Trahern company will return to Nashville for an-
> other season at the Orpheum. Al Trahern has certainly lost nothing of his
> well-established reputation as a manager. [*Billboard,* 3 June 1911, 14]

By mid–March 1912 a clear change in Trahern's practice from previous summers on Long Island took place. Rather than forming a company to present conventional dramas and comedies over his traditional circuit, Trahern experimented with various forms of entertainment, including musical theater. In one trial effort, Trahern established a four-person tabloid stock company to perform shortened plays and variety entertainment nightly, based exclusively at the Lyceum Theatre in Patchogue, with "motion pictures to support the programme." This quartet presented the tabloid play *Sweethearts* as their premiere offering (*Mirror*, 27 Mar., 10). Although tabloid companies are traditionally associated with short musical performances, this apparently was not the case with Trahern's small troupe. In addition, Trahern created a musical stock company consisting of 25 individuals to begin in mid–April its first season over the established circle circuit. This new venture obviously planned to showcase the talents of Trahern's wife, Jessie Mae, and in due time the success of musical stock on the Long Island circuit was touted:

> Jessie Mae Hall recently played a four weeks' season of comic opera, making a decided hit as Arline in *The Bohemian Girl.* She also scored as Serpolette in *The Chimes of Normandy*, Bettina in *The Mascot,* and in the title-role of *Olivette.* Miss Hall's ability in dramatic work is well known, and being possessed of a highly cultivated soprano voice, forms a combination very essential in the present day of musical stock and comic opera. [*Mirror,* 12 June 1912, 17]

However worthy (or questionable) the endeavor, the public clearly refused to support the venture. As the *Suffolk County News* reported, "Manager Trahern, whose policy is always to please, has decided at the request of his many patrons to replace the Opera Co. with Dramatic Stock again..." (3 May 1912, 5).

Despite this miscalculation, Trahern's firmly established reputation for circle stock on Long Island, in addition to his overwhelming popularity in extended stock engagements (such as in Nashville), seemingly boded well for the future. Then, unexpectedly, a headline in the fall of 1912 proclaimed "Trahern Bankrupt." Listing liabilities of $7,160 with no assets, Trahern sought legal refuge from 43 creditors. Chief among the liabilities was $1,800 owed to the trustees of the Odd Fellows Lodge in "Greenpoint, Long Island," for the unexpired lease of the Auditorium Theatre—an obvious misprint, actually referring to the theater in Greenport used in his summer 1912 circuit. Other major creditors and the amount owed included the Metropolitan Printing Company ($348); the National Printing and Engraving Company ($191); the American Play Company ($102); along with Grayton Hedges (should read Dayton) ($705) of Patchogue, New York (*Clipper,* 5 Oct., 3).

While no contemporary explanation has been discovered for Trahern's dramatic change in fortune, Long Island theater historian Harold Smith con-cludes that because of intense competition for patrons, "Trahern was run-ning into troubled waters. His lavish operetta productions and his battles for audiences ... caused him to overextend himself" (*Long Island Theatres,* 35). As a result, in less than a year after declaring bankruptcy, Trahern had largely abandoned Long Island circle stock and taken a position with the vaudeville magnate Benjamin Franklin Keith–undoubtedly necessitated by financial concerns.[18] The *Clipper* reported:

> Mr. Trahern is widely known as the only manager who successfully piloted dramatic stock companies for six consecutive summer seasons of twenty weeks each on Long Island.... Mr. Trahern has disposed of his circuit of the-atres on Long Island and will devote his entire time in the interests of Mr. Keith's Greenpoint Theatre. [6 Sept. 1913, 3]

Following his management of the Greenpoint Theatre in Brooklyn for 20 weeks during the 1913–14 season, Trahern was placed in control of a vari-ety of Keith theaters, including the Crescent, the Gotham, the Bushwick, and the Bronx.

It might appear that with his involvement in Keith's vast entertain-ment empire, Trahern's career entered into a distinctly new phase. To the contrary, his work for Keith funded a return to running his own theater company as early as December 1913 with a midwinter circle tour of *Life's Shop Window* on Long Island (*Suffolk County News,* 19 Dec., 1).[19] Even while maintaining employment under B. F. Keith, Trahern launched a successful seventh summer tour of Long Island in May 1914 (*Suffolk County News,* 22 May, 1). The *Clipper* noted in 1915 that Trahern again traveled Long Island on a circle circuit,[20] while the *Dramatic Mirror* reported that the Traherns, following more than a decade of married life, terminated their personal and professional union. In January of that year, Mrs. Trahern received a decree of absolute divorce with the privilege of resuming her maiden and professional name–Jessie Mae Hall (24 Mar., 6).

By May 1915, Trahern had once again married his leading lady–this time that role being played by Rita Knight. Yet this marriage proved to be a most unhappy one, as it ended in divorce in roughly one year (*Long Islander,* 2 June 1916, 4). Following this second dissolution decree Trahern traveled to Kansas City for what would amount to a three-year hiatus from Long Island. During this wartime period, entertainment activities in the communities normally played by Trahern mainly centered around amateur play performances, local dances, and motion pictures, with only a limited number of professional touring productions.

While absent from the area in 1917, Trahern faced a direct challenge when Russell Parker–a former employee of B. F. Keith and also the Tra-hern Stock Company–announced the establishment of a circuit of theaters

Capitol Theatre

RIVERHEAD
FRIDAY, OCT.   21

The Famous and Original

TRAHERN

STOCK COMPANY

(NEARLY 2000 PERFORMANCES ON LONG ISLAND)

WHERE THE TRAHERNS PLAY	WHERE TO BUY TICKETS
Monday - - - - - - Sayville	- - - - - - - - At Lemperts
Tuesday - - Bridgehampton	- - - Phillip's Jewelry Store
Wednesday - - - East Hampton	- - - - - - - At Box Office
Thursday - - - - Greenport	- - - - Harry Merrill's Store
Friday - - - - - Riverhead	- - - - Barth's Drug Store
Saturday - - - Southampton	- - - - Corwith's Drug Store

"BERTIE'S CAVE WOMAN"

A Western Comedy Drama in Three Acts By Ted and Virginia Maxwell.

Detail from handbill later in Trahern's tenure on Long Island, promoting "NEARLY 2000 PERFORMANCES" following the circle stock format (courtesy of the Patchogue-Medford [New York] Public Library).

in the largest towns of Suffolk and Nassau counties.[21] Certainly Parker's proposed circle operation owed much to Trahern's refinement of the practice. The *Clipper* noted that "the plan of Mr. Parker has created a good deal of interest in theatrical circles, as it will be remembered Al Trahern made considerable money for many years on a circuit of stock theaters on Long Island."

But in addition Parker planned an original twist. Whereas Trahern played only during the summer months, Parker intended to perform throughout the year. The report concluded:

In announcing his plans, Mr. Parker said: "I expect to interest lodges in the various towns in my plan to the extent of covering any possible loss. In return, they will receive a percentage of the gross receipts. The Moose Lodge at Huntington has taken both that town and Riverhead." [10 Jan. 1917, 13]

Despite seemingly well-developed plans, corroborating evidence that Parker did, in fact, establish and maintain this circuit remains lacking. It is probable that the influence of ongoing hostilities in Europe prevented Parker from capitalizing upon Trahern's absence. In fact, during periods when Trahern vacated his control over the Long Island theater scene, rival companies were quick to surface but traditionally would fail to tour for any extended period of time. For example, the 1913 summer season (following Trahern's bankruptcy) witnessed the J. A. Driscoll Stock Company successfully fill the void for only a few months, followed by the Lorch Stock Company, destined to suffer the same fate as the Driscoll organization.

In the fall of 1919 Trahern returned to Long Island from having spent the elapsed time principally in Kansas City, St. Louis, and Cleveland (*Suffolk County News,* 19 Sept., 1). Successful summer circle tours during 1920 and 1921 followed, and although Trahern became ill early in the 1922 circle season, suffering from pneumonia and complications, the company continued to perform during the early stages of his recuperation. Following a sudden turn for the worse in July, however, doctors declared Trahern a hopeless case—"two weeks, maybe longer" (*Suffolk County News,* 21 July, 1). Yet such dire predictions were premature, and while he was slowly regaining his health, Trahern's spirits were buoyed by two major benefit events in the fall of 1922 staged to help defray the expenses of his illness and his move from Long Island to the warmer climate of southern California.

While recovering in Los Angeles Trahern not only maintained connections with show business through management positions with the Orpheum Theatre in Los Angeles and the Santa Monica Amusement Pier, but having once again formed a stock company, in 1924 Trahern married his then current leading lady, Gladys Mann (*Suffolk County News,* 4 July, 1). With renewed body and spirit, Al returned with Gladys to Long Island in 1927 for 25-plus weeks of circle stock, after an absence of nearly five years. The following two years witnessed the continuation of circling on the island, with the 1928 circuit composed of (in order): East Hampton, Bridgehampton, Riverhead, Sayville, Westhampton, and Greenport (uniquely under canvas) (*East Hampton Star,* 27 April, 1).

During the 1929 season Trahern again resorted to an unusual circle arrangement, as *Bill Bruno's Bulletin* reported "the country's only combination house and tent show" played in

> theatres on the first five nights in the week and finishes under canvas at Riverhead on Saturday. The tent is permanently located in that town and is a 65 x 150 top, with raised flooring, opera chairs and a commodious stage, the outfit being arranged to remain permanently all summer. [30 May, 2]

Extensive editorial support from Riverhead's *County Review* concerning Trahern's initial application to pitch his tent in that community argued: "The fact that the Trahern Players play in a tent does not by any stretch of the imagination discount them as earnest and worthy contributors to the welfare of the community" (28 Mar. 1929, page unknown).

Also in 1929 rumors surfaced that Trahern's entire circle stock ensemble might be engaged for the making of sound motion pictures by a production company in the extensive network of East Coast film studios at that time, but no evidence indicates this came about (*BBB,* 13 June, 7). If such a scenario were true, it would possess a good deal of irony. This is due to the fact that during this period Trahern continually lost performance sites to the film industry because the investment in sound equipment forced theaters to raise rental fees, which small touring companies could not meet, thus effectively forcing Trahern into new performance venues such as the tent of recent seasons.

Bill Bruno's Bulletin reported that Trahern explored the state of Nebraska during the summer of 1930, intent on operating a stock circuit there the following winter, but once again this appears unfounded (19 June, 3). In late 1935 Bill Bruno implied continued Midwest involvement, claiming that Trahern "in recent summers has been active in the west" (meaning west of his traditional Long Island territory) (*BBB*, 21 Nov., 7). In fact, the Traherns are known to have done some rep work in the Wausau, Wisconsin, area during the mid–1930s. Yet despite these indications, no evidence has come to light to document Trahern operating a circle in the Midwest during the Depression era. Like so many others, 1929 appears to have been Trahern's last extensive touring season, inevitably leading to his withdrawal from the theater scene. A 1936 feature article on the Traherns reported that recent activities had included chicken farming in the Midwest, along with the management of a Greenport (Long Island) hotel (*Suffolk County News,* 20 Nov., 1). Following a number of years of employment as a clerk of the Suffolk County Supreme Court, Al Trahern died of a heart attack on 4 January 1946 at his home in Riverhead; he was survived by his wife Gladys.

In viewing Trahern's career as a whole one sees that while his fortunes varied greatly over the years, his career unquestionably demonstrated remarkable resilience and longevity. Throughout his active guardianship on Long Island, Trahern pledged to bring recent New York and stock successes to the public. Written accounts record hundreds of different plays presented or announced for performance on Trahern's circle circuits. These plays—which included scripts by playwrights ranging from Augustus Thomas, Clyde Fitch, George Broadhurst, David Belasco, and Bronson Howard to T. W. Robertson, Victorien Sardou, and Dion Boucicault to Charles F. Harrison, J. Hartley Manners, Robert Sherman, and Lem B. Parker—demonstrate the blend he desired. And while his productions were extensively and consistently praised for their wholesomeness and amusement, on occasion Trahern received reminders of the preferences of his Long Island audiences, as in this editor's comments in 1915:

> The metropolis will always afford an audience for problem plays like *The Havoc* but out this way most people prefer the comfortable old fashioned shows that have a happy ending and don't leave a bad taste in one's mouth. Not that there is anything particularly bad about Henry Miller's play. On the contrary, the lesson it teaches is a valuable one, but it was plainly to be seen that, though well acted, *The Havoc* did not make the hit with our people that many of Mr. Trahern's former productions have done. [*Suffolk County News,* 8 Jan., 1]

Yet Trahern's use of circle stock ultimately did more than simply supply him with an effective way to tour the communities of Long Island. His pioneering efforts provided countless smaller rep and stock companies during the first half of this century with the model of a flexible touring method uniquely able to adapt to various needs and requirements as they arose, whether in times of plenty or hardship.

Although Trahern now may rightfully be credited with the extensive early implementation of circle stock on the East Coast, the likelihood of his also being responsible for introducing circle stock to the Midwest remains a possibility. Bred in the Kansas City area, Trahern never forgot his roots, maintaining professional ties with his native region throughout his career. For example, once having resigned from B. F. Keith's employment late in 1914, Trahern managed the procurement of talent in New York City for a "homecoming" week in Kansas City during the Christmas season. These performers, originally from the area, staged a benefit show aiding the Kansas City Chapter of the Red Cross (*Clipper*, 26 Dec., 10). The *Kansas City Star* reports,

> The following telegram was sent at noon by the performers to Al Trahern, who has been managing the New York end of the benefit:
> The bunch assembled at breakfast–fifty of us–has just pledged a toast to you. The benefit is a tremendous success. Kansas City gives you credit. The Bunch. [22 Dec. 1914, 1]

Other reports found in print also connect Trahern with the Midwest at the time of the development of circle stock in the area. In 1916 Trahern served as the business manager for a Dubinsky Brothers Stock Company, newly installed at the renovated Tootle Theatre in St. Joseph, Missouri (*Clipper*, 26 Aug., 13). Early in the following year the *Clipper* names the "Trahern Circuit Players" playing theaters in Kansas. However, financial difficulties reportedly soon forced the company to disband (7 Feb. 1917, 13).

Despite various suggestions of Midwest involvement, it remains certain that the majority of Trahern's professional career was centered in the East and that any performances sponsored by Al Trahern in Kansas during 1917 are not the first use of circle stock in the area. It is reasonable to believe, however, that Trahern's close family and professional ties with the region make him a candidate for being a force in the introduction of circle stock to the region where it flourished–the Midwest.

Trousdale Brothers

Although Benjamin Vernon and Al Trahern possess strong claim as the earliest practitioners of the form, veteran circle performers nearly unanimously cite the four Trousdale brothers of Iowa as the founding fathers of

The Trousdale brothers of Iowa (from left): Winn Walter, Merle Mortimer, Earle Eugene, and Boyd Buckmaster (courtesy of the Museum of Repertoire Americana).

circle stock. The Trousdale family, involved in popular entertainment and theater from 1896 to 1935, remains to this day a mainstay in the annals of Midwest theater history. Hailing from Estherville in the northwest corner of Iowa, the brothers–Merle, Earle, Winn, and Boyd–started their formal career in theater as band members with the "Ideal Dramatic Company" in 1898. This company included

> fifty actors and entertainers playing a tent setup in several northwest Iowa towns. The season was cut short when a windstorm demolished the tent. After the troupe disbanded, the Trousdales formed their own "Dramatic Company" to finish out the summer. They appeared throughout northwest Iowa, in local opera houses and school auditoriums, or wherever an audience could be gathered. [Andrews, 24]

Following the financial failure of this first Trousdale Dramatic Company in Rock Valley, Iowa, the brothers tried their hand at various types of popular entertainment, including Swiss bell ringing, animal acts, medicine shows, minstrel shows, and vaudeville. Shortly after the beginning of this century, the brothers focused their efforts on dramatic offerings produced under the family name. Through such touring productions, the brothers–each eventually heading his own Trousdale Brothers Company–made their mark, primarily performing one-nighters. Several of their one-night-stand presentations received both popular and critical acclaim, among them: *The Man on the Box*, based on the popular Harold McGrath novel; *Madame X*, by Alexandre Bisson and adapted by John H. Raphel; and *The Aviator*, featuring an actual Bleriot monoplane, moving across the stage on wires.

It was not until 1913–following extensive experience filled with both successes and failures in their joint and individual careers–that the Trousdales first experimented with circle stock as a touring and scheduling method. This initial involvement with circuit touring began during the summer of 1913 in Clear Lake, Iowa. After a successful winter tour of *Madame X* in one-nights, the family gathered in Clear Lake, a frequent summer meeting place for the Trousdale clan. While recreational activities and family outings filled their days, adult family members played in neighboring towns at night. According to Earle Trousdale:

> We rented a large cottage for the entire company and the ladies took turns in cooking. We only played three nights a week ... the rest of the time we fished and swam and just had a good time. We changed the play every week and we had a hard time getting the people out of the water long enough to rehearse ... some coming in their bathing suits. [qtd. in Latchaw, 113]

The weekly rotation for this summer season, involving all of the brothers and their families, included Britt on Wednesdays, Garner on Thursdays, and Clear Lake on Fridays. From early June through late August 1913 they performed on this small circuit, after which the company resumed touring *Madame X* as a one-night production, traveling to seven Midwestern states.[22] Following the close of the second tour of *Madame X*, the brothers decided to begin playing circle stock in earnest.

Three of the four brothers each began a separate circle rotation with the coming of the new year, 1914.[23] All three consisted of one-week circles of six nights each, all in the state of Iowa. Winn's circle traveled to the towns of Lake City (Monday), Ida Grove (Tuesday), Sac City (Wednesday), Rockwell City (Thursday), Manson (Friday), and Fonda (Saturday). Boyd's circuit encompassed Mason City, Osage, Charles City, Waverly, Corwith, and Belmond or Britt on Saturday. Merle's towns included Marion, Anamosa, Monticello, Vinton, Garrison or Waverly on Friday, and La Porte City. One might note that on occasion the community of Waverly served as host to two different Trousdale companies: Boyd's on Thursday and Merle's on Friday–a good show town indeed. According to the 1910 Federal Census for Iowa, the largest of these communities were Mason City, with a population of well over 11,000, Charles City, with nearly 6,000, and Marion, with 4,400. The smallest communities included Corwith, boasting of 455 citizens, while Garrison trailed slightly, with only 438. The remaining communities averaged around 1,200–3,000 in population.

In 1936 Winn Trousdale recalled these early days of circle stock:

> As far as I know, we were the first to open a circle stock–or "circuit stock," as we called it at that time. I opened one the latter part of December twenty-two years ago–on December 27, 1914, to be exact.... In that original company were Grace Lyman, Marlyn Fink, Jessie Egan, Roxa Gaylord, Walter Fane, Jay Coggshall, Ed Silvers and myself.

The theatres in the towns played were all upstairs houses.... All the towns were good ones and the business all winter, in spite of unusual cold and snow, was very good.

Some weeks later, in January, Boyd and Earle saw the possibilities in this new form of repertoire and each opened a circle stock, the former in Minnesota and the latter in southern Iowa.... As for who might have originated the idea: I can't recall whether it was mine or if one of the others first thought of playing on a merry-go-'round. At any rate, we were pioneers. [*BBB*, 17 Dec., 27]

Our Name is a Guarantee of a Good Show

Every Performance Guaranteed

The BEST of Shows at LOWEST of Prices

See Us Every Week You May Like the Next Show Even Better than This One

Watch for the Play Next Week

Handbill attributed to a Trousdale circle stock company (courtesy of the Museum of Repertoire Americana).

Regrettably the accuracy of this remembrance falls short in two major areas, no doubt due to the fact that Winn Trousdale recalled these events well over two decades after the fact. Records show that the Trousdales established their initial circuits in early January 1914, with perhaps a few trial performances in late December of the previous year. This predates the time frame recalled by Winn above by one full year. Moreover the placing of Boyd's circuit in Minnesota and Earle's circuit in southern Iowa is without basis. Boyd placed his original circuit in north central Iowa, while Earle did not run a circle stock company in 1914 at all. Although the Trousdales were certainly pioneers, as Winn suggests, it is important to note that their initial success in circuit playing relied as much on their reputation for presenting quality one-night engagements as it did on the innovation of circle stock. For example, the *Waverly Democrat* (1 Jan. 1914) reported:

On next Wednesday evening, Jan. 7, Boyd B. Trousdale, who appeared here last season in *The Man on the Box*, will open a series of engagements at the opera house. Every Wednesday evening he will appear in a new play. Special scenery will be carried each week, and the prices are within the reach of all—25 cents, ANY SEAT. Just the same as you would pay a dollar to see. Opening play, a great comedy—*Is Marriage A Failure?* [5]

The support given by local newspaper editors throughout this first full season of circle stock offered by the Trousdales remained uniformly positive, although the amount of coverage varied from one community newspaper to another. The *Vinton Review* devoted more than the average amount of space to this new venture, coverage that seemingly reflected strong support and acceptance for Merle's troupe in the community. Prior to the first performance in Vinton by this group, the *Vinton Review* reported:

> The company will also appear at the Opera house every Friday night during the balance of the season and will present a new and different play at each visit. The price of admission is an inducement to every one and will, no doubt, pack the house at every visit. Children 10 cents and adults 25 cents. This company is making a weekly circuit of six towns and the Opera House management consider themselves very fortunate in securing the Trousdale Bros to add Vinton to their list of towns and the theatre goers should take advantage of the opportunity and pack the theatre at each visit. [8 Jan. 1914, 4]

A few weeks later when the company performed *The Chauffeur* in Vinton, the hometown newspaper announced that the "play has been played in the cities at $1.00 and $1.50 prices. Now you can see the same show for 25 cents ... and have your seats reserved–it costs you nothing, only your time" (22 Jan., 1). Still later in this season the *Vinton Review* maintained its enthusiastic support by stressing that "the plays offered by the Trousdale Bros. Company are the best that have ever been seen in this city and especially at these prices. The popularity of the company is growing each week" (2 Apr., 4).

After two additional return visits, the local editor urged that the visit of the Trousdale Company become a part of the public's weekly routine:

> It seems to be the verdict of all theatre goers that the Trousdale Bros. company [Merle Trousdale, manager] is getting better at each visit and the opera house is practically sold out every Thursday night to witness these excellent plays offered at the small prices of 10 and 25 cents ... no one can go wrong in seeing these productions offered by this company, in other words it will pay you to get the Thursday night habit. [16 Apr., 4]

All three Trousdale circle companies experienced successful initial seasons, with each troupe building a loyal following. In late February 1914 Winn exchanged circuits with Merle, taking over the circle that included Vinton so that Winn could be closer to his wife, awaiting the birth of a child in Cedar Rapids. In late March following the birth, the brothers returned to their original territories, presumably to rekindle each circuit's loyalty to its original company.

During summer 1914 the brothers and their families (except Winn, who remained with his wife and new daughter in Cedar Rapids) reverted to the abbreviated circle stock based in Clear Lake, which they successfully played the previous summer. The performance schedule remained Britt on

Wednesdays, Garner on Thursdays, and Clear Lake on Fridays, with additional towns played on an irregular basis.

The following fall companies managed by the brothers toured in both one-night and three-night stands, throughout Iowa and Illinois, while relatively good weather prevailed. But by January 1915—and the onset of the severest period of a Midwest winter—Merle (united with partner Edward C. Horne) returned to the eldest Trousdale's old circle with a Trousdale-Horne Company. Likewise, Winn journeyed again to his original circle, and Boyd to his. Only Earle continued one-nighters, said to be still performing *The Rejuvenation of Aunt Mary*. Thus during the late winter of 1914–15, three companies under the Trousdale family name once again practiced circle touring.

But by the end of spring 1915 the use of circle stock by the Trousdale family waned. When the pressures of attempting to raise a family on the road became unmanageable, Winn left show business never to return to it. Over the years he purchased hotels in various Iowa communities and from 1915 on remained an innkeeper.

Merle, the eldest brother, left the road from 1915 to 1921, during which time he tried his hand at both newspaper and hotel businesses. Later, during the mid–1920s, he managed Iowa's famous Cherry Sisters (billed as "America's Worst" vaudeville act), continued with his trained animal acts, and worked as an advance agent for his brother Boyd. By 1929 his only theatrical effort remained an occasional dog show.

Earle, the second oldest, left show business in 1917 also to enter the hotel business, while Boyd, the youngest, continued in show business, eventually completing well over 30 years in total. Boyd used circle stock occasionally in the 1920s, but for most of his remaining career his companies performed in permanent stock engagements.

Although they practiced the touring method of circle stock for only a short period of time (roughly 1913–15), the Trousdale brothers nevertheless hold an important place in the development of the method. Because of being early practitioners of circle touring in the Midwest—an area where circle stock would eventually flourish more than in any other—they demonstrated for the observant the advantages of the system and the strong community support that it generated.

An Era of Circuits

Even though individual circuits existed for virtually every type of amusement touring America near the turn of this century, each fashioned itself in essentially the same manner. These circuits—ranging from vaudeville and burlesque to one-night theater companies—carried entertainment units to the remote reaches of this country, normally in the form of entire productions. They traveled over an organized route of performance sites, followed by another unit and then another—essentially a linear sequence of shows over the same track. Having traveled the path—composed of as few as ten to as many as 50 or more stops—units normally ventured on to different routes, or disbanded, or (more rarely) prepared a new production to offer for immediate bookings on the same path. Such circuits were obviously designed to minimize expense, travel time, and disruptions, while maximizing efficiency and profit. In virtually all respects, circle stock followed a methodology identical to these various chains, except that the number of stops regularly remained fewer and each company routinely started over on the chain once a complete cycle had been traversed. Placing the history of circle touring in relation to that of para-theatrical chains and legitimate theater circuits clearly demonstrates that circle stock did not evolve in a vacuum but developed during a period characterized by a multitude of touring systems and structures.

Vaudeville Circuits

Vaudeville historian Douglas Gilbert places the beginning of the first vaudeville circuit or "chain" around 1880, organized by Harry Miner and Thomas Canary. This pair maintained a joint management and booking office, while also operating both Miner's New Bowery Theatre and the Eighth Avenue Theatre in New York City. "That their enterprises were ... extensive is indicated by their announcements guaranteeing ten to sixteen weeks' playing time for 'first-class talent'" (Gilbert, 14).

While Bernard Sobel also cites the efforts of Miner and Canary in the nineteenth century, he names Martin Beck as the individual who "perfected" the procedure of a "linked chain or circuit of consecutive bookings" eventually adopted by the entire industry (*Vaudeville*, 77–78). Beck began his career in San Francisco, connected with the Orpheum Theatre there, and eventually headed the famous vaudeville circuit named for that very theater. By 1905 Beck's Orpheum circuit included 17 houses reaching from the West Coast to Chicago. Later Beck linked his growing enterprise with that of the established Kohl and Castle circuit—a major Midwest chain based in Chicago—thus significantly strengthening and expanding the Orpheum empire.

Taken as a whole, the staggering size and complexity of the numerous vaudeville circuits existing during the first decade of this century bear little resemblance to circle stock. One traditional story set around 1910 helps illustrate the abundance of vaudeville circuits, especially the "two-a-days," and the confusion they could create. It concerns an actor who, when booked to play a circuit with which he was unfamiliar, asked, "What is it? Smalltime, medium smalltime, big smalltime, little big time, medium big time or big time?" (DiMeglio, 20).

Throughout vaudeville's history, the size of circuits serving the industry did, indeed, vary. The noted Gus Sun circuit covered well over 100 theaters in nine states and Canada, whereas the Wells circuit in the South controlled only 11 theaters (DiMeglio, 174). But even as an untypically small vaudeville circuit, the Wells route covered distances far greater and involved more theaters than was to be seen in the first fledgling circle circuits.

Burlesque Wheels

Burlesque in America near the end of the nineteenth century had not yet had recourse to the vulgarity of the striptease–a phenomenon of the 1920s and the 1930s. The burlesque show at this time consisted primarily of slapstick comedy sketches, unusual variety acts, female chorus numbers, an occasional travesty on politics or a current play, and the parading of shapely beauties on stage known as the "leg show." Yet the comedian reigned supreme, liberally supported with double entendre. At the turn of this century, following roughly two decades of the initial growth and development of burlesque in this nation, a movement surfaced to improve and refine burlesque's haphazard techniques of scheduling and touring. First efforts resulted in the creation of the Travelling Variety Managers' Association in 1900, uniting the established producers and theater owners (Sobel, *Burlesque*, 81). This organization–the first true cooperative venture in burlesque–made improvements in travel arrangements, establishment of territories, and other logistical aspects of touring.

But with increasing rivalry and hostility between two factions of this group, an inevitable split occurred. In 1905 two "wheels" or circuits evolved, with the old-line producers and managers combining under the name of the Empire (or Western) circuit and many younger, more powerful burlesque show owners forming the Columbia (or Eastern) circuit (Sobel, *Burlesque,* 82; Conner, 158). The creation of two megacircuits, according to Ralph Allen, marks the beginning of the golden age of burlesque. Although the designations might suggest distinct geographic territories, Irving Zeidman reports that in the heated rivalry between the two circuits,

> every city in the East was tapped for possible theatres. But neither of them went beyond the Midwest. The West Coast, San Francisco, was exceeding the wildest burlesque imaginings with its Barbary Coast dives. Burlesque there could only be anticlimactic. [54]

With the creation of the Empire and Columbia wheels, the burlesque industry clearly demonstrated its tremendous size and popularity. In these wheels, performing companies originated at each member theater and appeared there for a set period of time. Following this, the company started on the rotation of the wheel. With the total number of theaters on these circuits reaching 40 or more and with a company performing in each theater for the maximum of one week, every franchised show could be guaranteed nearly an entire year of work in order to complete a single rotation of a large wheel.

Again, the sheer size of such circuits separates them from the eventual scale used by the circle units. Yet these wheel circuits, unlike most other circuits of the period, did literally follow a circular pattern. In describing this pattern, an image used later to characterize circle stock is seen first depicting the burlesque circuits: Walter K. Hill, a press agent for the Columbia circuit once remarked, "Shows follow their leader as the spokes of a wheel revolve around its hub" (qtd. in Zeidman, 53).

Airdome Circuits

Circuits were also established to route talent to the hundreds of airdomes once dotting the Midwest landscape. As an open-air theater, the airdome usually consisted of "an area surrounded by a temporary wall of canvas, metal or wood without any roof covering, with the ground for the floor where the seats were placed," often situated on a prominent vacant lot in a town's business district (Mickel, 212). A covered stage area accommodated live performances by rep companies or vaudeville troupes, or possibly a simple projection screen for silent pictures. According to the scant historical research completed on them, the airdomes developed during the mid- to late-1890s and flourished until World War I, reaching their greatest period of expansion around 1908 to 1909. Eventually street noises from an ever-increasing number of automobiles, in addition to the high demand and, hence, high values placed on their prime midtown locations, forced the airdomes out of business (Slout, *Theatre in a Tent*, 25).

From the editorial page of *Billboard* in the fall of 1909 came the optimistic, but certainly not prophetic, assessment: "The airdome is a branch of the amusement business that has come to stay." Although providing a slightly romanticized view of the airdomes, this editorial does depict many of its chief characteristics:

> With the stage erected out-of-doors, and with no roof except the sky, and with the moon furnishing most of the light necessary, the airdome proved to be the ideal place to spend the evening, furnishing an opportunity to enjoy the entertainment without courting suffocation. With no expensive building to rent and vacant lots being cheap, the airdome immediately proved to be not only a more comfortable place of amusement, but an

Exterior of an upscale airdome theater found in Atchison, Kansas (courtesy of the Museum of Repertoire Americana).

inexpensive one for the promoter. This is the reason why there will be more airdomes next summer, and they will be erected and conducted on a scale more elaborate. [25 Sept., 16]

Numerous airdome circuits developed to supply and route entertainment, with the Bell-Ballard-Olendorf and the Crawford circuits out of Kansas City considered the most prominent. Many smaller airdome routes also developed. For example, 1910 marks the formation of the Missouri-Kansas Airdome Association representing 12 airdomes in the two states, organized primarily to gain strength in numbers and "to put the airdome theatres and repertoire companies playing over the Association houses, on a paying basis." Reportedly the burlesque wheels provided the model for this 18-week circuit. In fact, *Billboard* explicitly states that the Missouri-Kansas airdome circuit planned to operate in the "manner of a burlesque wheel, a sort of a co-operative plan by which every manager of a theatre also owns a traveling company, which plays one week in his theatre and one week in each other theatre on the circuit" (5 Feb. 1910, 16).

Once again, the size of the circuits and the considerable distances traveled in touring prevents the airdome circuits from striking more than a general similarity to circle stock.

Airdome crowd, possibly in Beatrice, Nebraska, circa 1911. Building to the left is said to be the local opera house (courtesy of the Museum of Repertoire Americana).

Additional Circuits of the Period

Other para-theatrical institutions also developed circuits that routed talent. Tent Chautauqua circuits, like many other similar circuits, developed during the first decade of this century. The entire Chautauqua movement dates from 1874 when the Rev. John Heyl Vincent and Lewis Miller founded the Fair Point Sunday School Assembly beside Lake Chautauqua in the southwestern corner of New York State, which developed into the noted Chautauqua Institute.

Similar enterprises in theme and purpose soon spread across this nation, and in their effort to emulate the original assembly they also adopted the title of Chautauqua. Devoted to educational and religious purposes, these seven- to ten-day gatherings also accepted "elevated" entertainment. Near the turn of the century, inspirational lectures, informative talks, and music provided the main staples for an assembly. In the declining years of the movement in the late 1920s and beyond, theatrical performances and motion pictures obtained respectability and helped the assemblies stay financially solvent. Otherwise the event still consisted largely of music and educational speakers.

These assemblies, which attempted to model themselves after Vincent and Miller's original creation, are normally divided into two groups. One group includes the so-called independent or permanent Chautauquas that developed within only a few years following the founding of the original assembly. Such offspring called themselves permanent Chautauquas because they annually convened at an appropriate setting (usually near a lake or stream) on which a large permanent structure (usually referred to as a tabernacle or pavilion) was built for their mass gatherings. In addition, these permanent assemblies optimistically were expected to last in the community where they were established for an indefinite period of time.

Over a quarter century passed, however, until the Chautauqua movement took to the road in the form of circuits. Keith Vawter, a partner in the Redpath Lyceum Bureau with his headquarters in Chicago, is credited with the effort to mobilize the Chautauqua movement. Under Vawter's leadership, Chautauqua entered new territories and brought its mission of education and culture, with the addition of appropriate entertainment, to the smaller centers and rural areas of this country, all under canvas. Historian Theodore Morrison summarizes the stages through which Vawter journeyed to make circuit Chautauqua a success:

> In 1904 he organized a nine-day program and tried to sell it at reduced rates to local independents. Their resistance made this first venture a financial failure, and Vawter saw that he must either give up or venture on a business of his own without regard to the independents. In 1907 he took the field again, this time successfully, though it was not until 1910 that he fully established the plan that led to the spectacular growth of the circuits. [178]

The initial circuit of 1904 involved 14 towns spread across the entire state of Iowa, also including one performance site in Minnesota and four in Nebraska. From this beginning the circuit Chautauqua movement grew steadily, reaching its zenith during the mid–1920s. As Morrison reminds us, "To literally millions of Americans, 'Chautauqua' has meant these circuit companies rather than the institution in New York" (vii).

Lastly, even the highly popular outdoor amusement parks at the turn of this century developed circuits for the routing of talent. Similar to the talent appearing on the airdome circuits, the amusement parks booked primarily vaudeville and variety troupes, along with touring rep companies. For example, during the summer of 1906, the North Brothers Comedians played the Breinig circuit of parks through the states of Indiana, Illinois, and Michigan (*Clipper*, 23 June, 488).

Early Theatrical Circuits

In his detailed study on the economic history of the American theater, Alfred Bernheim traces the rise and dominance of theatrical circuits in the late nineteenth century. Bernheim demonstrates that circuits developed following the demise of this country's resident stock company system in the midnineteenth century. With the ensuing growth of the traveling "combination" companies—a star performer supported with an entire ensemble—Bernheim notes significant development in the process of building theatrical circuits beginning around 1870.

These early circuits were essentially cooperative enterprises organized for the purpose of taking advantage of joint action. With the ability to have a single spokesperson for a circuit, such advantages included increased bargaining leverage as a group and reduced time and labor in the booking process, which translated directly into savings for all members of the cooperative. At first, geographic proximity forged the common link for members of theatrical circuits, helping ensure ease in plotting a logical route for a touring company. The concluding quarter of the nineteenth century witnessed rapidly increasing numbers of such circuits, especially among those venues catering to the one-night-stand companies.

By their very existence, circuits acknowledged a movement in the American theater toward the concentration and centralization of artistic and financial management. Eventually centralized ownership or management of circuits led to the dominance of particular managers, who increasingly wrested power away from the group. Slowly over a period of roughly 25 years, the establishment of circuits and booking agencies led toward the placing of theater power in the hands of the few.

Theatrical Syndicate

Near the end of the nineteenth century, this consolidation of power reached unequaled heights with the creation of the Theatrical Syndicate in 1896. Composed of Charles Frohman, Al Hayman, Marc Klaw, and Abraham Erlanger from New York, plus Sam Nixon and Fred Zimmerman from Philadelphia, the Syndicate reigned unrivaled in power for over a decade while dictating the course of the theater world.

Circuits provided the raw material from which the Syndicate built its empire. In Bernheim's estimation, "It was a supremely logical development. It was the inevitable next step in the theatrical history of this country. The circuits and the booking agencies that preceded it were its forerunners causally as well as chronologically" (46). Unquestionably, the early combination and one-night chains prior to the turn of the century were of vital importance to the Syndicate.[24]

The image of a "circuit" is misleading when called upon to describe the true strength and backbone of the Syndicate, however. Rather, the image of passage through a narrow corridor is somewhat more helpful in reconstructing the Syndicate's methods, because the Syndicate put to use its holdings in theater property in a way unlike any other management organization of the period. Although the Syndicate controlled the bulk of first-class theaters in the major metropolitan centers, the fact that it controlled the theaters in communities located between such theater centers provided its true source of power. Without access to these smaller towns, non–Syndicate companies simply could not afford the long jumps from one chief city to another. Thus the Syndicate actually needed to own or manage only a percentage of this nation's theaters in order effectively to dominate the business of touring theatrical productions–to monopolize "the road."

Although the control of key theaters in towns strategically located between population centers was the base of its power, these venues did not make money for the Syndicate. Members of the Syndicate built their fortunes from lengthy runs in the major theaters under their control. Performances while touring between major metropolitan areas only helped defray travel costs. Simply put, the power of the Syndicate accrued in large part from controlling the so-called one-night-stand houses, not from actually developing and touring one-night companies to the far reaches of this country. This responsibility fell to a level of theater entrepreneurs below that of the Syndicate.

The Syndicate maintained its unchallenged influence and control of the road from roughly 1896 until 1910, utilizing a key characteristic of circle stock touring: the regular use of theaters within a region. Yet the Syndicate did not always send companies in a prescribed sequential order over the chain of theaters under its control, as one might imagine. Instead, the Syndicate used its power to move companies on and off routes as it so desired. As Bernheim suggests, the Syndicate played the American theatrical scene like a giant game of chess. In this fashion, the Syndicate

> juggled routes almost at will, changing the tours of attractions to suit the interests of its members. If a Syndicate play was enjoying a successful run at any theatre its stay would be extended and other plays would be side-tracked. If, on the other hand, a Syndicate theatre stood empty, any attraction might be called to fill in the time irrespective of its other engagements. In short, the attractions and theatres of the country were puppets, and the Syndicate ... pulled the strings. [59]

Although the Syndicate is correctly remembered as a tremendous power maintaining control over hundreds of theaters and the routes connecting them, the methods employed by the Syndicate to use and maintain those vital routes were decidedly not linear or sequential. In fact, in conducting its business the Syndicate cannot be described as either regular or logical. More often than not, its routing of theater companies followed the Syndicate's business-instinct whims. Yet the belief that the Syndicate

maintained systematic control over its theater holdings undoubtedly provided an impetus for businessmen of the entertainment industry to emulate
what was, in fact, largely only an image. As such, contrary to the Syndicate's
actual practices, circle stock companies relied upon orderly, sequential
movement around their circuits.

The Shuberts

An exploration of this prominent circuit era would not be complete without a look at the rival theatrical monopoly created by the three Shubert
brothers: Sam, Lee, and Jacob. Chronologically, the Syndicate predates the
Shuberts: by the time Sam Shubert had acquired his very first theater in
1897 (the Opera House in Utica, New York), the Syndicate had already cel-
ebrated the initial anniversary of its founding. Even so, the Shuberts eventually acquired a status equal to the Syndicate and then superseded it, both
organizations operating in a very similar fashion. Up until 1905 the Shuberts maintained a close business relationship with their eventual rivals, as
Shubert productions played theaters controlled by the Syndicate, and Shubert theaters obtained talent through Klaw and Erlanger's exchange, the
segment of the Syndicate controlling all of that organization's bookings.

In 1905 the Syndicate feared the rising power of the Shuberts, and
open hostilities broke out between the two, leading the Shubert organization to sever all relations with the opposing side in July of that year. Even
though Sam, the eldest Shubert, died in a railroad accident in May 1905,
the two surviving brothers set out to conquer the Syndicate. With determined effort, they achieved a rapid rise to power unparalleled in American
theater history. In August 1905 the duo controlled some 30 theaters, and
with their holdings continually increasing, by the end of that calendar year
nearly 50 theaters carried the Shubert identification. By the end of 1906 the
brothers booked or controlled outright nearly 60 theaters, although as Bernheim points out, "the Syndicate could count the theaters it booked in hundreds, while the Shuberts still counted theirs in tens" (67).

Regardless of the disparity between the two, the fact remains that in
under ten years the Shuberts had built a formidable theatrical circuit, still
growing and developing. By about 1910 the Shuberts acquired status equal
to the Syndicate and proceeded to surpass it. Apart from size, however,
Bernheim concludes that the Syndicate possessed more vision and con-
structive genius than its competitors:

> Once the Shuberts achieved the position they sought, they conducted their
> enterprises in essentially the same way as the Syndicate conducted its. They
> devised nothing new in the way of circuits, booking offices, theatrical sys-
> tems. They followed a model; they enlarged its scale; they did not alter its
> proportions. [67]

One-Night Production Circuits

Bernheim suggests that following the turn of this century little is heard concerning circuits because the Syndicate had "obtained sway over the theatre." While the power of the Syndicate cannot be denied, the idea of circuits certainly had not dropped from the scene. Circuits continued as a topic of attention in the trade publications, so much so that the image of a "circuit" or "wheel" could not have escaped the notice of anyone interested in the techniques of theatrical touring at the beginning of the twentieth century. In virtually all cases, these routes chained one-night productions and were controlled by small-time theatrical entrepreneurs, competing with and also emulating the monopolistic control of the Syndicate. In nearly all cases, however, the one-nighter circuits organized theaters of little interest to the Syndicate because of their remote and isolated locations. This linking of theaters in areas outside the control of the major national circuits closely simulates circle stock. For example, the *Dramatic Mirror* recorded in 1904 ambitious efforts toward a circuit in downstate Illinois to capitalize on touring companies out of Chicago:

> Theatre managers in the cities of Aurora, Elgin, Joliet, Ottawa, Streator, Kewanee and Galesburg, Ill., at a meeting in Aurora last week, took steps toward organizing a theatrical circuit.... Mr. Williams [of Streator] said that the past season had been unsatisfactory both to managers and to theatre goers, and that the prospects for next season are not assuring if the conditions continue. By organizing a circuit of the cities they represent, they shall be in a position to offer practically a week's engagement, with short jumps, to companies as they start out from Chicago. They should be able to get better terms from the companies and better attractions. [25 June, 7]

A similar cooperative circuit developed by East Coast managers took shape in 1905. In describing the venture, the editorial staff of *Billboard* used a familiar image for the time:

> And now we are to have a stock "wheel." The eastern stock managers held a meeting in New York last week to consummate plans for the project. An organization was effected for one year, sixteen managers being present, each representing a company that will be a part of the organization. The purpose is to form a circuit of these houses over which the various companies will tour, the bills being changed as often as policy requires.

The techniques and methods planned for this "wheel" were not new, being modeled largely on the system used for burlesque at the time. The *Billboard* editorial, however, suggests that this particular method of touring in conjunction with permanent stock companies was indeed novel. Even so, the editorial stresses that these companies

> will not be materially different from the numberless organizations that tour the country from season to season. They will be repertoire companies

> playing over a circuit. The circuit itself is the important factor. The compa-
> nies will be limited to the houses in the circuit. They will not be permitted
> to play at theatres not in the combine. Nor will these theatres be allowed to
> offer attractions not belonging to the organization.
>
> Of course it will be called a syndicate by those antagonistic to it. [20 May,
> 10]

One wonders if this description of "repertoire companies playing over a
circuit" appearing in 1905 motivated Al Trahern, at that time nearly two
years away from beginning his initial circle stock efforts on Long Island.
Nevertheless, we see that one response to the Syndicate was the formation
of smaller syndicate-like routes specializing in one-night stands.

A feature article in a *Billboard* of early spring 1906 carries the title "Circuits / Growing In The One Night Stands / Managers are Hustling to Get
Into Line—Activity Greater Than Ever Before." Furious efforts to organize
this lucrative area of the theatrical industry took place on various levels—
from the ultrapowerful conglomerates to smaller state and regional agencies, from the country's great industrial centers to isolated rural areas. *Billboard* reported that "there is hardly a town that has not received overtures
to become a part of some circuit or to at least form a booking arrangement
with some agency" (21 Apr., 3). These efforts in organizing smaller communities were largely not in the hands of powerful agencies or partnerships
but in the hands of what *Billboard* called "fellows with ambitions." Additional efforts to establish circuits in the "very small towns" reportedly were
not successful, due primarily to an inability to link this size of communities
together profitably. To overcome this problem, agencies typically representing a large number of smaller hamlets booked for them one-night
attractions, often charging participating theater companies a fee equal to
two and a half percent of the organization's gross from the tour.

In September 1906 *Billboard* reported circuits continuing to grow rapidly among the one-nighters, claiming

> before a year shall have gone by every one night stand of any prominence
> east of the Mississippi river will be identified with some circuit or other. The
> promoters of these circuits are working all the time, and because they do
> not see fit to report their progress weekly through the dramatic press is no
> reason for thinking they are inactive. [29 Sept., 4]

While the growth of these one-night circuits flourished, a few observers saw
the difficult lessons and troubles that lay ahead, as reported in December
1907:

> Managers who have been playing the one-night stand circuits, organized
> within the past year, claim that the owners of those circuits have killed the
> goose that laid the golden egg by over-booking. Towns that were only good
> for one attraction a week, but very good at that, now get six shows a week,

and none of them get more than carfare to the next town. Many managers claim that they will not play these one-night stands next season. [*Billboard,* 14 Dec., 4]

The one-night circuits developing at this time varied considerably in the number of theaters included in the arrangement. An "Iowa-Illinois Circuit" consisted of 25 of the "best show towns" in the two states (*Billboard,* 27 May 1905, 11). Other circuits easily totaled 30–70 communities and even higher. In addition, the size of the territory covered could be considerable. Frank Livingstone, manager of the Livingstone Stock Company at the Lafayette Theatre, Detroit, announced in the fall of 1905 plans for a circuit of theaters stretching from New York State to the Pacific coast, reporting:

> We are already in practical possession of a New York house, and are negotiating for two in Chicago. Kansas City and eight other good houses in good cities will be on the circuit.... Our idea is to move the companies from one theatre to another. This will give the patrons a variety of plays and actors drilled in the parts they assume. It is something of an innovation, but it is sensible and will succeed. [*Billboard,* 30 Sept., 11]

Amidst such plans for large circuits, often encompassing several states, one can find examples of much smaller chains seemingly similar to circle stock. In the summer of 1906 the Ruble Theatre Company announced

> a complete circuit of theatres in Nevada, to be known as the "Nevada Mining Camp circuit," embracing Tonopah, Goldfield, Manhattan, Bull Frog, Ely, Austin and Eureka. There are over 150,000 people in this district, and things theatrical are booming. Other houses will be added by next fall, making a circuit of real opera houses in a territory hitherto untouched by recognized companies. [*Clipper,* 2 June, 406]

Thus a route of only seven theaters was established, although its organizers hoped for continued growth.

A brief entry in the *Clipper* during 1906 refers to a small circuit in southern Illinois, the size of which makes it sound very much like a circle stock operation, although one must assume it merely linked one-night stands. In this instance, a letter from a theater manager in Marion, Illinois, complained, "I note that you have never made mention of the fact that right here in Egypt there is one of the best seven night circuits you have ever had the pleasure to report, and it will be appreciated if at this time you will kindly mention the same" (13 Oct., 906).[25]

While many of these circuits remained quite large, the smaller ones indeed resembled the circle circuits that flourished in years to come. With management control over a string of theaters, usually through exclusive booking rights or possibly even through actual ownership, the one-night circuits of this time supported a flow of performing troupes over the route— a flow as constant as the market would bear. Yet performances often did not take place according to a regular pattern, because the vast majority of those managing the circuits did not also control the performing units. Management merely did its best to contract for as many companies as possible to perform over the route and then take a percentage of profits from these organizations.

Trahern's circle stock techniques improved upon this situation by maintaining management control over the majority of venues performed in (a situation not known to be true with Vernon), while also maintaining artistic and business control over the production unit. With control over both of these crucial elements–theaters and performance companies–Trahern could guarantee regular appearances over his circle stock circuit.

By the fall of 1908, with Trahern in his second season of circle stock on Long Island, reports from the Midwest continued to show various small circuits developing. These include a route developed by the Rice Stock Company of Fort Wayne, Indiana, scheduled to "play regularly once a week in Anderson, Ind., alternating between Lima [Ohio], Ft. Wayne [Indiana], Muncie [Indiana] and Anderson" (*Billboard,* 17 Oct., 48). While certainly marking the establishment of some type of circuit playing, it is not clear on what schedule the company performed in each city.

By 1911 Frank Readick of Chicago organized the Tri-City Stock Company and installed it in the area referred to as the Quad cities. The performance schedule included the Burtis Theatre in Davenport, Iowa, on Monday and Tuesday; the Illinois Theatre in Rock Island, Illinois, on Wednesday and Thursday; and the Moline Theatre, Moline, Illinois, for "the balance of the week." Concerning plans for the venture *Billboard* reported:

> The company has been assembled in Chicago by Mr. Readick and rehearsals are now in progress. The opening bill will be *The Sign of the Four.* The bill will be changed each week, only royalty plays being presented. A scenic artist has been engaged and every effort will be made to present each play in the most adequate manner possible. Popular prices will prevail. [4 Nov., 6]

In succeeding years theater companies from various regions toured using a variety of plans–some performing in classic six-day circle stock, others in several different variations. For example, *Billboard* reported a mixture of several different types of circuit playing in the 1915 season. In January, E. Forest Taylor reported his nine-person ensemble, appropriately called the Rotation Stock Company, already touring on a route of Idaho towns (2 Jan., 44). A few months later one learned that "a stock company has been organized in Lewiston, Ill. [to] play two-night engagements each week in Lewiston, Havana, and Beardstown" (24 Apr., 19). Later that summer, plans called for a traveling stock company to operate in St. Louis. Preparations called for "three well-known hippodromes" in the city to be leased, with the company to perform at each hippodrome two nights a week, and a new program to tour each week over the "miniature circuit"

(26 Dec. 1914, 3). And in September 1915 a seven-person group entitled the "Circle Stock Company" established itself in Kansas City and reported "very fair" business (25 Sept., 16).

Clearly, by the end of 1915, with the Trousdales already leaving the practice of circle stock, with Al Trahern's re-entry into circle stock on Long Island, and with the rapid adoption of the method throughout the nation, circle stock had arrived and would continue to make an important impact on the American theater scene for years to come. And as tempting as it might seem, the creation of a hierarchy of influences upon the early practitioners of circle stock best remains unexplored, even if it were possible.

Rather it is important to grasp that circle stock stands as a testament, not to star personalities, theater structures, or cultural institutions, but to grass-roots managerial expertise and savvy, managers who understood local needs, customs, and mores. Ultimately these early circle circuits were established on a scale that one manager and one stock company could create and maintain. For men such as Vernon, Trahern, and the Trousdales, circle stock allowed for a managerial independence plus security of territory and income quite suited to this era of circuits. In later years, this managerial importance continued, but circle stock increasingly demonstrated the determined efforts of troupers compelled to survive and perform against overwhelming odds, to keep on bringing the show to town.

3

Maintaining Body and Soul

W HEN ASKED WHY THEY CHOSE TO USE the circle stock format of touring, veteran performers routinely answer that it "paid our expenses," or that it "provided a vehicle to keep working," or that it simply allowed them "to eat." Circle stock did, in fact, provide a less expensive way of touring than other related methods, not only under normal conditions but especially in times of need. Hence it could flourish when other forms of scheduling went broke. But since veteran performers repeatedly cite circle stock as a way "to hold body and soul together," one must investigate not only financial motivations but also personal factors that made circle stock a system that fed artistic and social yearnings of the participants as well.

Financial Motivations

A significant part of the financial savings provided by circle stock took place in lower transportation costs. Rather than moving an entire production a lengthy distance to a new town each night (as did one-night-stand companies) or each week (as did week-long rep companies, whether performing in theaters or under canvas), circle stock troupes based themselves in one community and made daily excursions to an evening's performance site, normally returning home each night. Whereas it is true that circle troupes traveled just as frequently as one-night organizations, and up to seven times more frequently than week-long rep companies, the cost advantages available in circle stock touring accrued from the major differences between it and other forms of touring.

Not only was the length of circle stock jumps almost always shorter than travel in other types of theatrical touring, but due to the smaller size of circle companies—in personnel, scenery, and equipment—travel required fewer vehicles. In tent show touring, the necessity of transporting a large canvas theater with all its furnishings, not to mention accompanying items such as chairs, bleachers, and multiple sets of scenery, involved numerous vehicles and considerable expense. Alfred Bernheim notes, while discussing tent rep in his 1932 work on the economics of the American theater, "The average jump of 50 to 100 miles involves an outlay of $75 to $250" (100). And while one-night productions or week-long residencies in theaters did not require the transportation of a structure in which to perform or seating equipment, these types of units traditionally transported a respectable number of cast and crew members, in addition to a large array of scenery and properties specifically designed for the tour. In 1921 *Billboard* judged the merits of circle stock travel against the train transportation still used by many touring organizations, especially one-night productions, and concluded, "The economy of this system [circle stock] is apparent. The jumps are small and the need of sleeping cars, et cetera, is obviated" (12 Nov., 26).

In contrast to the demands of more elaborate touring methods, most circle stock troupes relied upon only one large car (possibly with a small trailer) to transport the essential elements: cast members, scenery (usually backdrops), costumes, and a few props—all for only one show. In addition, the company's familiarity with the terrain and the people of the countryside provided circle stock with a decided advantage. Long-distance touring frequently confronted unforeseen problems and detours.

Regretfully, to date, sufficient financial records have not been uncovered which would allow one to contrast with certainty the transportation expenses for various modes of theatrical touring. But even if such records did survive, a comparison of travel costs could be misleading because a true comparison would require that other budget variables remain constant, which was by no means the case. Lacking evidence to the contrary, we must accept the nearly unanimous testimony from veteran troupers that travel costs for a circle operation remained less than similar expenses for other touring patterns.

But lower transportation expenditures were not the only area of savings. Reduced costs in technical areas also made circle stock attractive to a fiscal-minded manager. Performance facilities varied greatly on a typical circle, often ranging from a platform in a simple meeting hall, to the small stage of a motion picture house, to much larger stages in the old second-story opera houses. Because of this diversity, circle stock relied upon minimal scenery and props to maintain flexibility. "Diamond dye" drops could easily be hung from the ceiling and a simple throw cover could quickly transform two folding chairs into a settee.[1] With such simplicity, lower costs were typically seen in the areas of scenery and props. Interestingly enough, few records exist suggesting that the diminished reliance upon scenic elements caused a negative response from circle stock audiences. At any rate, many of the people in these small, rural communities may never have seen anything more elaborate on a stage anyway.

Because circle stock companies established headquarters in a community for an extended period, housing arrangements (which often included cooking facilities) could be made for a longer term than one-night productions or week-long rep companies, normally resulting in lower personal expenses for the performers. Like lodging, most expenditures for consumables also could be made in bulk. However, not all of these purchases were made in base communities because companies found it advantageous to obtain goods and services needed for the day-to-day running of the troupe in each and every community on the circle. In doing so, the actors maintained visibility and also came to know the townspeople both in performance and in public. Frank Wiziarde, an experienced tent rep and circle stock veteran, explains the plan he followed:

> You tried to do certain amounts of shopping, like groceries, gas, and so forth [in the towns]. In other words, to be seen; to let it be known what you were doing there, because you were becoming a part of the business in that town. And they liked to feel that the money wasn't all leaving.

Because circle stock required a small capital investment and low operating costs, it provided an answer to the needs of various units in differing financial conditions—namely individuals seeking to establish and manage their own theater company on a limited budget, groups experiencing financial problems stemming from poor business, and also troupes that fell victim to natural disasters.

Due to the low amount of funds needed to establish a circuit, even meager savings could be enough to launch one's own circle company. As previously cited, Maude Gentry recalls, "Get six people or so together, with a few scripts, [and] a car," plus some modest operating capital, and a circle company usually took shape. Often performers left a tent season or even another circle tour expressly to form their own circuit company. In September 1936 Roscoe ("Nig") and Jessie Allen finished the summer season with the No. 2 Neal circle in Colorado only to travel directly to Dodge City, Kansas, to organize and manage their own circle company and to perform on a circuit of towns successfully played the previous winter (*BBB,* 1 Oct., 1). In some instances, upon seeing an apparent need for entertainment and also the ease of establishing a circuit, the circle industry gained enthusiastic participants from professions outside show business. *Bill Bruno's Bulletin* records the intriguing story of one convert to circle stock from the agricultural community:

> William C. Hart, manager of the Alva Sales Pavilion in Alva, Okla., is a live wire who recently proved to his own satisfaction that show business can be done when one goes after it right.

Mr. Hart for several weeks attended the performances of the Morris-Davis company at Capron, Okla., there being no theatre available for the company in Alva. But he saw possibilities for such a company in his hometown, so built a stage in the pavilion, with dressing rooms added, bought scenery, interested ten merchants in sponsoring the show and booked it for Sunday nights. The engagement was a success with [the] result that sixteen more merchants were added and the company forced to play both Saturday and Sunday nights to accommodate the crowds. Which caused the Morris-Davis company to change their headquarters to Alva from Zenda, Kansas, and to further rebook its circle of towns. Business continues to be capacity on the two weekend nights played, with more merchants joining in the sponsoring of the show. [14 May 1936, 2]

At times members of a rep or stock company that had closed for any number of reasons would elect to continue as a new entity. For many groups, the simplicity of circle stock's financial concerns greatly influenced these newly resurrected companies to choose playing on a circuit. Records show that on one occasion members of the Christy Obrecht Stock Company, following the close of their season, quickly reorganized as the Capitol Players to play a circle of northwest Iowa communities centered around Sheldon (*BBB,* 26 Nov. 1936, 1).

Without question, circle stock provided many a performer desirous of becoming his own boss with a real opportunity. Even so, large numbers of actors using their savings from a previous tent season to become managers presented some real problems, as evidenced by Bill Bruno's concerns in the fall of 1936:

Now that the [tent] outfits are being "put in the barn," many an actor is being stung by the circle bee. [The tent] Season has been the best in years and that is an added incentive. If all the actors turn managers, how are they going to fill casts? And the danger is that there will not be enough towns to go around. So most of the newcomers will probably sneak into the territory of the manager they worked for the past summer and mess it all up. [*BBB,* 17 Sept,. 3]

On occasion *Bill Bruno's Bulletin* reported a "shoestring" approach to establishing a circle company taken to the extreme, as in this account of an aspiring manager with nothing to offer but some personal dreams:

Don Carlos was in the village Saturday, having come to get a cast for a circle somewhere in the west. Having the idea (only), he required an agent with car to finance himself while booking towns and soliciting merchants, a director with scripts, a comedian with two sets of dye scenery, and a leading team with a 7-passenger car to haul the company to the base in the west. [19 Nov. 1936, 1]

In the following issue, editor Bruno found it necessary to assert emphatically the truth of the whole Carlos affair:

A number of letters received question the authenticity of last week's item relative to the would-be manager who had only the idea with which to open a circle. It was considered an exaggeration. But, unfortunately, it wasn't. And, more unfortunately, there were actors who gave the venture consideration. Perhaps you'd be surprised to know that many circles have been opened on no more than Carlos offered—just the idea. (*BBB,* 26 Nov., 3)

Although the opportunity to elevate oneself to the ranks of theater management could be accomplished through circle stock, the process became a frequent subject for both humor and genuine concern. Early in the fall of 1936, after surveying the approaching circle stock season, Bruno summed up the problem succinctly: "If all the circles planned for next winter were placed end to end, there would still be too many of them" (*BBB,* 20 Aug., 3).

Circle stock also provided refuge for different types of touring companies plagued with economic difficulties. Because circle stock represented a quick way to cut losses and to begin generating income again, frequently various types of rep companies resorted to circle stock to make ends meet. In some instances the financial problems arose from poor business at the box office, as in late 1929 when the Lanshaw Players opened a circle in central Kansas after struggling for three weeks with three-night stands in western Kansas to "far from satisfactory results" (*BBB,* 31 Oct., 4). A few weeks later the Pearson-Gotchy company resorted to a circle in central Iowa, "having found three night stands anything but profitable" (*BBB,* 14 Nov., 4). These experiences, in addition to similar ones throughout the rep field, prompted Bill Bruno to editorialize in 1929,

Several optimistic managers of small shows have this winter season again attempted to put over three night stand shows and as is the result in ninety-nine out of a hundred cases where this is attempted, have failed.... It has always failed in the smaller towns, but still managers will try it.

In a few cases the managers realized that they were up against a losing proposition and booked a circle, which in almost every case proved successful ... and it is entirely probable that others—even those attempting week stands in the small towns—will follow their example. [*BBB,* 14 Nov., 6]

At times the need sounded more urgent, as in the case of the Larry Nolan Players, who "after seven weeks of three nights and week stands to from poor to fair business" opened a circle in Colorado following a "weeks layoff for preparation" (*BBB,* 30 Jan. 1930, 3).

Thus circle stock provided a reliable safety net for a manager in need, irrespective of the reason. The Joe Marion Show provides a vivid example of fortunes turning for the worse after ending a circle stock run, forcing the troupe to return to circuit playing. The show, having finished more than one year on a circle in central Nebraska, lasted only two weeks under canvas.

The opening occurred in Columbus to three nights of bad business in spite of the fact that Marion and his company were great favorites in the town and had usually played to big business in the theatre. The show moved to Norfolk for a week, but business is said to have been so very bad that Marion closed after playing Thursday night of last week and is reported to have gone to headquarters in York for the purpose of lining up another circle until his Fair dates start next month. [*BBB,* 17 July 1930, 2]

Management also resorted to circle stock following various disasters outside the company's control. Rep veterans resolutely agree that of all the challenges faced by tent show managers, none greater existed than the danger of high winds and violent storms. And when the destructive forces of nature did strike, circle stock often rose from the debris—as in the case of Harry Dunbar, who lost his tent while performing in Brush, Colorado, on 31 May 1930,

the top being reduced to ribbons by a wind storm that reached almost cyclonic proportions just after close of the matinee performance. Not only was the top completely demolished, but even the equipment was ruined and to such extent that Dunbar has abandoned further tent operation for the summer, having cancelled all booked dates. [*BBB,* 12 June, 2]

With items worth salvaging stored in Brush, a few performances took place in both Brush and Fort Morgan while Dunbar reorganized his Colorado circle from previous seasons. During the remainder of the summer the company circled out of Fort Morgan. With traditional trouper determination, Dunbar finished his account by stressing, "We can't quit, because a quitter never gets anywhere." Soon after reporting on Dunbar's misfortune and following a similar "blow down" in Huntington, Oregon, *Bill Bruno's Bulletin* recorded that Don's Comedians were attempting to recover from their calamity by organizing "a circle of towns for the balance of the summer" (5 June 1930, 3).

Throughout its history, the economic soundness of circle stock provided a major incentive for adopting this method of management. But since the practice of circle touring stretches from the first decade of this century through the 1950s, turning to this technique might signal anything from a businesslike move to maximize profits by reducing expenses to that of desperate performers attempting to avoid unemployment and soup lines. Regardless of the motivation, the financial benefits offered by circle stock remained constant, although with such clear-cut economic advantages, one might question why circle stock did not come to dominate the touring rep theater system. Certainly for some performers and companies, its general dependence upon the people and towns found in America's rural areas did not elicit a positive response. And strictly from an economic angle, while circle stock provided the safety net of a solid and stable format of touring, it could not generate large amounts of income primarily because of the low admission prices it charged and the small centers of population it based its existence upon. In the estimation of circuit pioneer Winn Trousdale, "No manager ever made a fortune in operating them ... but the circles have served their purpose" (Mickel, 25).

Tied closely to these clear financial advantages of circle stock are a series of operational advantages that also added to the fiscal strength of the method, albeit in less direct ways but nevertheless further enhancing the system's attractiveness.

First, circle stock provided a technique to maintain together a veteran company through lean times. Throughout most of its history, circle stock aided countless performers in subsisting through the long months of winter until the beginning of the more lucrative tent season in the late spring. In using a circle company of veteran performers to bridge the two distinct seasons, managers discovered that the start-up of the profitable summer tent season could, on occasion, be accomplished without the loss of a single night, requiring no "dark" time for organization and rehearsal. When managers accomplished such a smooth transition, they often notified the trade publications and crowed a bit. Such events occurred more often than not because performers frequently stayed with a single company for many years—flowing from the tent season to the circle season and returning to the tent season—a pattern repeated again and again. Dale Madden, Sr., proudly notes that the Madden and Stillian Players "once operated with the same cast for seven years, winter and summer." In limiting turnover with companies, circle stock frequently supported more profitable types of performing.

Normally troupes that alternated between the tent and circle seasons were personally led by their managers through the winter circle campaign. Contrary to this practice, various performers recall that the management of the Roberson-Gifford tent rep company encouraged a core group from their summer canvas season to use the company's scenery, scripts, and props during the winter months, at which time the actors performed under their own management. By allowing this small unit to play circle stock in the winter, the Roberson-Gifford management helped ensure that a nucleus of their top performers remained together, ready to return to performing under canvas for the following summer.

The support that circle stock could provide, however, worked in areas other than merely personnel. A typical tent season required a minimum of six or seven bills to make up a week-long repertory, but the season normally used more than that number because plays that did not go over well with the summer audiences were dropped and replaced. To the benefit of a future tent season, a considerable number of scripts and specialties could be tested first before receptive audiences during a winter circle season.

Dot Sund of the Sun Players believes that circle stock allowed her

Sun Players, 1956, heading directly to circle stock following the tent season (collection of the author).

husband, Jess, and her to "see what bills would go best with the audience; what kind of reception we would get." At the conclusion of a typical Sun Players' winter circle season, "we would be up in our seven shows" to open the tent campaign. She further adds, "We didn't have to have a two-weeks rehearsal as we were already up in the shows." Concerning the use of circle stock to develop and practice new material, Frank Wiziarde recalls the opportunities it provided for those performing specialty acts:

> Of course circle stock was a field day for specialty people—the people who did between-the-acts song and dance, monologues, etc. It was a good spot to break in new material, to try out material; to be able to project what you were going to do new for the new season. And it was a lot of fun, I mean, you had a chance to "do your thing" without too much criticism. It didn't make a whole lot of difference—people loved it.

Similarly, Dick Elsenpeter, who performed with such circle companies as Tilton's Comedians and the Roberson-Gifford Stock Company under the stage name Dick Ellis, feels circle stock played an important role as a necessary "testing ground" for new material. He remembers that in "the old days, you'd run it up [on the circle] and then if it 'played,' you'd play it in permanent stock. Or when you went into the summer, include that in your [tent] rep."

For some companies, instead of playing circle throughout the entire winter, circle stock represented only a short preparation period prior to opening under canvas. In this respect circle touring provided an economical method to shape and prepare a largely new company for the rigors of the summer season. In 1937 the Orpheum Players of Ohio planned on seven weeks of circle prior to a mid–May opening in the tent (*BBB,* 4 Mar., 1). That same year the Crago Players planned on six weeks of circle work prior to going under canvas for the summer (*BBB,* 11 Mar., 4). Periodically trade ads for companies emphasized that their use of circle stock prepared them for summer business. A 1940 ad for the Wallace Bruce Players of Kansas states, "Circle now, tent in summer. NOTE–Bills we play on circle will use in summer rep" (*BBB,* 18 Jan., 2). With sights on a slightly different goal, Kelly Masters once played circle for four weeks prior to opening a permanent stock engagement in Columbus, Mississippi, where he planned on presenting two bills a week (*BBB,* 18 Feb. 1937, 1).

The ease in changing the location of a circle company is the basis of yet an additional operational advantage found in circle stock. In times of falling box office revenue, the relative speed and simplicity with which a company could abandon a circle helped a manager maintain the troupe's profitability. When an area was "played out," a change in headquarters soon followed. This might mean moving only to another section of the same state, or moving farther. Unless the circle utilized a large two- or three-week circuit, the distance of such a change remained relatively short because the geographic territory needed for a circle normally remained considerably smaller than that required for a tent rep company. Jess and Dot Sund confess that when once considering a difficult lengthy jump across several state lines into Nebraska to set up a circle, knowing the new territory and potential audience took precedence over the distance. In planning the move, the Sunds were obliged to "get a map out" and study it for an appropriate base town and surrounding communities. As for the people of the general area, no decisions had to be made: "There's Bohemians over there. They're good show people; very faithful to you."

Some companies even capitalized upon changing locations, regularly moving between two or more bases, literally creating a "circuit of circles." Once the LaThey-Rush troupe in an area around Texarkana, Texas, established three two-week circuits, each with a different base, therefore requiring a new bill only every six weeks (*BBB,* 2 Apr. 1936, 3). In a different fashion, Kelly Masters at one time established five two-week circles in Mississippi, playing each in successive rotation. In this way, he claimed, "We do not show them to death and the customers seem glad to have us come back" (*BBB,* 5 Aug. 1937, 1). In yet another variation, B. L. Dickson, whose circle territory included Minnesota and South Dakota, maintained the policy of remaining no longer than ten weeks on any of his four established circles, thus making a single rotation of Dickson's total circuit 40 weeks in length (*BBB,* 7 Jan. 1937, 1).

Yet the advantageous uses of circle stock theater went far beyond an ability only to prepare for other forms of touring. Some groups found circle stock so much to their liking that they exclusively followed circuit playing.

The number of theater companies that elected solely to play circle stock, either on a partial year or full year basis, definitely grew as economic conditions worsened during the Depression era and as the investment necessary for canvas touring became too prohibitive for most.

The success of units that employed variations of the basic format, such as presenting both a show and a dance, led many groups to follow suit and pursue only this style of circle stock. Widely known companies from the show-and-dance ranks included the

Publicity photograph of Dick Elsenpeter, new to rep and circle touring; circa 1945 (courtesy of the Museum of Repertoire Americana).

many different units of the "Happy Bill" Balthazor Radio Players (also found in print as Balthazer) and the ubiquitous "Big Ole" troupes of northern regions of the Midwest.

Especially noted for playing conventional circle stock for extended periods of time were the Henry and Ruby Neal Players, who specialized in circle touring in the 1930s throughout Colorado and Kansas. During the final years of the circuits in the 1950s, Tilton's Comedians faced the challenge of playing circle year-round with few exceptions.[2] The following schedule, based on records compiled by company member Don Weage, substantiates frequent changes in circuits which owner/manager Mid Tilton apparently found necessary to maintain the troupe's profitability.[3] For one uninterrupted period of nearly 19 months, performances were based out of the following communities: East Peoria, Illinois (November–December 1949); Ashkum, Illinois (January–February 1950); Sandwich, Illinois (March–April 1950); Wisconsin Rapids, Wisconsin (May–August 1950); Mason City, Iowa (September–December 1950); and Fort

Dodge, Iowa (January–early May 1951). Weage also notes that contrary to the usual pattern of this period, Tilton's Comedians did appear under canvas during late May to September 1951 and from May to mid–September 1952, taking advantage of a talented ensemble at that time. Following each of these two departures from manager Tilton's basic practice, the Comedians returned to circle stock.

Due to these financial and operational advantages, circle touring developed a reputation for being hale and hearty—an ability to provide a continuing source of employment and income through both flush and lean times. Circle stock frequently demonstrated that, with proper effort and good conditions, circuits could be maintained for seemingly indefinite periods.

Some extended circle tours were legendary, dutifully recalled in "Remember when..." columns, such as Jim and Hattie Dougherty's three continuous years of playing one circle of wee Minnesota towns (*BBB*, 17 July 1930, 5). Veteran performer Jay Bee Flesner recalls that the Jack and Lucille Collier Players trouped 105 consecutive weeks out of the small burg of Goff, Kansas, in the 1930s. *Bob Feagin's Bulletin* reports that other companies, such as the Town Hall Players of Wisconsin, reached an impressive four years of nonstop circle performances primarily because of moving their base from one community to another (5 Feb. 1941, 1).[4]

Hardly less impressive are such recorded runs as 42 weeks for the Hazel Hurd Company in Texas (*BBB*, 27 June 1929, 8); or 47 weeks for the Christy Obrecht circle stock in Minnesota (*Billboard*, 24 Dec. 1927, 32); or 52 weeks (and "STILL GOING STRONG!") for the Joe Marion Players in Nebraska (*BBB*, 29 May 1930, 16). Normally periods of employing circle stock were shorter. Depending entirely upon the needs of the company, from 16 to 24 weeks of circle touring could be considered average during the late fall and winter months, before playing under canvas during late spring, summer, and early fall.

Whether it merely prepared the way for other forms of touring or made a go of it for an extended period of time, circle stock met real economic needs of performers attempting to maintain their livelihood through varying and frequently difficult conditions. The flexibility of the circle touring format unquestionably provided managers with an ability to respond effectively to demands of the marketplace.

Interpersonal Motivations

Whereas the primary motivation for circle stock always centered upon financial considerations, a second major area of influences can be described as interpersonal. These elements remain very vivid in the minds of many veteran troupers; yet however much, they cannot be accurately measured in terms of profit or loss.

While numerous tales recount the hardships and difficulties of circle touring, for many troupers circle stock held a particular charm. Playing circle demanded of the performers many long hours of line study, rehearsal, travel, set up, performance, and tear down, which placed one in nearly constant contact with the rest of the company. Undoubtedly the everyday camaraderie of a circle troupe enabled many to make it through such challenging times. A member of a circle unit (established along commonwealth lines) wrote to editor Bill Bruno in early 1930 primarily describing the season but also highlighting a feeling experienced by many other circle performers:

Bob Feagin, rep performer, playwright, and founding coeditor of *Bob Feagin's Bulletin* (courtesy of the Museum of Repertoire Americana).

> While we have not gotten rich we have managed to make a fair salary, which you must admit is better than waiting around Kansas City through the winter. In addition, it has been one of the most pleasant engagements I was ever on, the people being, all of them, real troupers. [*BBB*, 27 Feb., 7][5]

Similar testimonials of troupers rank circle stock high among their best experiences in the profession. Wendell Poe joined the Roberson-Gifford Stock Company playing circle stock in 1949 and soon discovered "a special family." He recalls, "With few and minor exceptions, we all worked well together. We ate together, laughed together, cried together, rode to the towns together, put the set together together," concluding, "It really was a marvelous experience." Reflecting on her circle experiences, Noreen Depenbrink states that "despite all the hardships we sometimes had to endure, I'd do it all over again." Dick Elsenpeter goes so far in his appreciation of circle stock to refer to it lovingly as a "lazy" method of performing. Though the rehearsal and performance process demanded considerable

Gladys Feagin, rep performer and founding coeditor of *Bob Feagin's Bulletin* (courtesy of the Museum of Repertoire Americana).

time, "when you learned your part, you had the time free to yourself then." He elaborates:

> Once you were into circle stock and you got your first rehearsal under the belt, I could usually go and learn my lines in the whole play that night. From then on your rehearsals were just honing; putting the lines into place. After the second rehearsal usually you knew your part, and so therefore you could work on your method of acting. I remember a fellow actor who just thought this was wonderful, what a training ground. Every night he would do the part a little bit different, emphasize this word or that word; inflections would change. He really worked at his craft. Therefore I say it was a lazy method. You could learn the lines and then you were free to work at your craft, and really that's something!

From a rather practical viewpoint, Jay Bee Flesner suggests that the labor necessary to run a circle stock—"working together from 11:00 A.M. to midnight, six days a week"—in itself produced a cooperative attitude. According to Flesner, "There had to be camaraderie, there had to be fellowship, they had to get along. Anybody that couldn't get along with others, they didn't stay very long." Whatever the cause, for many performers the circle stock experience worked exceptionally well, and the remembrances are particularly sweet.

However, in reviewing the testimony of these veterans concerning the fellowship they experienced when performing circle stock, one should not believe that the method itself provided for a friendlier working environment than, say, week-long rep or one-night productions. Certainly these positive remembrances rely in large part on the composition of individuals within a company. Also the coherence among individuals that frequently takes place when a group is faced with a difficult task—many circle experiences certainly seem to fit into this category—could be responsible for these positive reflections upon circle stock.

This bonding notwithstanding, for some the memories of circle stock are rather bittersweet. Barbara Brooks Emory, while appreciating her circle experience, relates it to living in "a tight little world of our own." Outside of contact with the community during the performance, the "towners" (read townspeople) for her sake "didn't really exist." She concludes, "In fact, the outside world hardly mattered. It was usually a quite congenial group, with an occasional 'beer bust' in someone's room, practical jokes and always a card game going on somewhere." Don Weage found circle stock to be "an odd, unpredictable and sometimes unique way of life," concluding that "for some unfathomable reason, we loved it." He continues:

> But all of the hardships (and they were considerable) we were willing to put up with because it gave us the opportunity to do what we wanted to do for a couple of hours each evening. Looking back on it, I find it a little difficult to understand. But of course, the things that a twenty year old and a twenty-five and even thirty year old understands are not necessarily the same as those which a sixty year old understands. Perhaps it would be more accurate to say that the things which a twenty-five year old values are not necessarily the same as those which are valued by a sixty year old.

This special attachment can be found among many who experienced circle stock, and for some it still remains difficult to explain. Possibly fondness grows from remembering not only the everyday companionship among a company but also occasions of special fellowship—much like that of the Gould Players in Michigan celebrating Thanksgiving in 1924 at the farm of manager Lloyd T. Gould.

> Dinner was served at noon to the members of the company and a few guests. In the evening the entire group motored to Belding, the regular Thursday night town in their circle stock route, where they played to a capacity house. After the performance everyone went back to the farm, where the radio entertainment, dancing and visiting took place until the wee small hours. [*Billboard,* 13 Dec., 58]

A few years later, a report on the 1927 Christmas party of the Chick Boyes Players records an appropriate festive mood, even though Mrs. Boyes was hospitalized at the time:

> A lovely Christmas banquet was enjoyed by the Chick Boyes Players at the Home Bakery on Christmas eve. The members of the company gathered after the show at Bruning [Nebraska] and following an exchange of presents were served a delectable three-course supper. The opening of the comical gifts provoked much mirth from the crowd and was fully enjoyed. The banquet table was beautifully decorated with a Christmas tree and streamers leading to each place. A row of candles down the center of the table served to accentuate the Christmas spirit. After all had partaken to capacity the gathering broke up, each delightfully applauding the party. [*Hebron* (Nebraska) *Register-Champion,* 29 Dec., 1]

On occasion the citizens of rural America showed their thanks for the contribution that circle stock made to their lives in a way that they possibly do best—with a small-town gathering filled with food and fellowship. Once, following the completion of their circle season during the mid–1930s,

Florence Boyes, wife of Chick Boyes and featured performer with the Chick Boyes Players (courtesy of the Otoe County [Nebraska] Museum of Memories).

the Tilton-Guthrie Players were honored with a "farewell party and pot-luck supper" in Buda, Illinois. A meal of "baked ham, supplemented by covered dishes and delicacies" started the festivities.

> After the meal L. C. Stutzman, on behalf of the sponsors, expressed praise for the kind of entertainment the show people had furnished and invited them for a return engagement another year. Mr. McClure [representing the company] and Mr. Tilton made appropriate responses and voiced their appreciation of the way the people of the town had made them feel at home among friendly neighbors during their stay here. [MRA Collection, unidentified newspaper clipping]

The evening's program also included a lengthy vocal serenade of the company by community members, with the rest of the time spent in "visiting and playing games." Before the affair ended, the men of the company returned the favor with a series of vocal selections as a farewell tribute.

Such special occasions were not a guaranteed part of the circle stock experience, but many records of such events exist. Yet regardless of the personal feelings and experiences of the troupers off stage, the public's interest mainly centered on the performances by these professionals, typically reacting to a company's efforts in a very positive fashion. Repeated evidence of the consistent and often overwhelming appreciative response to the circle stock troupes supports the obvious conclusion that few, if any, other forms of live entertainment visited these small towns and hamlets. The circle companies met a real need of rural America, and the public in return showered the performers with both applause and loyalty.

Dick Wolever relates an experience in which a community's response demonstrated such a genuine outpouring of support. For a few seasons in the 1930s, Wolever and his brother, Jack, operated their own tent show in Kansas during the summer. In the winter they circled out of their hometown, Fredonia. Once, having an open date, the brothers decided to play the nearby small town of Longton, Kansas, with a population of 800–900.

> We got in late the first time we played it. We had to go find the man who had the power company and put up a deposit and have him turn the lights on. We had to have people bring in wood for a wood stove and the theatre was not really dirty but dust over everything and we didn't have time to clean it.

That evening the brothers had no idea of what size of audience to expect, although they had advertised well in the area. Wolever estimates about 150 people attended the performance and apparently enjoyed the show. With this beginning, the two decided that the town would be tried at least once more.

> So the next Wednesday we went a little early so we could get things in order. When we got there we found out the electricity was on, donated by the power company. We met the mayor, a very nice man, and they had gotten together and the theatre was spotless. They had washed all the glass in the box office and everything was spotless. They had gone back stage and cleaned it up beautifully.
>
> About 7:30 P.M. they started coming and by 8:00 P.M. we couldn't get any more people in. There must have been 400 or 500.

From that point onward, Longton became a regular stop on the circle for the remainder of the winter; "Standing Room Only" audiences soon became the norm. But the community's positive response did not end with each performance.

> They would meet us as we came into town; they wanted to carry your scenery, your luggage, your wardrobe, anything you had. You couldn't give them a pass; they wanted to buy their own tickets so we would be sure to come back. And it was very gratifying because everything we did they loved.

Similar demonstrations of support for circle stock were not infrequent, coming in a variety of forms. A unique response is recorded by editor Bob Feagin concerning the Guthrie Players under the management of Bill Guthrie:

> While visiting with Bill in Peoria he showed us something that we have never seen before in all our years of trouping. On the last performance, on the circle, Bill was handed a formal petition with 500 signatures, requesting the return of the company next season. That's leaving 'em right, Bill. [*BFB,* 16 Apr. 1941, 1]

To many citizens of countless small rural communities, the weekly or bimonthly visit of the players evolved into an event of importance in their lives. Typically a strong relationship developed between the circle company and audience members. Frank Wiziarde believes this bonding was crucial, as the primary factor in a successful circle was your "regulars"—just like those who tune in on the same television program every week, you had the same people who would show, I mean irregardless. They were fans and they had their personal favorite.

The general consensus among troupers is that circle stock, because of its regular visits to the communities of a circuit, created a stronger and closer relationship between the townspeople and the performers than in any other form of rep theater. Indeed, no other theatrical touring method of the era made as frequent and as consistent stops in the communities of the rural countryside as did circle stock. As one experienced performer suggests, "We were a bright spot in their weekly existence." As early as 1921 *Billboard* recognized the impact of this repeated exposure of the circle performers to the public: "Audiences come to know and admire their regular entertainers and increase their admiration for the members of the company the more and the oftener they see them" (12 Nov., 26).

As community members took interest in different members of the company, food frequently became a gesture of support and appreciation. Invitations for a good home-cooked meal were often extended to the performers. Dave Koch (who used the stage name Dave Castle) recalls from his circle experience in the mid–1950s that a free meal for the performers could garner the hosts "some free tickets," along with the much sought after ability to say "we know those actors." Mercedes Brunk deliciously remembers that when the Collier Players performed in a Wisconsin tavern during the 1930s, a special treat often awaited them. Normally following each performance the tavern keeper's wife invited the company to her kitchen, warmed by her large wood cooking stove, and once there the performers beheld a long table laden with "the most wonderful German food and loads of wonderful Wisconsin cheese."

R. Norton Walther (known in the business as Buddy Norton) still fondly recalls that in the 1930s, while a young actor doing juvenile parts (along with dancing and comedy specialties) on the Frank Wilder circle in Minnesota, he received a most heartwarming going-away gift shortly before his final departure from the headquarters town. When he was ready to leave his hotel for the train station, a farm family who had taken a keen interest in him "came in from the country and they brought a suit box filled with sandwiches, cookies and all kinds of homemade goodies that they had made for me." His was undoubtedly a long train ride made more pleasant through the kindness of some who were no longer strangers. Such demonstrations of support were tangible signs of the importance of the players to the communities.

Although financial considerations undoubtedly took precedence, we should not underestimate the impact of audience support and response in motivating both the establishment and the continuance of circle stock operations. Certainly from a performer's standpoint, the eager and attentive circle stock audiences that jammed the hall or opera house every time the company appeared were deeply appreciated. Countless pairs of eyes intently trained on the performers clearly indicated that they were cherished members of each and every community they played in. Dick Elsenpeter once voiced concern to his friend and fellow circle performer Don Weage that no one from their cast of Tilton's Comedians had ever "made it big." Elsenpeter still distinctly recalls Weage's reply: "Dick, we *did* make it big. We were stars, do you realize that? When you stepped on stage they applauded. Do you realize what that is?" Reflecting on the reply, Elsenpeter concludes, "So as far as being successful, we were as successful as anybody could be."

Certainly a good part of the general public's positive response to circle stock developed out of the high image it consistently maintained in their eyes. During the circle era the reputation of a company maintained great importance, and appropriateness, decency, and cleanliness endured as absolute standards strictly adhered to, leaving virtually no room for suggestive double entendre or innuendo. Most companies followed the old trouper's adage: "A hell and a damn never brought anybody to the theater, but it has kept a few away."

A positive word from the local newspaper editor many times provided a circle's best advertisement, with every company working to develop and maintain a cordial relationship with the area press. The Chick Boyes Players stands as one of the Midwest's perennially successful groups in this regard. Note, for example, that the positive editorial support that consistently greeted them throughout the state of Nebraska during the 1924-25 winter season centered largely on the question of economical and appropriate family entertainment:

> These are all good clean shows, put on by a good clean company and are worthy of your patronage. When in the cities you pay two or three dollars for a show and you will not get a bit more enjoyment out of it than you will at a Chick Boyes show. [*Weekly Arbor State,* 12 Dec. 1924, 8]

> Most everyone is glad when the time rolls around for them to show up. They have shown by past performances that putting on poor shows is entirely out of their line of business. We can always rely on "Chick" and his people to put on something worth twice the admission price. [*Sutton News,* 2 Jan. 1925, 1]

> This popular company is composed of ladies and gentlemen and all who attend their plays here can do so with the satisfied feeling that nothing will be said or done to offend. [*Harvard Courier,* 9 Apr. 1925, 1]

> Before the last act [of *The Rose of Killarney*] Mr. Boyes appeared and thanked the audience for its patronage during the past season.... Mr. Boyes stated that their plays would continue to be clean, and added that when the company couldn't secure clean plays they wouldn't secure any. [*York Daily News-Times,* 23 Apr. 1925, 3]

Upon the return of the Chick Boyes troupe to Hebron, Nebraska, on their winter circle of 1925-26, the public responded by packing the theater and the local editor greeted them with acclaim: "Chick's people won a place in the community during the past two years, and folks have been looking forward to their coming" (*Hebron Register-Champion,* 3 Dec. 1925, 1). Following yet another successful season, Chick Boyes particularly pleased the public by mounting a traditional favorite of the rep companies and audiences alike, *Saintly Hypocrites and Honest Sinners.*

In addition to offering the kind of productions desired, local editors appreciated the economic benefits brought by the players to their cities and hamlets. The *Sutton News* outlined the impact of the Boyes troupe in this fashion:

> The regular appearance of a company of this high character is a distinct asset to a town. Folks come for many miles to take in the Boyes show each time they made their appearance in Sutton. That's what we want–to make Sutton headquarters for a continually enlarging territory. We certainly hope to have the Chick Boyes Players back with us next fall, as they make a valuable contribution to Sutton. [30 Apr. 1926, 1]

One reason for the consistent success of the Chick Boyes Players and many other similar companies involved their efforts to make the community feel, if for only the day they visited, that the players "belonged" to them. This closeness could be accomplished through various methods. Players did try to be visible in a town on performance day and to reserve some purchases (food, gas, auto maintenance) for businesses there. Soldiers returning to a circle company from the Second World War were often instructed by management to wear their uniforms for a number of rotations of the circuit. This helped announce that a veteran held a position in the company and drew upon patriotic fervor.

Many companies attempted to cement the union between actors and towners in more specific ways. For example, some troupes adopted the practice of giving free dancing lessons to the community. The children of Lew Henderson recall that the periodic addition of dance instruction to the schedule required the company to arrive at the performance site early. As the children of the area left school they came directly to the theater for their one-hour lesson, which on occasion included both tap dancing and acrobatics coaching. The wife of Dale Madden, Sr., described by her husband as "a fine dancer, a lovable woman, and a great favorite with the customers," also frequently conducted dance classes in towns in which the Madden and Stillian Players performed. Madden remembers that this practice provided both a "boon to business and good feelings." Obviously such instruction served dual purposes: it advertised the company by making their presence known, but just as important it helped link the community to a company.

One method Chick Boyes and others used for uniting troupe and town involved the audience in play selection. An undated program from the 1930s used on a western Kansas circle operated by Chick Boyes devotes two of its four pages to information for the audience, including a questionnaire seeking choices of plays to be performed:

> It might be interesting to you to know that this is the tenth consecutive season for the Chick Boyes Players of circle stock. The Chick Boyes Players is the oldest established circle stock company in the middle west. We want you to feel that this is your company, a home company owned by home people.
> A partial list of the plays that will be selected by you for presentation are given in the following list. Check off the plays that you would like to see and leave the programme at the box office. In this way, we may be able to offer the plays that you will like.[6]

Following this introduction, a list of 14 plays included a blend of rep standards and newer scripts, among them: *Six Cylinder Love, The Bird of Paradise, The Awakening of John Slater, Pollyanna, Why Men Leave Home, Little Peggy O'Moore, Is Zat So?,* and *Getting Gertie's Garter.* The questionnaire continued:

> All suggestions to Plays that you would like to see will receive our attention. Get the Habit of seeing each one of the plays that will be presented here every other week.... Theatre parties given special attention. It's a nice way to entertain your friends.

Newsy information about the company and cast members filled the final page of the program. At one point the audience was reminded, "Any question relative to the plays or players may be asked," along with assuring them that the questions "will be answered upon next week's programme." This final page concludes with one of Chick's typically pithy thoughts and certainly a motto for the entire circle stock profession: "Remember: Pleasing You Keeps Us In Business." Without a doubt such sentiment always remained an essential part of the business strategy employed by any successful circle stock manager.

In many respects, the story of circle touring remains a rather simple one. Circle stock provided one vehicle through which countless small groups of dedicated theater professionals brought entertainment to the hinterlands, often bonding actors with the audience to a most significant degree. Hardships were ever present, to be sure, but they were overlooked or overcome because of the driving force of performers wishing to practice their craft before appreciative audiences. Normally the general public consistently returned to the troupers' periodic appearances, drawn back partly by the glamor and charm of it all, partly by the personalities of the performers involved. But of equal or greater importance remained the common link between performer and audience–the circle stock performance.

4

Satisfied Patrons Always Come Back

R EP PLAYWRIGHT AND PLAY BROKER Herschell Weiss offered
in a 1930 advertisement an appropriate motto for the circle stock
performance: "A Play is the merchandise a manager sells to his
patrons and Satisfied Patrons always come back" (*BBB,* 6 Mar., 10). For the
purposes of this investigation one might want to exchange the word *play*
for *performance,* for as professionals, circle stock troupers sold an entire performance, not just a play. Interspersed throughout the play were vaude-
ville-like acts, presented by the cast during scene or act breaks. In addition,
a musical overture or even a short musical production, complete unto itself, might begin the festivities. Yet it was largely the play per se that drew
the audience to the performance.

This exploration attempts to describe the circle stock performance—
how plays, specialty acts, and additional musical entertainment were chosen to provide the kinds of entertainment desired by the audiences.
As such, the descriptions are not based on a literary or cultural consideration but rather center on the down-to-earth business decisions faced by circle stock managers as they planned their programs. Clearly the performance catered to audience desires, and the box office provided the
company with the all-important reading of the public's interest and
response. Simply put, the circle stock performance required a positive
reception because the company's existence relied upon the continued
patronage of the public. As one veteran manager was fond of saying, "The
only reason for bad business is the audience doesn't like what you're
doing." In the following, the important elements of the circle stock performance will be investigated, beginning with a company's primary concern—
the choice of plays.

Play Selection

To date, little research has been conducted concerning the plays used by tent rep and circle stock companies. Long considered of little importance, these plays are now attracting increased interest. William Slout's research, entitled "Traveling Repertoire: From Shakespeare to Sherman" (1987), outlines recent explorations into the plays of rep. Primarily based on information recorded in *Billboard* between 1915 and 1929, Slout's findings reveal, first of all, the sheer quantity of drama used by the rep companies. Even though the majority of managers did not regularly report their season's repertory to *Billboard,* Slout found published "correspondence by over 200 different shows, which included announcements of plays being used; and which, throughout the decade and a half, amounted to well over 1,000 play titles" (11).

In studying this literature, one finds little evidence that the various forms of touring rep preferred certain kinds of plays over others. Veteran performers consistently reject the notion that any substantial differences existed between the plays used in tent or house rep and those used in circle stock; a shared pool of drama existed from which all of these varieties of small-time show business drew. For as previously noted, during its existence circle stock maintained a symbiotic relationship with tent rep, as a significant number of companies continually flowed from the outdoor tent productions into the indoor circle season and back again to performing under canvas.[1] A different repertory for each form of touring would have made such transitions considerably more challenging. At the center of what remained constant during these changes in touring styles were the plays themselves. Still, subtle differences did exist. Companies operating as show-and-dance circles, for example, often cut their plays significantly to allow additional time for the dance to follow.[2]

Because the majority of circle stock companies presented a different bill each week, the demand for scripts remained constant, bordering on the voracious. The plea for more scripts made in early 1928 on behalf of the entire industry by Paul English (then president of the Tent Repertoire Managers Protective Association) had certainly been heard before:

> I have just finished my fifth week of circuit stock and have played *Other People's Business* and *The Push* successfully. These two plays are splendid bills and I can cheerfully recommend them, but we cannot all use these plays as many repertoire companies play the same territory. I have read several plays, and very excellent ones, from the pen of the smaller playwrights but could not use them on account of their having been played to death in my territory. Now a word to the wise is sufficient. Mr. Small Playwright, why not progress? Get more plays and do not rest and expect your few good ones to last eternally. [*Billboard,* 3 Mar., 31]

This same appeal, in various permutations, echoed throughout the history of rep. Indeed, the demand for scripts even captured the notice of the news media. For example, note the comments as early as 1915 made by the editor of the *Vinton* (Iowa) *Review* when reviewing the Trousdale-Horne circle's production of *The Man From the West,* a comedy drama:

> The play is entirely different from any that has yet been offered by this company. In presenting a different play each week, it is necessary to offer plays of a great variety, and this company is always endeavoring to please every person who attends every play. [25 Feb., 5]

Through unrelenting effort the industry struggled forward, obtaining scripts to maintain its needs through whatever means necessary. In many instances, today these plays receive low marks for literary and artistic merit, but in their time they provided a sufficient response to the ever-pressing question "What is our next bill going to be?" Regardless of current critical opinion of these plays, it is important to discover what elements within them caused their wide acceptance by audiences. To answer these questions one needs to understand what kinds of plays a circle stock manager used and where he secured such scripts. In such an exploration one will notice both professional and amateur contributions, as well as both legal and illegal means of obtaining them, all of which are part of the varied tapestry of circle stock.[3]

In a panel discussion on the plays of rep held at the Museum of Repertoire Americana, veteran troupers once faced the question of what the general public found appealing in the plays they presented.[4] Two performers who responded found themselves at odds over an answer. Jay Bee Flesner felt the appeal of such plays rested in the familiar:

> The same things that interest the Iowa farmers today: mortgage on the farm, income, pregnant daughters, what kind of a crop they were going to have, everyday things glamorized for your audience. They didn't care about Broadway, they didn't care about New York City. The most popular plays were those that had the same problems that those Iowa farmers have out there today.

R. Norton Walther begged to differ, finding the appeal of the plays in the escape that they offered:

> A lot of them wanted to get away from those things that they put up with every day. They wanted to go see glamor and all of the stuff that Broadway shows and dress-up shows had. They wanted to get away from the everyday life.

However disparate these two viewpoints appear, they are not mutually exclusive. The plays of rep typically reflected the audience's need to see both a representation of life as they knew it and a representation of life that they dreamed of and for which they longed. Within this wide range, the plays of rep continually copied the virtues and morals of small-town America, reinforcing what was believed to be the wholesomeness of rural life. Not confrontational drama in the least, these plays carefully mirrored the audience's values, interests, beliefs, prejudices, concerns, and even their fantasies. At the same time, these plays demonstrated surprisingly varied plots and environments, since "an interest in local color themes encouraged settings of tropical islands, the north woods, western ranch lands, exotic Arabia, as well as the familiar and comfortable village and farm" (Slout, "Traveling Repertoire," 18–19).

An analysis of the various kinds of scripts offered in catalogs by play brokers to the circle troupes reveals some of the tendencies of the industry.[5] Relying on the classifications used by the firms themselves, one typically finds that the single largest category of scripts in such play catalogs–often composing 50 percent or more of the total offerings–is that of "comedy" and "comedy-drama." The second largest area, representing roughly 10–15 percent of each catalog, is normally found under the rubrics of "melodrama" and "melodramatic-farce." Other significant classifications (each one representing up to 10 percent of the offerings) include "drama," "mystery," "rural comedy," and the special category of "small cast" scripts. Classifications used even less frequently include "western," "tabloid," "farce," and "musical comedy." As these figures suggest, the primary purpose of rep theater was clearly understood to be entertainment. Even so, some managers staged productions not easily included in such categories. Today veteran troupers still identify Richard Henderson as a noted rep manager who obtained wide renown for frequently performing his version of *Faust* and also for staging on occasion a nine-person adaptation of *Othello.*

Perhaps the surest method to reveal the characteristics thought most desirable in these scripts is to observe the way in which they were marketed. For example, note some of the colorful copy advertising *A Texas Cattle King,* by small-time playwright Otto Johnson:

> Managers! Attention! Here's Your Bank Roll! ... 3 Acts, one exterior set; full cast 6–3, consistently doubles to 4–2. No steal, no hash-up, no trash, no filth. Feature Indian character, roaring Irish comedy male and female. Every character strong enough to feature. [*BBB,* 19 Dec. 1929, 4]

Beneath the surface hype, one can detect many of the major elements making a play desirable for use on circle stock. These include (1) manageable length, (2) simple scenery requirements, (3) ability to reduce the cast requirements, (4) original plot line, (5) cleanliness, (6) good solid characters, and (7) flexibility.

The length of the plays selected for presentation on circle stock affected not only the performers but the audience as well. Throughout its history, three-act plays remained the standard on circle stock, with the entire performance lasting from one and a half to two hours. This length of performance aided the majority of companies because they returned to their home base following each performance. As for audience members, a two-hour performance provided for an enjoyable evening of entertainment without keeping them up excessively late. This always remained especially important for the farm families in attendance, as an early rise the following morning would be required, as on all the other mornings of the week. Playwright John Lawrence once offered a highly specific prescription for the length of circle stock plays: "The first two acts should run approximately thirty minutes each and the third act about twenty-five minutes" (38).

Yet playwrights not well versed in the needs of the industry—once they realized that plays shorter than standard New York practice were required—sometimes overcompensated and skimped on length. By the early 1940s playwright Al W. Clark, reporting on the recent submissions of scripts to circle stock and tent rep companies, complained of the short length of the plays received, as "several came in of thirty or less typewritten pages to be played in three acts." This Clark found unacceptable since "sixty to eighty pages is the requirement" (39). Similarly Clark labeled the submission of one-act plays to touring companies as totally inappropriate, suggesting that such scripts be sent directly to a publishing firm.

In terms of scenery requirements, simplicity remained the most important criterion. The frequently cramped or virtually nonexistent backstage areas of the performance sites used for circle stock severely limited the ability to change scenery. Physical conditions normally dictated the use of plays with only a single setting.⁶ Restraints placed upon multiple settings also carried over to furnishings and stage effects.

> It is well not to specify any particular style of furniture or to call for too many special effects, otherwise some of the "Circles" will shy away from your play. You must understand that there is not much left for the managers after they pay the necessary expenses, so you had better omit rising moons, banquet scenes requiring perishable properties, Queen Anne furniture, and such. [Lawrence, 39]

Cast size limitations, possibly as much as any other aspect of circle stock, reflected an ongoing effort to save on costs. Yet in reducing the size of a company to its bare essentials, a manager faced the challenge of balancing the effect of minimizing expenses while still maintaining some sort of artistic integrity. Playwrights met this need by adopting new formulas to follow in writing for rep. So in the early 1930s when so many small circle companies struggled to exist, playwrights specifically emphasized "short cast" bills, a large percentage of them written for only three men and two women ("3-2"), along with similar male to female ratios such as "4-3" and "5-3." By 1929 the Don Melrose Exchange already offered "a weeks

Repertoire of Short Cast Plays that can be played with a cast of 3 men and 2 women and no doubles. All in One Set" (*BBB*, 25 Apr., 9).[7] As conditions worsened during the Depression era and as companies generally reduced in size in order to lower costs, such scripts greatly increased in demand and a larger supply followed. By the fall of 1940 the Bulletin Play Service announced an entire catalog of "new short cast plays of no mean proportions." Listing over 20 new plays with promises for additional entries, all of the plays required "no cutting, being written strictly for 4 and 2 and 3 and 2 casts" (*BBB*, 8 Aug., 3).[8]

Eventually a script calling for seven to eight cast members became accepted as the standard maximum for use on most circle stocks. In consequence, John Lawrence urged aspiring playwrights to maximize the flexibility of a script by arranging the characters "so that either a male or female can do the third woman part" (37). Maintaining flexibility within a script helped ensure its marketability.

As for content, the circle stock performance followed unquestioned standards of cleanliness within the industry. When giving advice to prospective playwrights outside of circle stock's active participants, Lawrence felt the need to remind would-be dramatists to keep their plays clean:

Advertisement publicizing Don Melrose's collection of short cast scripts, from *Bill Bruno's Bulletin,* 25 April 1929 (courtesy of the Museum of Repertoire Americana).

> You must remember to avoid any suggestive dialogue or situations. Also refrain from using any profanity as a large number of the performances are given in school auditoriums and a good percentage of the audience consists of school children. [37]

In similar fashion, Al Clark's advice excluded any plays "based on sex or with a sex angle." In concluding some remarks on the topic of decency and decorum, Clark placed his warning in easily understood terms: "You're not supposed to ruin little Nell in small towns" (39). In another forum Clark further warned:

In the average "circle" town the whole family turns out and no father wants to take his children to see and hear a show composed mainly of smut. If you cut out the suggestive scenes and lines [of "Broadway" plays] you have nothing left but the title. [*BBB,* 19 Dec. 1935, 22]

This is not to suggest, however, that sex did not provide a potent selling force in rep plays, for as Jere Mickel reminds us, "Puritanism encourages the prurient mind" (67). For instance, J. S. Angell advertised for the 1930 season a new play, *Today's Virtue or A Flapper's Confession,* by his daughter Ruth Angell Ross. A straightforward advertising headline drew attention to the play: "Managers! If your territory demands a play bordering on sex, here it is." The play's description provided a strange blend of traditional selling points mixed with the sensational:

A play that can be featured. It deals with sex from a different angle. No children allowed unless accompanied by parents. A play that ALL will like. It has plenty of Sensation, Comedy and Heart Interest. [*BBB,* 3 Apr. 1930, 8]

Oddly enough, the use of suggestive sounding titles in rep went largely tolerated, essentially because the plays themselves never fulfilled the promise. Plays such as *Where's My Teddy, Getting Gertie's Garter, Up in Mabel's Room,* and *Why Girls Walk Home* were, in fact, bland admonitions to the straight and narrow. When Al Trahern produced *Up in Mabel's Room* on Long Island in 1921, a local editor playfully argued for the proper nature of the play:

Built up around a dainty article of women's wear, it caused much discussion at first as to the propriety of the play, the final decision resulting in its favor. There is really nothing suggestive in the piece unless the mere exhibition of the aforesaid dainty article of women's wear may be termed such; but then, like garments (it is said to be a chemise) are to be seen nowadays in most any clothing store window. In point of fact it simply shows how much real honest-to-goodness fun may be gotten out of so simple and innocent a garment as a woman's—ahem. [*Suffolk County News,* 10 June, 1]

Such titles, however, did cause concern at times, as seen in the following event involving a local newspaper editor reacting to the featured plays of the Davidson Players during one of their tent seasons. Recalling the previous year's feature play with a suggestive title and the current feature play with a similarly styled title, the concerned editor exclaimed, "What are you going to have her take off next year?" (*BBB,* 18 July 1929, 5). At the very least, confusion did present itself with such like sounding titles: "*Twin Beds* should not be confused with *Parlor, Bedroom and Bath* nor *Breakfast in Bed,* both of which have already been produced by the Trahern Company" (*Suffolk County News,* 28 Apr. 1922, 1).

Apart from cleanliness, flexibility provided the most important criterion for the success of a script on circle stock. Because the strength of a company rested squarely on the talents of the individual members of the troupe, a script allowing for a diversity of abilities quickly became more likely to be used. As previously noted, such flexibility included ways easily to change the cast size or to alter the scenic requirements. But just as important, a carefully constructed and balanced script also provided the flexibility of highlighting a character within the play according to the strengths of a particular company—the claim present in the often repeated phrase "Every character strong enough to feature."

In addition to these characteristics, as a rule rep playwrights desired to instill in their efforts the quality of "afterdraft"—the ability of a play to draw the audience back to subsequent performances. In tent or house rep, the sole importance of afterdraft existed for the duration of the stay in that community, be it six or seven days. But in circle stock, the concept of afterdraft extended over a longer period of time, in a sense reaching multiple months or even years.

Unidentified character actress with the Chick Boyes Players (courtesy of the Otoe County [Nebraska] Museum of Memories).

Collectively these desired characteristics developed through the years in part owing to the practical and financial constraints placed upon circle stock. Those playwrights actively associated with rep knew of the elements the industry required, and in writing such plays they literally created a "formula" to follow. The same considerations explain why so many performers and managers also wrote scripts. While the preceding presents a general outline of the plays suitable for circle stock, three categories of plays—Broadway releases, Toby plays, and war plays—require a closer examination.

Broadway vs. Midwest Plays

In the early years of its existence, circle stock relied heavily on the dramatic offerings from permanent stock, which in turn depended mainly on recent releases from Broadway and on older scripts with small royalties. Early circle companies prided themselves on using the most popular releases available, frequently claiming in their advertising, the "Latest in Royalty Plays." Scripts from New York City and other prestigious metropolitan centers–often referred to as "city fare"–proved to be an ideal source for material at the time, lending both allure and artistic credibility to these early circles.

In 1914, for example, when announcing an upcoming performance by Boyd Trousdale's circle company of the *Power of Politics*, a four-act political comedy, the background of the playwright received prominent attention in the local press:

> This play is fresh from the pen of Mr. D. G. Esrom, the popular playwright who has turned out numerous of the big successes now being produced in the larger cities and promises to be one of the best and most interesting plays presented at the opera house this season.
> Mr. Trousdale is the first to procure playing rights of this wonderful play.... The Trousdale players have a number of pleasant surprises in store this season in the way of new and up-to-date royalty plays, and the theater goers of Osage should encourage the weekly visits of this popular company. [*Mitchell County* (Iowa) *Press*, 28 Jan., 8]

Later that season, an article publicizing an upcoming production by Boyd's company took a similar approach:

> *The Country Boy*, a play that is scoring such a success, and reaching such a sensation in New York, Chicago and the larger cities this season, will be presented at the Sprague on next Tuesday evening. ... The play is new and thoroughly up-to-date; full of heart interest and abounds in wholesome, clean cut comedy. The dramatic situations are telling, the climaxes full of force and meaning. [*Mitchell County* (Iowa) *Press*, 4 Mar., 8]

Yet it was not always possible to secure the rights to such recent popular plays, especially following the onset of difficult economic times. When such scripts could no longer be afforded–a situation faced by many managers during the 1920s and the 1930s–circle stock resorted to plays written largely by Midwest playwrights, primarily because they cost less. And even when recent Broadway scripts were available, plays written by regional authors often emerged as more popular. In 1929 Bill Bruno recorded that

> one of the most successful of the midwest showmen wrote us that "he was playing and paying for three New York plays in order to get prestige with the theatre men, but found it necessary to use three midwest plays in order to put his show over." Figure that out for yourselves! [*BBB*, 19 Sept., 7]

Ted North once wrote to playwright Bob Feagin stating, "Used your *Governor's Lady* last summer in rep. I can truthfully tell you that it pleased as well, or better, than anything else I used, including the so-called New York plays" (*BBB*, 28 Oct. 1937, 4). Although lured away from using scripts by Midwest playwrights on occasion, the majority of circle stock performances relied upon material that originated in America's heartland.

Toby Plays

Of the many "featured" roles in the circle stock repertory, the Toby character–the unsophisticated yet clever, red-headed, freckle-faced country boy–came to have a life of its own, and over time Toby plays maintained a sizable part of the large body of drama from which circle stock managers made their selections for upcoming swings around their circuits. While surely entertaining and thoroughly enjoyed by circle stock audiences, the genre of Toby plays has aroused continued discussion and dissension. Of considerable dispute among veterans and historians of the rep era is whether the Toby character made an essentially positive or negative impact on the indus-

Sid Kingdon as Toby, circa 1934 (courtesy of the Museum of Repertoire Americana).

try. Controversy centers upon instances of too much reliance upon the Toby play within a company's repertory and the excesses in characterization that frequently transformed many plays into mere excuses for Toby's exaggerated shenanigans. While a small amount of support for Toby plays made it into print during the circle stock period, vehement attacks against Toby scripts make it clear that some leaders in the rep movement were alarmed.

Publicity photograph of Chick Boyes as a traditional G-string character (courtesy of the Otoe County [Nebraska] Museum of Memories).

One of the few voices in support of the use of Toby material is found in a December 1939 article in *Writer's Digest,* entitled "Circles Like Tobys and G Strings."[9] Writing advice to would-be contributors to the circle industry, playwright John Lawrence saw the Toby play as an excellent opportunity to capture the circle stock play market: "A door that has opened slowly during the past few years now stands wide open to playwrights whose Broadway ambitions do not extend to a nonstop flight."

Estimating that there were over 150 circle companies in existence at the time, Lawrence asserts that, with a body of properly written plays based on either the Toby or G-string characters, it "will be possible for you to lease at least one script to practically every [circle] company" (36). Although genuinely supporting Toby plays, Lawrence does suggest that an aspiring playwright's best bet for his first offering to the circles lies in melodrama. But a perusal of Lawrence's article reveals that in his opinion scripts involving Toby and G-string characters remained the most popular plays on the circles.

In consistent opposition to the boosters of Toby, Bill Bruno found Toby plays an improper offering to the circle managers, and a destructive one at that.

> There is little doubt, however, that a certain type of manager who has become an addict to these most terrible baboons will gladly accept any play that will give him all the comedy and allow him to hide his more or less natural talents under a red wig. These monstrosities are the real reason (of course, we expect nobody to side with us when we make the statement)

why show business is in its present pitiful condition.... When the Tobys have been ousted, show business will resume its dignity and become profitable once more.

Bruno concluded this tirade by suggesting that aspiring playwrights attempt to write a far more humane comedy for "the tent and circle market":

> Write human being comedy that is funny and not offensive. Write heart interest with action. Not necessarily melodrama, but plays that are fast-moving and will hold an audience's attention without dragging in comedy by the horns to wake the customers from their sleep. [*BBB*, 14 Dec. 1939, 6]

Still, the very passion with which Bruno and others attacked the Toby genre gives ample evidence that rep managers did not pay particular heed to these objectives. By early 1941 rep playwright Al Clark published a follow-up story to Lawrence's advice to playwrights, also found in *Writer's Digest*. Clark discovered that many plays submitted by aspiring authors at that time using Toby and G-string characters showed "little or no conception" of these character types, and he suggested that the individuals responsible for these efforts purchase examples of such plays and study them.

The trick to writing good Toby plays, Clark believed, was to make the character more "human." Nevertheless, Clark realized that comedians specializing in the Toby character were likely to exaggerate and distort even the most naturally written Toby.

> No matter how human you write your Tobys some comedians will, by personal application of the part, change that character into a most peculiar type of prehistoric man, the like of which you, in your wildest imagination, could never have conceived. Pay no attention to this! Your play is good, your conscience is clear and that rustling noise in your R. U. (Right Upper) vest pocket is caused by the check you received for the lease. [40]

In consequence of what he saw as the widespread debasement of the Toby character, Clark ultimately advised playwrights to avoid the form altogether. Based on his own experience and observation, Clark believed that the "higher class comedies" rather than the Toby shows "will live longer and in the end make the writer more money."

All this is not to suggest that Toby comedians of exceptional talent did not exist. Theater scholars such as William Slout, Jere Mickel, and Clifford Ashby document cases of extreme refinement in the portrayal of this role. Still, the current view tends to support Bruno's condemnation of Toby.

The most outspoken assessment of the Toby character to date is found in Slout's 1972 work, *Theatre in a Tent*. After tracing the origin of the character and his "gradual take-over" of the tent movement, Slout concludes:

> It might even be suggested that Toby was in part responsible for the decline of tent shows. His strong rustic heritage expressed through the antic of low comedy did not allow tent drama to progress with changing times. The

Neil E. Schaffner in Toby role, 1928 (courtesy of the Museum of Repertoire Americana).

rural setting endured, since it was necessary for Toby's bucolic comedy, into the age of H-bombs, jet planes, and massive urban problems. Tent shows were unable to get off the farm. Toby further deteriorated tent show quality by his refusal to stay within the play. Exuberant Toby comedians committed all kinds of improvised tomfoolery, leaping out of character, stopping the play completely to carry on some discourse with the audience, and even running up and down the aisles. Such behavior pushed the play into secondary importance; and when the drama is lost, so are the actors and their audience. [111]

How thoroughly Toby came to dominate the circle stock repertory is difficult to determine, primarily because of the lack of reliable company production histories. Without such records, one must turn to information from the trade publications. Yet the same financial troubles of the 1930s which forced a great number of circle troupes to rely more heavily on the Toby plays also obliged the ensembles to pirate plays extensively and, hence, to supply the trade papers with inaccurate information regarding their play selections, if they supplied information at all.

One element distorting the view of the part Toby played in rep theater is the extensive use of Toby material by the few remaining tent companies during the period following the Second World War. The resulting print and electronic media coverage of the heavy reliance on the Toby character at this time should not be taken as representing the entire history of either tent rep or circle stock. As Slout reminds us,

> Contemporary journalists, in their enchantment with the Toby character, have tended to over-emphasize him. The ability of Neil Schaffner, one of the last of the Toby comedians, to secure space in newspapers and national magazines, did much to enhance the image of Toby in modern tent companies. From contemporary articles, it is easy to assume that the modern

> Toby show is typical of the tent shows of yesteryear. ... However, many of the repertoire companies used no Toby bills. [*Theatre in a Tent,* 111]

Although confusion about the importance of the Toby character to rep theater might be present in the minds of those making only cursory investigations into the subject, those who played an active part in the rep field take a more balanced approach. One has only to suggest to a gathering of veteran troupers that the various branches of rep theater relied too heavily upon the Toby plays for the bulk of their performances to receive a resounding and unequivocal answer. While admitting the great popularity of Toby, former circle stock performers reject the notion that Toby plays deleteriously predominated in the offerings of rep.

War Plays

World War II was an important influence on the body of plays available for production on circle stock. Shortly following the attack on Pearl Harbor, a somber and realistic Bob Feagin recorded his shock concerning America's swift entry into the war:

> We are at war. That fact has struck a lot of us with a stunning impact. We still feel as tho we dreamed it, and it cannot be so. But it is. It is here. The opening phase has been bad–and shall get worse before it gets better. But it WILL get better–never doubt it.

Yet Feagin knew from past experience that a country at war still needed entertainment:

> It is not our province to discuss the war.... But it is our province, as your editor, to discuss its results on our business.
> No one can foretell, with any accuracy, what this will be. The only thing we can go by is the effect of other wars. As we mentioned, last summer, the effect has always been to boom show business, AFTER the first shock wears off. ENTERTAINMENT WILL BE IN DEMAND. Whether WE provide it, or the movie interests remain to be seen. [*BFB,* 10 Dec. 1941, 3]

While dutifully accepting the gravity of the situation, Feagin believed that as a war-weary public sought entertainment rep would experience a resurgence of growth and prosperity. Looking ahead to the summer of 1942, Feagin urged a patriotic theme:

> Last summer war plays were taboo. America was, at that time, still doing her ostrich imitation with her head buried deep in the sand. The audience didn't want to hear the word "war." It will be different this summer. Give them all the flag waving you can without becoming monotonous. They'll eat it up. If you are using a presentation don't overlook the old George M. Cohan numbers. They're unbeatable. [*BFB,* 28 Jan., 3]

Circle stock managers apparently agreed, and during this period of growing global conflict and eventual involvement of the United States a large number of patriotic plays for the circle stock and tent rep market were prepared, and true to the period, several of them were Toby plays.[10] Among them were Russell Murdock's *Toby and the Nazi Spies* ("Every person that can read a newspaper is a potential PAID ADMISSION"); L. Verne Slout's *Toby the Yankee Doodle Dandy* ("The *COMEDY* with a Jap heavy"); and Bob Feagin's *Toby at Pearl Harbor* ("He's in the Navy now!").[11]

Additional patriotic bills included D. Harvey Atchison's *The Great Secret*, which dealt with a Japanese spy system in this country; Russell Murdock's *Men Against Democracy*, advertised to "knock the Hit out of Hitler"; Al W. Clark's *Hitler's Secret Weapon*; and Warda Hatcher Magoon's *Wings Over America*, edited by Bob Feagin and described as not a war play but a "story of intrigue in one of our defense plants." Advertising for this script also carried the guarantee "There is not a line in this play that can offend our German-American Citizens"—an important consideration in much of the Midwest.

Play Brokers

One important source for scripts produced by circle stock companies—from the specialized war plays and Toby offerings to the traditional melodramas and comedies—was the play brokers and playwrights who specifically catered to the rep field.

Although many managers and actors wrote material for their own use on circle stock, certainly the greatest amount of new material introduced on the circuits was originally secured from professionals in the field. In his advice to aspiring authors, playwright John Lawrence noted several reasons why these agents played an important part in the total process of preparing the circle stock performance:

> First: Probably ten or more companies change their base ... weekly as a result of discontinuing unprofitable towns and adding new ones. Consequently, to keep your mailing list accurate you have to correspond with them almost weekly. Secondly: The agents know from experience what managers can be trusted and to whom it is necessary to send the scripts C.O.D., and there are quite a number of the latter.

Lawrence particularly recommended the use of Kansas City play brokers, while cautioning that their commissions reached 40 percent or more of the royalties—"larger than the agents for big productions."

> Kansas City is the center of a great number of "Circles" and there are days when as many as fifteen or twenty managers visit the agents for the sole

purpose of looking over plays, so you may be assured that in all probability the first day your play arrives, there will be at least one manager who reads and (if it suits him) leases it. [40]

The list of play brokers who actively serviced the rep industry is a relatively short one. This group slowly evolved over the years, yet a handful of companies remained prominent in the field, confirmed by high profiles maintained in trade publications. For instance, although a total of 18 play brokers and playwrights advertised during 1929 in *Bill Bruno's Bulletin,* four clearly topped the group: the Karl F. Simpson Theatrical Exchange of Kansas City; the Murdock Play Bureau of San Antonio, Texas; Harrison & Colegrove of Denver; and playwright Neil Schaffner, at that time of Fort Dodge, Iowa. Two other companies deserve mention, namely, the Coburn Play Bureau of Kansas City and the International Play Company of San Francisco, California.

By 1936 the field (although noticeably diminished by the Depression) continued to be dominated by the Simpson Agency. Other prominent entities included Wayne's Theatrical Exchange and playwright Don Melrose, both of Kansas City, along with playwright J. S. Angell of San Diego. Companies making their presence known through large (though infrequent) ads included the E. L. Paul Play Company of Kansas City and the Unity Play Company of Little Neck, New York, on Long Island.

Three years later, in 1939, the field continued to dwindle and appeared fairly divided between the Wayne Agency and the Simpson Agency (now listed as the Karl F. Simpson, Jr., Company), along with playwright Bob Feagin, who had consistently increased his influence in the rep industry over a number of years. The A. B. C. Theatrical Agency of Kansas City also made its presence known at this time.[12]

By 1941 *Feagin's Bulletin* (published by Bob and Gladys Feagin) relied upon essentially four advertisers of any consequence. The Simpson Agency (now bearing the Agnes Simpson Agency as its title) and the Wayne Agency, still both of Kansas City, dominated the field. Along with them, playwrights Bob Feagin and Neil Schaffner also actively advertised their work at this time. This handful of agencies and playwrights, each in vital ways helping continue the existence of circle stock and tent rep, supported *Feagin's Bulletin* through advertising until it ceased publication in early spring of 1942.

Although only a small group of play brokers and playwrights actively aided the Midwest rep industry, this limited number of sources should not suggest a reduced number or variety of plays offered to the companies. Both the very large holdings of such play brokers, along with access to script companies based on either coast, ensured a wide array from which to choose. For example, the Century Play Company of New York City, although not closely connected with the rep business, offered nearly 500 plays throughout the second and third decades of this century (MRA

Promotion for Neil Schaffner's response to the controversy surrounding a
new marketing system sweeping rural America in 1930, from *Bill Bruno's
Bulletin,* 6 Feb. 1930 (courtesy of the Museum of Repertoire Americana).

Collection), while the Simpson Agency of Kansas City offered more than
1,500 plays during the mid–1930s (*BBB,* 4 June 1936, 6).

As for royalties, few play brokers offered special rates for circle stock
during the 1920s in either the trade publications or their own catalogs; thus,
stated royalties were considerably higher than would be found in following
decades. For example, the International Play Company's 1928-29 catalog
placed a range of $20–$200 for their royalties, adding that "special royalties" were quoted upon request (MRA Collection). In other instances, advertisements avoided quoting amounts, preferring instead such phrases as
"Royalties you can afford," "Moderate Royalty," or "Special Low Royalty,"
at the same time requesting a written inquiry. It is apparent that fees for
performances during this era were determined largely on an individual
basis, therefore a wide range resulted.

By contrast, royalties charged the circle stock field during the height of
its existence in the 1930s varied within a considerably smaller range. A full-
page ad for Karl Simpson in 1936 offers plays for lease at $5–$30 for an
entire 20-week season in rep, in addition to "Circles $5, $7.50, $10," which
presumably covered a circuit lasting a single week (*BBB,* 4 June, 6). That
same year the Wayne Theatrical Exchange advertised royalties for a one-
week circle at $5–$10 (*BBB,* 29 Oct., 4).[13] With few exceptions, a $5–$10
range represents the average for circle stock royalties during the early to

mid–1930s. However, as the decade progressed and economic conditions worsened, stated charges generally decreased. By 1939 playwright John Lawrence offered his plays, "script, parts and royalty," for one-week circles at $3–$5 (*BBB,* 2 Nov., 2).

Sometimes the fees charged for plays used on circle stock seemed high when compared with those quoted for lengthy rep seasons. For instance, in 1929 the Coburn Play Bureau advertised a new play, *The Little Imp,* at "$30 for 30 weeks, $25 for circle stock" (*BBB,* 3 Oct., 9). In the case of the first quotation, $30 authorized 30 once-a-week performances, while the $25 fee for circle stock understandably covered only seven or fewer presentations. In the same ad, *Gossiping Neighbors* commanded "$20 for 30 weeks; $20 for circle stock." In similar fashion, Russell Murdock's *Know Your Groceries,* advertised as "A Three Act, Snappy, Dressy, Toby Comedy of the Love Story of an American Girl," quoted the following royalties: "In Repertoire, $30; One week Circle, $15; Two week Circle, $30; Two-a-week Stock, $15; One-a-week Stock, $30" (*BBB,* 14 Nov. 1929, 7).

It is certainly possible that these charges were set high to discourage production by circle organizations. Or perhaps these figures merely represent inflated charges existing prior to the onset of the hard realities brought about by the 1929 stock market crash–changes that did not sweep the Midwest but only continued the slow dissolution of the already weakened agricultural economy of the area. However tempting, the argument that circle touring was capable of withstanding heavier royalties than other similar forms of theater stands without merit.

Even though the demand for new material remained consistently high, plays were periodically withheld from production by circuit companies. Herschell Weiss held back *Those Show Folks* from circles during the winter of 1929-30, planning instead to distribute it the following summer tent season (*BBB,* 6 Feb. 1930, 3).[14] With the release of *Glamour School,* by Buddy Ross, through the Bulletin Play Service of Kansas City came the announcement "Available only to one manager in each territory [of tent rep] and will not be released to circle stocks" (*BBB,* 4 Jan. 1940, 6). The most plausible reason for withholding scripts from production by circle companies centers on the fear of overexposure for the material. Although any one circuit covered a rather minimal area, a play performed by many circle companies could quickly receive a wide amount of exposure in the rural heartland. Obviously some play brokers felt that such extensive usage lessened the play's attractiveness to tent companies whose tours covered much larger expanses, easily passing through the territories of several circle troupes where the play might already have been performed.

In their efforts to fulfill the demand for scripts, some play brokers looked for material outside traditional sources. In 1940 a large ad placed by Al Wilson in *Bill Bruno's Bulletin* claimed an apparently new source:

> Attention! For several months I have been dealing with several Hollywood writers for new material for the Repertoire and Circle Stock Managers and I am now able to offer HIGH CLASS PLAYS of the BETTER TYPE at a reasonable royalty for SEASON or WEEKLY CIRCLE ... ALL STAGE SUCCESSES THAT HAVE BEEN PLAYED BY STOCK COMPANIES ON THE WEST COAST and cut to fit your cast by the AUTHORS. [4 Jan., 7]

Perhaps West Coast writers, previously not looked upon for new material, now could provide the industry with an additional source to draw upon for scripts. Wilson's advertisement implies that these playwrights were screenwriters, and the use of such writers in 1940 coincides with a year of significant retrenchment in Hollywood (after the extravagant film years of the 1930s), causing extensive layoffs and cutbacks at the movie studios (Higham and Greenberg, 7). Under these circumstances Wilson no doubt found unemployed film writers quite willing to offer plays to the rep stages.

Although little more is heard of this source for scripts, some suggest that film writers had indirectly supplied material for rep stages for years. One veteran of 25 years in Midwest show business claimed that many rep scripts in 1930 were pirated from popular motion pictures by "well-known writers":

> The author goes to a picture show and then rushes home to write a play. The natives are quick to take exception at being bored with a poorly written and acted steal of a well mounted talking picture played by a wonderful cast which they failed to go in raptures over at the first showing. The public respects and appreciates originality, is disgusted with the copyist, and when all is said and done "The play is the thing." [*BBB*, 19 June, 7]

As the demand for plays continued to grow and economic conditions declined, the number of plays written by rep performers, especially managers, greatly increased. Entries in *Bill Bruno's Bulletin* such as the following became decidedly more frequent: "Will N. Rogers has joined the ranks of the Midwest playwrights, having devoted his vacation to the finishing of two plays which he will release in the near future" (26 Sept. 1929, 10). In 1936 Robert La-They, a well-known rep performer, announced the completion of *Meal Ticket*, making it available to both the circles and the tents (*BBB,* 20 Feb., 6). The following year we learn that Clyde McWhirter of the Rod Brasfield circle had "turned playwright, his maiden effort, *Quarantined,* having been very well received" (*BBB,* 11 Feb., 4). A few years later, Mac and Maree MacDonald found time during the hectic pace of the Borgen circle in northern Minnesota to complete two short-cast plays for the circles, both scheduled to be leased through the Bulletin Play Service (*BBB,* 23 May 1940, 4). But despite an announcement in *Bill Bruno's Bulletin,* Maree MacDonald reports that such writing projects did not circulate and only gathered dust:

> My husband and I wrote three plays that the agents said were "first rate"
> but they were never used because no one had the money to lease them–as
> a result they were never copied. We used to laugh and say we would almost
> feel better to have someone steal them than not to have them used at all.

While these and other script efforts by performers are documented in
the trade publications, it is likely that the majority of plays written by rep
performers went unheralded. Likewise, while the voluminous contributions of rep manager, playwright, and performer Neil Schaffner have been
reiterated numerous times, one must believe that the efforts of other managers simply did not receive such attention and exposure.[15] Therefore while
the contribution of plays by individuals within the field should not be under-
estimated, one cannot accurately gauge the amount of these efforts.

On occasion hard-pressed managers advertised directly for scripts. In
1926 Everett Walker, leader of the Taylor Players No. 2 company, sought
in *Billboard* "five and three" bills: "For Rep. and Circle Stock, for the coming winter. Would like some new Toby bills, state your price for one bill a
week circle. Also price for rep" (24 July, 27). An ad once placed by Harry
Dunbar read: "Wanted!–Hokum Seven People Scripts that I haven't used,
with good story and lots of clean comedy and action" (*BBB*, 24 Oct. 1929,
11). Occasionally managers searching for plays became desperate. Probably owing to increasing financial difficulties, Jack Owens placed an ad with
Bill Bruno's Bulletin in 1930 seeking "Short cast manuscripts that are royalty
free; preferably for 3 and 2" (16 Jan., 12).

Script Alteration

Of the available scripts, many specifically written for the circle stock market, managers were frequently obliged to alter what they had chosen in
order to meet a company's specific needs. While requirements varied from
troupe to troupe, normally both the size of the cast and the technical elements of the play demanded reduction and alteration. Thus, cutting a script
down to include fewer characters, less scenery, and shorter playing time
often became an essential preliminary to mounting a play on circle stock.
Moreover, cutting could also prepare a script so as to demonstrate a particular company's strengths or to attempt to hide its deficiencies. While script
cutting likely existed throughout the history of circle stock, the onset of
severe hardships in the 1930s nearly made the practice obligatory.

Often plays were advertised specifically as easy to cut, thus providing
flexibility for the manager and also helping increase the playwright's
chances of leasing the script. Don Melrose's *Night Club Nellie* ("Feature
Ingenue Lead and STAR Toby") carried the following description: "Full
cast is 5 men, 3 women, but can be cut to 4–3, 4–2 or 3–2. It takes only

FIVE minutes to cut this play to any size cast. Director's instructions for cutting with every script" (*BBB*, 30 July 1936, 4).

Yet in the majority of cases play cutting remained a regular burden of the manager, without the aid of specific instructions on how to do so. Jay Bee Flesner, an experienced script editor himself, cites manager Jack Collier as a "master" of the practice. After purchasing two copies of a play along with a large notebook, Collier tore apart the scripts and carefully pasted them into the notebook, making each page available to be "whittled down." Collier himself affectionately called the process "Collierizing a Script."[16]

As Flesner boasts, "There is hardly a script written that a little judicious blue penciling won't improve; tightening it up, making it move faster." One common practice in editing a script, says Flesner, involved a simple stage prop:

> The telephone was a marvelous invention on the set. You could put a whole character on the telephone. He never showed up. He would call. I remember in one town, the town boys were helping us unload the scenery and one asked, "Is the villain going to be on the telephone tonight?"

Commonly found among veteran troupers is the belief that almost any script could be cut down to five or six people, with the often crucial addition of a telephone for the conveyance of threats. Flesner also recalls that in trimming down an older script written in five acts, one technique involved completely eliminating the third act. Experience had taught these script editors that the fourth act normally reviewed the events of the previous act through dialogue, making the action of the third act expendable.

Regardless of whether the manager found it necessary to reduce a script for production, titles of plays were often changed in hopes of finding ones more attractive to the public. With an eye on increasing box office income, managers often sought new titles suggesting or sounding like a popular stock or Broadway show. Such was the case when a pirated dramatization of John Fox's popular novel *Trail of the Lonesome Pine* appeared as *Tobacco Ridge* because of the popularity of *Tobacco Road.* Alternate titles recorded in the Chick Boyes ledgers include *Ozark Mountain Folks* for *Trail of the Lonesome Pine,* and *What a Woman Will Do* for Charles Harrison's rep standard, *The Awakening of John Slater.* As Don Weage remembers, a title change sought to "bring up something more appealing to audiences" and "to tie into something nationally, internationally, or locally." Under the best circumstances, this practice remained a largely innocent attempt to increase income at the box office, but for less honest reasons a title change might try to hide the true identity of the script, either to avoid royalty payments or to dupe spectators into viewing a play again which they had already seen.[17]

Play Piracy

The subject of the alteration of scripts and titles is closely intertwined with the practice of play piracy. Because of its illegality few managers admitted to such theft and consequently left behind few records by which to judge its prevalence. Yet the very frequency with which articles concerning piracy appeared in the trade papers testifies to the widespread nature of the practice.

One must remember that for the greatest part of its existence, circle stock struggled through economic adversity. While the 1930s obviously stand as the low point, the periods preceding and following the Great Depression were hardly lucrative for the majority of these small bands of performers. Because of the reliance of circle stock and tent rep upon the general health of the economy, troubled times on the farm also meant troubled times for the rep stage. Beginning in 1920 America's rural sector entered a period of prolonged economic hardship, as the booming wartime economy of World War I could not be sustained. During the war American farmers greatly increased production to help feed the hungry nations of Europe. But following the conflict, the withdrawal of government price supports and the continued high levels of production sent farm prices plummeting, as this nation entered into its greatest agricultural depression. Starting in May 1920 and culminating in 1921,

> prices received by farmers dropped at least 43 percent below their peak. Corn fell from $1.52 to 52 cents a bushel, wheat from $2.16 to $1.03 a bushel, and cotton from 35 to 16 cents a pound. [Chandler, 55]

Although this initial plunge took only a matter of months, during the extended period from 1920 to 1932 farm prices fell as much as 63 percent from their high mark (Meltzer, 123). For the American farmer, the era of the Great Depression essentially lasted well over two decades.

And even as the country slowly recovered from the Depression through the late 1930s and into the early 1940s, circle stock shared in the steady decline of the touring rep system in general. This post–Depression period, while not so clearly burdened with widespread monetary problems, nevertheless remained a period of struggle and hardship for all touring theater companies as they faced increased competition from radio, film, and eventually television. As an appendage of the rep theater system, circle stock declined as the main organism aged and weakened. Inevitably, then, throughout a large part of its history, circle stock managers sought to cut expenses. With the price of admission as low as ten cents, profit margins were thin indeed, and the nonpayment of royalties developed as the easiest ploy with which to control a tight budget. Expenses such as wages, transportation, food, lodging, and performance site rental could be trimmed only with great effort and never eliminated completely. Yet royalty payments could be ignored and this is what set the expenditure apart from the rest.

The widespread availability of scripts, which came into the possession of performers through sundry means, greatly fueled the play piracy problem. Many circle stock and tent rep veterans flatly state that before returning leased materials to a play bureau or directly to the playwright it was common practice to write or type out a duplicate of the script, thereby retaining it for possible future use.[18] Steps to obtain a sought-after script, one perhaps not yet released for performance, might involve no more than going to a public library and copying down the play. Simply buying a single script, as if to study it for possible production, became a common method to procure a desired play. Dick Wolever recalls that a single script from Samuel French during the 1930s cost 75 cents, asserting, "Of course we would pirate them. I spent many a night, all night long, cutting down and typing shows to six, seven, or eight people casts."

In the estimation of some veteran performers, because of the widespread flow of scripts among rep companies and personnel in addition to the numerous adaptations made to these scripts to suit individual needs, the idea of royalties held little credence. Perhaps Don Weage expresses this belief best:

> Plays we used were not something written totally by a person, or two or three given persons. They were, many of them, plays that kind of evolved, from one typing of the script to another.... Managers couldn't be accused of piracy themselves, because the play had evolved through a series of little piracy acts here and there—a bit swiped from here, a bit swiped from there.

In the final analysis, Weage emphasizes that even if the money had been available, payments for script usage in many instances would have been an impossible task: "If a manager had wanted to be scrupulously honest and pay royalties, in most cases he wouldn't have known who would really be entitled to the royalty."

The term *play piracy* does connote a rather sinister and ruthless activity, and certainly the playwright saw it in such light. But Iris Hollingsworth provides another defense (and perhaps rationalization) from the perspective of performer or management:

> We're talking mostly about the Depression years and times when no one had very much money. We were working very hard to even make a living for the people in the cast. And you cut expenses any way you could. It was not that you were a crook or anything; you were trying to get by and keep a troupe of actors working.

Although the inevitability of play piracy seems apparent from this distance, a war of words concerning the topic raged continually during a large part of circle stock's history. In late 1929 a lengthy article in *Bill Bruno's Bulletin* touted the efforts of playwrights and play brokers to address the problem by forming a Kansas City branch of the National Authors and Playbrokers Association, an alliance founded in the East some five years previously. The initial membership included Harrison & Colegrove of Denver and the International Play Bureau of San Francisco, in addition to the following play brokers all headquartered in Kansas City: Don Melrose, Herschell Weiss, the Murdock Play Bureau, the E. L. Paul Play Company, and the Karl F. Simpson Agency, representing playwright Robert J. Sherman. With newly hired legal consult, the association felt ready for action. Concerning the motivation for their actions, playwright Sherman attested:

> During the past two years unscrupulous managers have been pirating our plays, usually obtained from equally unscrupulous actors who had worked in them and copied them, until it is necessary that we make a determined effort to put a stop to the practice in order that territory leased to right managers be protected. While it is true that these piracy cases are few, the practice gives evidence of spreading and it is our aim to put an end to it before it becomes more dangerous. [7 Nov., 2]

In the battle against play piracy, rewards were offered up like ammunition. As early as July 1929 playwright Herschell Weiss announced a "standing offer" of a $25 reward for providing proof of his work "being pirated by anyone, anywhere, at any time" (*BBB,* 25 July, 5). An identical standing reward was soon made public for plays by Zane Coburn (*BBB,* 8 Aug. 1929, 8). By the fall of 1935 the E. L. Paul Play Company offered a modest $10 for information leading to the arrest and conviction of individuals pirating the organization's material (*BBB,* 31 Oct., 3). And by 1936 Karl Simpson, considered the foremost Kansas City play broker and agent, offered $50 for information concerning the unlawful use of plays written by "Robert J. Sherman, Neil Schaffner, Ted Maxwell, Zane Coburn, Russell Murdock, William Giles, Bob Feagin, [and] Jack Wolever" (*BBB,* 10 Sept., 3).

But such alliances and threats made little impact on piracy. The most active front line in these continuing hostilities always remained in the printed medium; thus *Bill Bruno's Bulletin* and *Feagin's Bulletin* provide a chronicle of the verbal assaults waged. For instance, fully a decade after Sherman's vow to "put an end" to play piracy before it spread, Bill Bruno had reason to editorialize,

> Those managers who are still stealing old plays and offering them under new titles are certainly not business men. Because one retitled play can kill all their hard work in building up their circle. And when it is taken into consideration that many new plays are being offered at three to five dollar royalties, it is nothing less than feeble mindedness to steal one of the old ones. Because if your circle can't stand less than a dollar a night for royalty on a new play, the towns aren't worth your time and that of the actors. [*BBB,* 9 Nov. 1939, 3]

And not all of the invective against piracy centered on the manager. Consider Bruno's message to actors in the profession the following year:

> And for the benefit of the actors who may suspect piracy of plays in which they are working on unreliable shows: It will be well to satisfy yourselves that the manager has rights to production; for under the copyright law you are held equally responsible with the manager when taking part in unauthorized productions. The law does not accept ignorance as an excuse, for you at all times have the right to assure yourself that the manager is protecting your best interests. [*BBB*, 23 May, 3]

Even as late as 1941 the verbal offensive against piracy still dominated *Feagin's Bulletin*:

> There are some Eastern play brokers that will demand $150.00 for a play for a weeks production. Useless to say that a circle, or repertoire show, cannot pay this. But the joke is that not many of these are pirated. The thieves pick on plays that can be leased at a maximum of $5.00 per week! And if that isn't petty larceny we've been studying from the wrong book.... And above all, let us not further dignify them with the title of "pirate." Let's give them their correct name—THIEVES. [28 May, 3]

Certainly a good deal of Feagin's frustration and anger stems not simply from his position as an observant journalist—Feagin was an active playwright and play broker himself. Once, in a lengthy editorial, Feagin carefully outlined the trouble created by the nonreturn of leased script materials, at one point threatening, "Unless it gets better playbrokers will have to circulate a blacklist of those that don't return plays when the lease has expired." At the time of this self-described "short sermon," Feagin printed his scripts and parts using a system of stencil masters reproduced by means of a mimeograph machine. Up until the previous summer (1941), Feagin prepared leased materials "by hand"—obviously typewritten with the aid of carbon paper. Needless to say both production methods are very labor-intensive. And when materials from a popular play failed to return, Feagin faced not only the loss of future royalties, but the added expense of preparing new copies of his most popular scripts, a situation he found the most difficult in his then seven years in the rep business.

In this 1942 *Feagin's Bulletin* editorial, following a series of insults and threats, Feagin attempts to present a more generous rationale against play piracy:

> We realize that this is not malicious intent on the part of most. It is just carelessness. We have been guilty of it ourselves. But here is what a lot of people don't realize; if this material CONTINUES on one-way traffic, about the third season (when a play is really going) you find that your play is like a python with his tail in his mouth. It's swallowing itself. And the more business you do the faster it swallows. [4 Feb., 3]

Later in 1942 Feagin reports that the larger play bureaus had finally actively joined forces with the Play Brokers Association in combating piracy:

> Heretofore these companies [play bureaus] have maintained a rather contemptuous attitude toward the "small fry" in rep and circle companies. But they are being hit where it hurts, in the pocket-book. High schools, that sometimes pay as high as seventy-five and a hundred dollars for the production of a play, are beginning to ask why these shows are being done in their communities ahead of them and at ten and twenty cents admission.
>
> The enlistment of these companies will aid immeasurably in the stamping out of this curse to our business. Maybe, before long, an honest manager can lease a play and actually get to use it first in his territory. [*BFB*, 18 Mar., 3]

As might be expected, advertising by play brokers did not shy away from the piracy question. A unique warning from the Harrison Play Bureau stated, "Warning! Play Pirates! 4,000 Amateur Clubs are watching you, so use your own judgment. We've caught three and our lawyers are going to the limit." At the very bottom of the ad, placed in parentheses, could be found the qualifying phrase "Not Intended for Honest Showmen" (*BBB*, 11 June 1936, 12). Paramount Productions of Sioux Falls, South Dakota, used the theme "WHY PIRATE when you can get good bills for next to nothing!" In one such ad, Paramount Productions offered three scripts, with "3–2" casting, for only $3.00 each (*BBB*, 4 Mar. 1937, 3). Simpson Agency ads on occasion carried the reminder "Our royalty is low and PLAYS THAT ARE PAID FOR just naturally draw business. It's the law" (*BBB*, 18 May 1939, 3).

While such ads cast piracy in a negative light, other advertisements commonly found in the trade publications remind one of the widespread availability of scripts. Ads often cited directors available for hire who also maintained a personal collection of scripts. An example reads, "At Liberty / for Dramatic Repertoire / Actor-Director with Short-Cast Scripts. Can take Entire Charge of Stage" (*BBB*, 27 Feb. 1930, 11). In such instances the desirability of a director was measured largely by the number of scripts he brought along when he joined the company. These ads, in addition to the long-standing tradition of changing titles of bills, certainly helped perpetuate the old yarn concerning an ideal, fictitious director whose "At Liberty" ad boasted of "one trunk of scripts, two trunks of titles."

As the repeated threats and entreaties show, there was relatively little danger of being caught performing unauthorized plays. Few performers turned in the names of offenders, since in doing so they might find themselves looking for a job. And attempts to police the industry posed nearly an impossible task. Occasionally, though, the piracy of a script was detected or, as in the following case, nearly so.

Dick Elsenpeter relates the unusual story of the dramatist of an evening's play arriving unannounced. This incident occurred when Neil and Caroline Schaffner attended a performance by the Roberson-Gifford Stock Company, a small circle company based in Girard, Illinois. The cast was composed of performers from the Roberson-Gifford tent company, whom the management allowed to use scripts, scenery, and other supplies during the circle season "to keep key players for the next season." Neither the tent show management, nor the group of actors, however, had paid royalties. Elsenpeter recalls:

> We were doing Neil's show and of course on circle you were rehearsing another play at the same time. So here they showed up and Mason [Wilkes] came around [backstage] and said, "Oh God, they're here and we have never paid royalties. And they're going to say 'Where did you get the script?'"

The fact that it came from a trunk housing the Roberson-Gifford script collection provided little comfort at the time. It was quickly decided that the play currently being rehearsed would be put on stage that evening under the guise of allowing the audience to receive a backstage glimpse of the rehearsal process. Wilkes's curtain speech began, "Many of you people come to our shows and you sometimes ask, how do you people get up in one play a week?" Following the appropriate introductory remarks, the company presented a "rehearsal," complete with the director providing blocking from the script and an off-stage cast member going out for coffee. Playwright Schaffner reportedly found the experience unique and innovative. The following week—with the playwright no longer present—the company presented the Schaffner play originally intended for that evening.

Although play piracy undoubtedly remained widespread, it should not be concluded that all circle stock companies, or for that matter all rep companies, engaged in play piracy. It is true that a vast number of companies failed to pay royalties in difficult times, but in all probability many other troupes found the idea of pirating material unthinkable. Obviously the answers to such questions lie in company business records. Unfortunately few ledger books—traditionally meticulous in detail—survive. Most were carted to the dump once they were considered no longer of value, others were burned by mourning widows, while still others were thrown out by children upon inheriting the contents of their parents' old Taylor theater trunks. Fortunately three extensive circle stock business ledgers from the Chick Boyes Players of Nebraska are available, covering the years 1925, 1936-37, and 1940-41.[19]

The ledger for 1925 documents manager Boyes following a two-week circle format from January until the end of April, and from November until the end of December. Normally a single entry is made concerning royalty payments. Other times a single figure is given for an entry labeled "Royalties/Scenery," but nevertheless an accounting for royalty payments is consistently made. When royalty expenditures are entered as a separate expense, two levels of payment are noted: $12.50 and $17.50 per week. When a single entry is listed for both royalties and scenery, the figure ranges from as low as $10 to as high as $150, with figures such as $27.50 and $52.50 per week being frequent.

The records of Boyes's 1925 tent season also exist (covering May through early October), but no entries can be found for royalty payments, either at the beginning or end of the season or pro-rated during the weeks of the summer. Although we do not know the names of the plays presented during the circle campaign directly preceding this tent season described above, the lack of recorded royalty payments for the summer suggests that the tent show line-up consisted of scripts carried over from circle stock, now being played without royalty payments.

When the business ledger covering an eight-month period from late September 1936 to early June 1937 is carefully examined, the purchase of scripts can be found a total of ten times. With these entries ranging from 36 cents to $7.60 it appears that scripts are being obtained, but no records indicate the payment of royalties. The 1940-41 ledger reveals only occasional royalty payments in circle stock, made to cover the production of a few specific scripts. Interestingly enough, the 1941 tent season, unlike the 1925 canvas campaign, does record some very modest royalty payments made at the beginning of the tour. Overall, evidence from these three sources suggests that prior to the Depression era Chick Boyes made a regular habit of royalty payments, but in following years such payments largely were not made, or were only made sporadically.

Although the nonpayment of royalties developed largely because of the easy availability of scripts and the economic hardships before, during, and following the Depression, a reason for the ongoing nonpayment of royalties might very well be the force of habit upon the human creature. As economic conditions in this country and in circle stock generally improved during the late 1930s and beyond, one must wonder whether the habit of not making royalty payments continued at a time when in actuality the expenditures could have been made. Once managers found it easy to forgo royalty fees, it is difficult to believe that such payments would ever regularly find their way back into the business dealings of circle stock.

Vaudeville Specialties

One vital segment of the circle stock performance—not part of the play itself, yet dovetailed into it—consisted of the vaudeville specialty acts, which traditionally took place during breaks in the play being performed. Never intended to complement or relate to the action of the play, specialties primarily covered scenic changes going on backstage. As such, the series of specialties within a performance collectively formed an important portion of an evening's entertainment, and often took on a special life of its own.

According to theater historian Jere Mickel's estimation, in addition to covering scene and costume changes, vaudeville specialties developed into a standard part of rep theater,

> an attempt by the rep shows to capitalize on the most popular entertainment form of the period.... Vaudeville brought some of the glitter, glamour, self-confidence, and specious cleverness of the cities to the rural audiences. [71]

Many veteran performers simply state that the specialty segments provided a little "variety" to the circle stock performance. Indeed they did, and especially during times when audience members carefully guarded their expenditures for all of life's necessities, including entertainment, specialties provided more entertainment value for the admission price.

Trouper Wendell Poe feels specialties also played a part "in timing the shows to about two hours in length." Because the playing time of scripts varied, specialty numbers could be increased or decreased, so that the total performance could reach a desired length, for delivering a performance of appropriate length and quality to their supportive and paying audience always remained important to these professionals. Good timing became a source of pride. "Timing was everything on those shows," notes Dick Elsenpeter. "You had a tempo and the tempo was set and it was just like a metronome."

Concerning the specialty act in circle stock, the advice from an experienced trouper to a neophyte thespian traditionally centered on keeping it short, for two important reasons. First, specialties needed to last only long enough to cover the preparation of the upcoming scene, so as not to delay the evening's play performance. Second, specialties needed to be brief in circle stock because of a performer's repeated exposure to a particular audience. In returning week after week, the young performer needed to learn to conserve his specialty material and not display it all in only a few performances.

Lengthy circle engagements required not only the careful conservation of specialty material but also involved the performer's rather limited free time in preparing and polishing new material. Without question, circle stock required versatile performers. In a small circle company a performer would normally have a "line" of characters to perform, such as leading woman, heavy, or ingenue, and in addition to that a full slate of specialties.

To obtain the flavor of the numerous types of specialty acts and the kinds of response they invoked, it is perhaps best to cite sample reviews of

Dick and Lee Elsenpeter performing a specialty number on Tilton's Comedians, circa 1951 (courtesy of the Museum of Repertoire Americana).

performances by the Chick Boyes Players in the late 1920s. A record of the first play in the 1927-28 circle season–*Is Zat So?*–provides unusually full descriptions of the company's specialty acts:

> The new people give a very pleasing diversion and add much to the quality of the show. The specialties were given by the new members of the cast. R. H. and Peggy Wachtel gave a "dirty cracker" skit after the first act; Harry

Murray sang a couple of numbers after the first scene of the second act that were pleasing to the ear and his voice is worthy of mention for singing songs of a popular trend for entertainment purposes; and the Locktee team gave a combination number after the second act consisting of singing, a fine exhibition of toe dancing by the lady member of the team and imitations by Gus Locktee. Their own particular number "Whistling Your Blues Away" was very pleasing as far as it went—the audience could have enjoyed more. Piano music was furnished by Jack Daul. [*Hebron* (Nebraska) *Register-Champion*, 20 Oct. 1927, 1]

A 1929 review of *In Love with Love*, presented by the Boyes Circle No. 2, managed by Ward Hatcher, contained this praise:

The orchestra played a number of new hits preceding the show, with choruses sung by Musical Slim—there's the boy that almost held up the show with his vaudeville. He coaxed, forced or scared music from a saw, toy balloon, wash tub, ukulele and others.

Billy Seldom gave a trumpet solo that was very good and for his encore was assisted by Miss Lilian LaVelle with a slip horn. Merle Flower delighted his audience with a soft shoe dance that was just a little different and entertaining. The Hatchers presented a comedy skit that demonstrated they had lost none of their former ability. [*Hebron* (Nebraska) *Register-Champion*, 24 Jan., 1]

With a premium placed upon the versatile performer, phrases such as "preference given to people who double" and "must double in brass" (i.e., requiring the playing of a musical instrument) are common in trade ads seeking both circle and tent performers. Because circle stock, by its very nature, normally relied upon fewer performers than tent and house rep shows, the necessary specialty acts divided among only a limited group added a considerable burden to an already heavy work load. Ads concerning the formation of or seeking additions to a circle company frequently demonstrate the need for performers able to fill the wide variety of elements within a show. Notice the requirements spelled out for the Tri-State Players performing on a one-week circle in Indiana:

People in all lines who double Orchestra or Specialties. Character Man and Woman who can do General Business, strong Ingenue or Soubrette who can be featured occasionally. Heavy Man who can play General Business, Comedian who plays Black, Toby or Light Comedy as cast. Musicians, especially Cornet, Piano, Trombone and Drums. Orchestra, no Band. [*Billboard*, 16 Apr. 1927, 31]

Understanding that the market required multitalented performers, individuals used their "At Liberty" ads to extol their wide-ranging abilities. Freddie and Lillyan Poole, known for their creative, though usually terse ads, on one occasion recounted their versatile talents at considerable length:

Publicity photograph of Musical Slim while appearing with the Chick Boyes Players (courtesy of the Otoe County [Nebraska] Museum of Memories).

Pooles are troupers that can really "troupe." Perfect characterizations in melodrama and comedy–thoroughly equipped, carrying $2,500 worth of wardrobe, wigs and working tools, car and baggage trailer–efficient stage, band and orchestra director with library, presenting plays and music that sell–both double b. and o., schooled in the standards and modern–single and double specialties, patter, musical, skits, sketches, chalk talks–truly repertoire's most versatile general business team. [*BBB,* 3 Sept. 1936, 3]

With some companies the challenge of supplying specialties was met in a special fashion. On the Lew Henderson show, with a household of talented offspring in addition to their versatile acrobatic father, the constant need for specialty numbers often drew upon this family resource. Although the children did not always perform on a regular basis, they quickly became audience favorites. So captivating were the specialty acts by the Henderson clan, that they often exercised considerable influence on attendance in the circle. Anna Hockett recalls audience members asking her father if the children would perform specialties again in one week. When told that they would not, but would perform on the following visit to the community, Henderson frequently received assurances from the inquiring individuals that they planned to attend only when the younger members of the family returned.

Advance billing prominently featured the inclusion of vaudeville specialties in the circle performance. In the early years of circle stock in the Midwest, Merle Trousdale's advertising proclaimed both traditional specialties and an untypical bonus: "New Specialties Between Acts–Also the 2-Reel Feature, 'The Hermit of Lonely Gulch' and the Pathe Weekly Educational." All this plus the play performance for an admission of only a dime or a quarter (*Marion* [Iowa] *Sentinel,* 12 Mar. 1914, 8).[20] The inclusion of mechanically produced entertainment undoubtedly led to problems on occasion: the editor of the *Sentinel* indulgently reminded his readers not to worry as the "machinery" was "now running perfectly."

Advertising heavily promoted the addition of specialty numbers to the performance. Phrases such as "Music–Vaudeville–Drama" nearly became a standard inclusion in ads, heralds, handbills, or posters. Chick Boyes on occasion liked to present his offerings in simple numerical fashion: "6 Big Vaudeville Acts Besides the 4-Act Play" or more often with the assurance "All New Specialties–Same Old Prices." Through the years the terms *vaudeville* and *specialties* in advertising slowly gave way to *vodvil,* a convenient, though rather unattractive, shorthand.

Veteran performers relate that companies particularly talented in the area of specialties would sometimes emphasize them to the detriment of the actual play. The quality of the play production might be damaged by spending too little time on its preparation or by cutting too much of the script to allow time for specialty acts. However, in viewing the total history of circle stock, no trend significantly to increase or decrease the number of specialties performed has been discovered.

Although specialties were thoroughly entrenched as part of the circle stock and tent rep performance, the mixing of dramatic and specialty talent did not sit well with some individuals. In his role as general spokesperson for the industry, Bill Bruno expressed his opposition to the heavy use of specialties and the "doubling" that it invariably required. Bruno voiced special concern over the rise of a new type of performer–one who sized up well to the need for specialty talents, normally playing one or more musical instruments, but who fell far from the mark in terms of theatrical abilities. On one occasion Bruno presented his argument in the following fashion, relying in part upon his typically underplayed humor:

> We have heard several good saxophonists who as actors were very accomplished saxophone players. We have also heard a number of actors who as saxophone players were really good actors. We have seldom, if ever, had the pleasure of hearing or seeing a successful combination of both.
>
> If the shows must carry orchestras, for presentations or otherwise, we suggest that they carry musicians; if the intent is to carry dramatic shows, let us suggest that they use actors ONLY. Our view is that the musicians are too generous in doubling; they keep actors who are really actors out of work and certainly do not strengthen the dramatic performance, nor are they paid a salary for doing parts. [*BBB,* 15 May 1930, 6]

This concern was not a passing fancy for Bruno but nearly a constant

Typical publicity photograph of vaudeville act appearing with the Chick Boyes Players during the circle stock era (courtesy of the Museum of Repertoire Americana).

crusade during the life of *Bill Bruno's Bulletin.* Remarking once upon the annual springtime urge of older performers to return to the road, Bruno took the occasion to drive his point home yet another time:

> Many of these folks have been out of the business since the days of acting went out and the new "doubling preferred" came in. They couldn't play an instrument or do a trapeze act—and went into the discard. ...and how it hurts to be told that your days of usefulness are passed. Because, heaven help them, they can only act. [5 May 1938, 3]

Dissatisfaction also occurred among actors who felt their dramatic skills overshadowed by specialty requirements. Victor Morgan ("Heavies, Characters, Gen. Bus.") and Margaret Dahlman ("Ingenue Leads or as cast") expressed their strong objections to the system through an "At Liberty" ad that reads in part:

> To the Manager (if any) who operates a Dramatic Show instead of a conglomeration of truck-drivers and baggage-smashers, WE GUARANTEE SATISFACTION.... Our Specialties are no worse than those of the average Dramatic actor. [*BBB,* 31 Oct. 1929, 9]

While the above ad appears to have been placed in good faith and with determined earnestness, Bruno's sense of humor surfaced in some make believe ads demonstrating his vision of the future dominated by specialty needs. Among them:

> Wanted–Man with troupe of seals for special feature act; prefer four seals who can double quartette and orchestra.
>
> Wanted–Character man to direct who can and will make Broadway productions with cast of musicians and specialty people. If can deliver the goods will offer old-timer board and room for the summer. [*BBB*, 29 May 1930, 4]

Despite Bruno's efforts to the contrary, specialties always remained an integral part of the circle stock and tent rep performance.

Presentations

In addition to the play and assorted specialty acts, the circle stock performance might even include a musical "presentation." In many respects the inclusion of musical presentations developed as an outgrowth and extension of the importance placed on specialty acts. If specialties brought the variety, glitter, and glamor of big-city entertainment to the rural setting, presentations attempted to do so one step better.

Although more frequently seen in tent rep, some circle companies used presentations. Consisting primarily of 15–30 minutes of musical entertainment to open an evening's performance, presentations traditionally were organized around a single theme supported with special scenery. Billie Schuller, a family member of the Lew Henderson Players, notes that their presentations, like their specialties, relied upon the abundance of Henderson children and included such themes as Circus, Collegiate, Dutch, Hawaiian, Indian, Mother Goose, Opening Night, Sailor, and Toy Town. The Hendersons used presentations extensively under canvas and when possible also on circle.

The Henderson's "Sailor" presentation, in front of the painted backdrop of a ship, employed songs such as "Minnie the Mermaid," "Barnacle Bill the Sailor," "Fifteen Years on the Erie Canal," along with a little hornpipe dance. In their "Opening Night" presentation, even Buster, the family dog, got involved. As family and cast members held up small tiles spelling out "Lew Henderson Co," the canine company member carried on stage a tile marked with a period to finish off the abbreviation.

Rep manager Neale Helvey also gained a widespread reputation for presentations. His "Holland" presentation is described by Jim Parsons as having

> a special back drop with fields of tulips on it. Also a bed of artificial tulips running the width of the stage were planted near the footlights. There was a large windmill set piece at the rear.

The company, both men and women, were costumed in special Dutch boy and Dutch girl costumes. The tabloid musical was extremely well done. It was all singing and dancing, wooden shoe dancing with both serious and comic numbers.

At the end to the tune of "Tulip Time in Holland," the full cast was on stage. They would come downstage on the second chorus, the lights would dim and all the little Dutch girls would advance on the artificial tulip beds with watering cans as the windmill began to turn and lights inside the artificial tulip beds went on and off in time to the music and the swinging of the watering cans. [qtd. in Mickel, 173][21]

Herald promoting the Lew Henderson Players while on circle stock in 1934. Note the bonus of an opening presentation entitled "Hello Everybody" (courtesy of Billie L. Schuller of Marquette, Michigan).

Following the lines of his arguments against specialties and actors being required to "double," Bill Bruno frequently preached against the use of presentations and what he saw as a further eroding of the proper position held by the dramatic performance.

> Managers are continually borrowing the other manager's ideas [on presentations] and if one show puts forth something new and is fairly successful with the venture, every other company attempts the same thing, whether framed for it or otherwise.... The great trouble this season is that not enough attention is being paid to the drama and plays. There is no denying that is what the patrons come out to see. If they want vaudeville, they have only to wait for the first medicine show to hit their town; if they desire presentations, they will drive to the nearest large city to see real presentations; and if they desire orchestra music, they will probably remain at home and get good music over the radio. [*BBB*, 8 May 1930, 6]

In the following issue of *Bill Bruno's Bulletin*, editor Bruno labeled his battle against presentations a difficult one, noting,

It is hard to convince managers that they can be wrong and the following from one of them will perhaps explain the position of the greater number of them, "When I see some other show getting money with a certain thing, I'm going to do that same thing." [15 May, 6]

The presentations used in circle stock and tent rep modeled themselves after the musical tabloid companies, often referred to as simply "Tab Shows," which flourished in America prior to the era of sound pictures. These short musical productions—always carrying a chorus line of girls, yet remaining prim and proper—provided live entertainment between the silent films. With an interesting twist of irony, Jere Mickel notes that the tab shows "were continued by the houses presenting talking pictures to add the element of living theater to their performances." Mickel concludes, "As used by the rep shows, presentations were staged to create for themselves and their audiences some of the growing glamour of the shows produced in Hollywood." But in this reasoning Mickel found a serious flaw—imitation. "They were trying to modernize the show in terms of other aspects of show business. Rep shows were really ceasing to be themselves" (172).

If not a presentation to open the festivities of a circle performance, undoubtedly some form of music preceded the beginning of the play. For instance, the Harry Masten Orchestra (specially engaged by Al Trahern for his initial season), was noted for elaborate musical selections entitled "descriptive fantasia," which combined instrumental sounds and effects. Extensively outlined in the evening's program, "Nigger in the Barnyard" (claiming to represent "life on a southern plantation in slavery times") is illustrative of one type of popular preshow music on circle stock in 1907:

> At dawn of day, the birds are singing in the trees near the rippling brook. Daybreak is announced by the rooster crowing in the barnyard as the sunrise is seen, in the distance Dinah is heard blowing the cowhorn. Footsteps of the darkies are heard as they sneak out to the barn to dance. A loud noise is heard which causes a stampede in the barn. A horse is heard to whinnie, then a mule to bray and a voice calling "whoa," and "Ba-a Ba-a." Then a hen cackles, a rooster crows and the bussing [*sic*] of bees is heard. The whistle is heard as a steamboat passes. At sunset the cow-bells are heard as the cows come home. In the evening by the moonlight the quartette is heard singing in the barnyard. As the clock strikes mid-night pandomoninum [*sic*] is caused amongst the animals. Cats, dogs, cows, horses, mules, and peacock, ending with a pistol shot. [Collection of the Author]

In later years, by banding together those members of the company who doubled on a musical instrument, many an overture on circle stock (lasting often 15 minutes and even up to 30 minutes) was scratched out, sometimes by only a five-piece orchestra. Veteran rep actress Caroline Schaffner goes so far as to assert that never did the curtain rise on a rep or circle show without some form of a musical introduction, even if it was contributed only by the company's piano player.

Photograph of the Chick Boyes orchestra in exotic costume; this was frequently done in this era for publicity (courtesy of the Otoe County [Nebraska] Museum of Memories).

In retrospect, one can truly sense the precarious existence led by these circle performers. Usually operating on a shoestring budget with slim profitability, their continued existence as a company depended upon their ability to attract an audience, entertain them, and draw them back to their succeeding visits to the community. Although they were obviously dedicated professionals, the challenge of preparing a different performance weekly–complete with play, specialties, and possible additional musical entertainment–always remained an arduous one, but one traditionally met with determined and devoted effort. Even so, the hectic pace of circle stock preparation and performance must often have appeared as a blur in the eyes of these performers. Upon reviewing a list of plays he performed on circle stock, Don Weage once remarked,

> Many of these titles bring back fond memories. Many others bring back no memories at all, because we did so many shows and did them so quickly and went on to something else so quickly that unless there was something unusual, interesting, or otherwise significant about a show they could slip from your memory so easily.

But for countless audience members, the plays of circle stock, indeed the circle stock performances in their entirety, were special events in their lives, events not soon forgotten.

5

*Controlling
the Grouch Bag*

I N EXPLORING THE MAJOR MANAGERIAL ISSUES of circle stock, four main areas of importance can be identified. The first involves the manager's leadership of the company, especially personnel matters and the rehearsal process. A second area concerns the methods used for the physical transportation of the cast and equipment. Important considerations here are the distances involved and the various weather conditions affecting company travel. The third division centers on the physical characteristics of the various performance sites used by the companies, including the scenic procedures employed on circle stock. Finally, the problems of competition and methods to maintain profitable circles will be considered. In this regard, while the motion picture industry undoubtedly presented the most significant challenge to circle stock, evidence suggests that local community events also acted as a rival.

Managers

Veteran troupers agree that attempting to describe a typical rep manager is a difficult task, as any two rarely seemed very much alike. Certainly the backgrounds of these individuals before assuming their leadership positions varied widely. Many, especially those controlling small circle stock companies, were successful actors who elevated themselves to a management level. A certain segment of this group could be described as disgruntled actors who found it difficult to work for anyone else. As such, they entered the management field to be their own bosses.

But in a significant number of cases, rep managers had little or no acting experience prior to assuming their leadership role. Noted family management groups in the rep field such as the four Dubinsky brothers and the seven Brunk brothers fit into this category. While it is true that some of the

112

brothers from these two families gained renown for both their administrative and acting skills, as a whole these men possessed virtually no acting experience prior to becoming managers.

Nor were all rep managers known for their cordial demeanor. Those who lacked the ability to get along well with their companies on an interpersonal level usually maintained a strict line of demarcation between management and employees.

Still, a number of positive characteristics are consistently attributed to successful rep managers. Chief among these are the possession of an astute business mind and also an ability—some troupers call it an "uncanny sense"—to maintain close contact with the general public's tastes and wishes. Additionally, a good manager kept a close eye on expenses and made efforts to maintain his "grouch bag"—traditionally a small concealed pouch, often made of chamois skin and kept close to the body, which provided a haven for money to use in emergencies. It received its name from the poor disposition of a manager or performer when forced by circumstances to withdraw hard-earned cash from it. In short, it was an important rainy day fund for those concerned.

One would be wrong, however, to imply that only male managers existed in the rep field. Women, such as the noted Hila Morgan, did acquire the leadership of companies and generally proved themselves highly adept in such positions. Where the contributions of women to management is most surely overlooked is in the vast numbers of husband-and-wife teams who owned and operated their own troupes. Even though in many cases the control of the company was attributed to the husband, one must not ignore the contribution of the wife to the administration of the operation. The children of Lew Henderson fondly suggest that while their father acted as manager of the Lew Henderson Players, their mother, Alice, frequently played the boss.

Because an individual could establish a company and plot a circuit with only a small amount of funds, circle stock probably witnessed the rise of more individuals from the general rank and file to the level of management than in any other form of popular theatre and entertainment. Of course to continue in the field, a manager needed a product that satisfied the public.

Bill Bruno reminded the many new, young managers (along with the experienced ones) of this fact as the industry approached the 1929 circle season:

> It will, as in other seasons, be a survival of the fittest. Anybody with a little capital can take a circle stock company on the road. The big thing is to know enough about the circle stock game to keep the show out. You've got to have A SHOW, brother, to continue on a circle successfully. [*BBB*, 1 Aug., 7]

The Company

In most instances the size of a circle stock ensemble remained reduced enough to hold down expenses but still sufficient enough to carry out the necessary operations of the company. During the depths of the Depression, many circle stock troupes consisted of only a handful of members. Other circle groups were as large as a dozen members, but only in unusual cases did the cast size rise above that total.

Generally managers located actors through "Wanted" ads placed in the various trade papers, while actors made known their availability by placing "At Liberty" ads in the same publications. Advertisements placed in the 15 October 1936 issue of *Bill Bruno's Bulletin* are representative examples of these two basic communications:

> Want People In All Lines for Circle Stock. Camden, Ark., base. Play school auditoriums. Merchants co-operate and auspices. Want young leading man, G. B. team and Comedian. $17.50 single, $30.00 double. Address Merchants Co-Operative Players, Camden, Arkansas.[2]

> Larry and Madlin Nolan AT LIBERTY. A-1 Comic, Toby, G-string or Light, can direct, 36, 5-11, 155. MADLIN—Leads or Ingenues, 31, 5-2, 103. Have best of wardrobe, study and appearance. Plenty of Specialties. Have been with the best. Prefer standard circle. Can join on wire. State salary. Have Packard Sedan. Wire care Western Union, Denver, Colo., or contact Karl Simpson, our exclusive agent. [2]

Perhaps these two advertisements require some interpretation. The first concerns a circle company operating with the financial aid of local merchants. Performers needed for this troupe included a male and female general business team, the "jack-of-all-trades" of rep performers. The "At Liberty" ad promotes a versatile team, complete with a wide variety of specialty acts and also a car. These performers were ready to join a company as quickly as a telegram instructed them to do so.

Yet a manager never knew what kind of response a printed call for performers would create. In 1942 rep manager Roy Lewis surely found great amusement in Eric Upchurch's response to the Lewis Players' ad in *Billboard.* A neatly typed letter from Atlanta, Georgia, found in the Museum of Repertoire Americana Collection, reads in part:

> I am not attractive in the least, my teeth are dull, my body is skinny, but I can act. I am not interested in the salary you pay, I am only interested in room and board, and for that, I'll act my heart out.... I am only seventeen years of age but carry a draft card because I told a lie about my age to get into Maritime school. I am six feet tall, have red hair, weigh 155 pounds, and by the grace of God am blessed with talent. No one told me I had talent, but I'm convinced I have because of the great desire to act.

Apart from the use of such "Wanted" and "At Liberty" ads, various booking agencies sought to place actors looking for employment in touch

Wanted Quick!

Actor as Cast

Preference given man who doubles brass in orchestra. Other Useful People write.

Goff's Popular Players

Cleveland, Oklahoma

A simple "Wanted" ad from *Bill Bruno's Bulletin*, 25 Apr. 1929 (courtesy of the Museum of Repertoire Americana).

with managers in need of performers. In 1936 ads for the highly successful Karl F. Simpson Agency of Kansas City (founded in 1922) emphasized the company's industry-leading rates: "1/4 of ONE Week's Salary has been our commission charge for booking people for the past two years. Why Make Them Pay More?" (*BBB*, 16 July, 2). Frequently such booking offices ran lists in the trade publications of performers successfully placed, providing publicity for the performer, company, and agency. In addition a manager assembling a cast relied heavily upon his prior association with individuals, direct solicitation, and also word-of-mouth advice from other managers and actors.

Managers routinely assembled circle stock companies of five to 12 actors. When managers created ensembles larger than this such companies usually attracted a good deal of attention but few of these groups survived more than a short period of time. One noted substantial circle operation took shape under the guidance of the well-known showman Harley Sadler. In 1938–a time of continued hardship for many groups–Bill Bruno delighted in the Texas-sized circle Sadler had formed:

> The folk down there know that when he [Sadler] offers them a show it's just what he aims it to be–A SHOW! He has never been guilty of chiseling. He might have opened on this present venture with ten people and traded on his past reputation. Which is not the Sadler style of showmanship. Instead he opened with 21 people and added vaudeville each week brings the number to 25. He spent quite close to $1,000 for publicity before opening. Nothing chiseling about that, would you say? [*BBB*, 24 Feb., 3]

At the same time, the popular showman Henry Brunk opened a 15-person circle in Oklahoma to equally enthusiastic praise from Bruno:

> He [Brunk] was wise–he didn't take it as an opportunity to chisel. He opened with 15 people, an acting cast and orchestra. The result? Splendid business and offers of enough additional theatres to put out three more companies. So what does that prove? You who have the chisel complex wouldn't understand the answer if given. [*BBB*, 24 Feb. 1938, 3]

Yet these circle ventures were short-lived, with the consensus being that both attempts were simply too large to survive on circle stock. Following only ten "very successful weeks" on a circle of four Texas towns, Sadler

A rather lighthearted "At Liberty" ad from *Bill Bruno's Bulletin,* 5 June 1930 (courtesy of the Museum of Repertoire Americana).

played some short engagements and then opened under canvas for a second consecutive summer of one-night stands (*BBB,* 24 Mar. 1938, 1).[1] According to Mercedes Brunk, her husband, Henry, "wasn't too happy" concerning this one-time-only venture into circle stock:

> We had been so used to having a big band and orchestra, but on the circle we had to cut to 15 people. We could only use a piano or organ. However, we did very good business. In fact, a number of times we had to do extra shows. We only worked a circle one winter. There wasn't enough money to be made to suit Henry.

Personnel Management

One of the chief managerial challenges of circle stock involved maintaining a cooperative working attitude among the members of the ensemble. Disharmony among a circle company, if not bringing about its demise, surely made the often difficult experience of circle touring an unbearable one. An individual who sowed discontent received an appropriate title: "dynamiter." Bill Bruno claims the term developed in the mid–1930s to describe troublesome instigators of unrest and dissension. Bruno explains:

> The "dynamiter" is that actor who is never satisfied with his job, the show, the management, plays or people. He knows everything!–except that he is a louse. Arriving on a new show, he (or she) immediately starts a whispering campaign against everything and everybody on the show. Especially

VERSATILE CHARACTERS and JUVENILES

WARDROBE EXPERIENCE ABILITY

Excellent Speaking Voice

MABEL SPENCER

PERM. ADDRESS

824 NO. FLINT ST. PHOENIX, ARIZ.

HEIGHT 5 FT. 4 IN. – WT. 136

Promotional postcard used by rep performer Mabel Spencer to tout her "line of business" and performance strengths (courtesy of the Museum of Repertoire Americana).

against the man who has his money invested and is to pay them a salary for trying to disorganize his show. These vermin are very seldom of value as actors and seem to imagine they are covering up their evident shortcoming by knocking everybody else. The manager who doesn't get rid of them the first time he discovers them at work has only himself to blame if he has trouble on his show all season. [*BBB*, 29 Oct. 1936, 3]

Furthermore, Bruno suggests a course of action for the dynamite problem: remove the source of friction as soon as possible.

The moment dissatisfaction starts among your people, find the dynamite and get it off the show. And do it QUICK! Such a course may put a hardship on you for a week or two; but you will be rid of continual and never-ending trouble when you get the disorganizer off the show. The sooner the better. [*BBB*, 17 Dec. 1936, 43]

In addition to the challenges presented by the sporadic dynamiter, the problems of what was known as contract jumping and advance jumping confronted a circle stock manager on occasion. As the titles imply, these two acts involved performers breaking a contractual agreement with a manager, often causing delays in scheduled rehearsals and openings, plus added expenses for both management and personnel. Whereas the following example probably involves preparation for the tent season, the result of such breaches of contract was similar for circle stock:

One certain company was all set to start its rehearsals last Saturday, when it was discovered that the leading team engaged during January was conspicious [*sid*] by its absence. Then on Monday word reached the manager that his leading people were rehearsing with another show not fifty miles away, where they had been offered a better salary. The manager of the first show is doing his utmost to replace the missing team, but with little success and will probably be obliged to open with a makeshift cast. In the meantime the balance of the company are forced to wait two weeks longer for the opening–while expenses continue. [*BBB*, 1 Apr. 1937, 1]

Advance jumping occurred when an individual or team failed to appear at an agreed-upon time and location after receiving money–usually under $25–to defray travel expenses in joining a company. Information concerning such incidents normally reached the trade publications in an effort to expose the guilty performers and to warn other managers, as in the following:

Claim is made that Harry Davis and Fern Sutton signed contracts to join the Harvey L. Twyman circle in South Dakota. The team asked for and received an advance of $25.00, were to join the show on the 6th and no word has been had of or from them since. [*BBB*, 16 Apr. 1936, 2]

Despite continued concern over contract and advance jumping, managers apparently never found a good way to put an end to these problems. Yet upon the return of his publication following five years of inactive status, Bill Bruno boasted in 1936 that his inclusion of notices that named such malefactors had done much to curb these abuses (*BBB*, 26 Nov., 3).

For the most part, rep managers dealt with their personnel independently without significant interference from union or governmental restrictions. When such limitations did eventually interfere with the prerogatives of managers, controversy ensued. One subject of heated debate centered on the requirement of special travel allowances to actors known as "fare on and off" payments, which originated from the rep field's connection with Actors' Equity.

Actors' Equity

Beginning in the early 1920s, Actors' Equity required managers abiding under Equity guidelines to ensure payment to actors for travel expenses when properly joining or leaving a show. Originally established to prevent performers from being stranded by unscrupulous managers, the system sometimes suffered from abuse, as shown in the following notice concerning some apparent circle companies:

A certain show recently closed after a season of twenty-two weeks and the actors on the show were paid fares back to the base, the amount including the excess baggage. Among the actors was one who was joining another company on the following Monday. The fare and excess was paid to the base in Kansas City, a matter of $16. Then the manager of the company the actor was joining paid the fare and excess on to the opening point—which happened to be within one hundred miles of the closing point of the other company—and this was a matter of $15. The actor received a total of $31 from both managers—and then cut across country to the opening point at a cost of in the neighborhood of $6.

All of which is in perfect accordance with the Equity contract but is the cause of a great deal of dissatisfaction among the managers. Nor is the above instance an isolated case. It is happening every week. [*BBB*, 6 Feb. 1930, 7]

To understand the "fare on and off" controversy, one must view the entire history of rep's relationship with Actors' Equity—a relationship that, even at its best, can only be described as tenuous.

Representatives of Equity first traveled throughout the Midwest, South, and Southwest rep territories in the early 1920s, actively pursuing actors (and even tent canvasmen) for membership. Veteran rep actress Caroline Schaffner recalls she joined Actors' Equity in 1921 while performing on a "tab" show. Mercedes Brunk states that representatives of the Kansas City Equity office "came out to Edgar Jones's circle show in the fall of 1928 and signed us all up," adding, "We had no choice." Although no definitive figures concerning Equity's success in recruiting rep actors survive, records from the organization's information organ entitled *Equity* and statistics by Alfred Bernheim make it clear that not all rep actors joined Equity (perhaps as few as one-third of these performers were union). A number of veteran performers similarly emphasize that not all rep shows in the 1920s were affiliated with Equity, but they do insist that the "standard" shows (i.e., relatively large, well-known companies possessing solid reputations) were 100 percent union (still perhaps only one-fourth of all rep companies were Equity). By all accounts, one must assume that a sizable number of companies were not bound by Equity contracts. On the other hand, it is probable that troupes not technically bound by Equity rules followed them nevertheless because of the widespread prevalence of "fare on and off" compliance.

Rep companies that were required to follow Equity guidelines during the 1920s were governed by two distinct contracts, both specifically written for the industry. One agreement covered tent troupes, the other covered a wide sweep of arrangements and was entitled "For Rep Companies Playing 75 cent top and in Permanent buildings" (MRA Collection). Circle stock companies submitting to Equity rules evidently abided by this covenant. Concerning the question of "fare on and off," the regulations are quite clear. If a manager canceled the employment of an actor, rules required the manager to pay, in cash, for the return of the actor and his baggage to his home base (normally Kansas City)—whether or not individuals actually

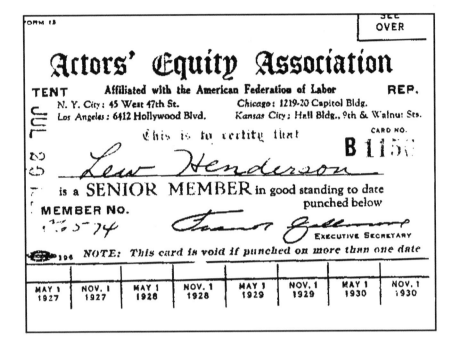

Actors' Equity Association

TENT   Affiliated with the American Federation of Labor   REP.

N. Y. City: 45 West 47th St.   Chicago: 1219-20 Capitol Bldg.
Los Angeles: 6412 Hollywood Blvd.   Kansas City: Hall Bldg., 9th & Walnut Sts.

JUNE 29 17

This is to certify that

Lew Henderson

CARD NO.

B 1150

is a SENIOR MEMBER in good standing to date
punched below

MEMBER NO.

1705-74

EXECUTIVE SECRETARY

NOTE: *This card is void if punched on more than one date*

MAY 1 1927	NOV. 1 1927	MAY 1 1928	NOV. 1 1928	MAY 1 1929	NOV. 1 1929	MAY 1 1930	NOV. 1 1930

A 1928 Actors' Equity card belonging to Lew Henderson (courtesy of Billie L. Schuller of Marquette, Michigan).

returned to their base. If it was the actor's own choice to leave the company, Equity's contract specified that departing individuals pay their own fare back to their base, and, in addition, required them to "reimburse the manager for any railroad fare for the successor" from the new company member's base to the point where the replacement joined the company.

While "fare on and off" generally met with wide approval from actors, it remained a sour point of contention for many rep managers in dealing with Equity. The problems that existed between the industry and the union centered on what many saw as Equity's ineffective use of funds, most pointedly the collection of dues from the Midwest region without any advantage other than the travel insurance represented in "fare on and off." Yet this benefit did not accrue directly from the dues of members because such payments came from management abiding by Equity rules. Strife also arose around a seemingly endless string of inconsistent and contradictory rulings from New York City involving disputes present in the Midwest rep field. Such concerns motivated many to call for "home rule" in the region, so that problems requiring arbitration could be settled quickly and fairly by a governing council composed of area troupers. Unrest with Equity, brewing throughout most of the 1920s, inevitably erupted in some attacks on the organization's leadership. The following diatribe against Equity in late 1929 represents Bill Bruno's early salvo in open warfare:

> All rulings east or west, and all dictation of policy in any quarter, are very evidently made by the wise men of the east. This is especially unequitable as Gilmore [Frank Gillmore, president of Actors' Equity] understands nothing of western conditions—and cares less. His concern in midwestern shows and actors is nothing beyond the $18 dues paid yearly by over 1,000 of them to keep up the office and the expense at New York, which gives nothing in return except the "railroad fare insurance" and yearly balls which none of the folks out here can or care to attend. [*BBB,* 12 Dec., 19]

Later in this same issue, Bruno presented a list of demands designed to give rep actors associated with Equity "control of their own affairs."

> The Midwest Equity members should be given their own council, elected by vote of midwest actors ONLY;
> The Midwest must be given a contract that will cover its own needs;
> The Midwest has never since the organization [began] been accorded representation in meetings of the New York body governing, and this must be extended them, the representatives to be nominated and elected by midwest vote ONLY. [20]

Shortly thereafter, successful rep manager Ralph Moody shared similar thoughts with the readers of *Bill Bruno's Bulletin*:

> I feel sure that if the New York officers realized the dissatisfaction among their members out here they would give some of their attention to them. Or perhaps they do not realize that they could not begin to exist should all of the midwest members withdraw from their organization. Perhaps they don't care, being too busy with "greater matters" to give attention to us "small fry." But they should remember that it was the peasantry which down through the ages overthrew thrones. [26 Dec. 1929, 6]

Although the leadership of Equity made some overtures to appease the organization's Midwest membership—including the establishment of a largely honorary position on the national council and filling it with the popular Texas rep manager Harley Sadler—the rift between the eastern and western factions of Equity remained throughout the lifetime of touring rep.

During the Great Depression, the union movement among rep actors fell moribund. Caroline Schaffner recalls that she remained a member of the union until "Equity itself, during Depression days, withdrew from the repertoire field." She stresses that Equity abandoned the rep shows in the 1930s of its own accord, because under Depression conditions few actors or managements could afford to abide by Equity's regulations. Indeed, with a scarcity of jobs, most troupers did not dare to be connected with Equity because that association often excluded them from work; veteran performers report that, in some cases, card-carrying Equity members assumed false names in order to take on desperately needed employment.

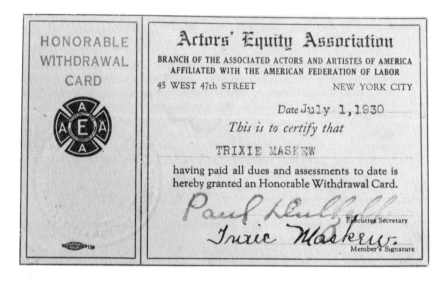

Trixie Maskew's honorable withdrawal card from Actors' Equity, 1930 (courtesy of the Museum of Repertoire Americana).

Whereas early on some rep companies proudly boasted of their association with the union in trade publications, later ads often emphatically insisted "No Equity."

Even though Equity's involvement in rep ended shortly after the onset of the Depression (the Kansas City Equity office apparently closed in 1931), *Bill Bruno's Bulletin* reported attempts to renew its association with the Midwest in 1936:

> We have it on the most reliable information that an effort is about to be made to have Equity again start its western collection agency for the universal good of the A.E.A. But we're not in the least frightened at the outcome of any attempt to again hook the western actor into paying tribute to the Gillmore gang. Their former record of mismanagement here in Kansas City should effectively put a stop to any attempt. It needs only an announcement that Frank Delmaine would return to take charge of the K. C. office to put the idea back in moth balls. And we doubt very much if the western actors would pay $18 a year for the privilege of working for the salaries now the rule. Just to show you how badly Ekkity has treated us, they have even taken the ninth or tenth vice-presidency from our own Harley Sadler! We don't want any more of Ekkity in the midwest. Nor do we need it. [12 Mar., 5]

In the face of such opposition, nothing came of Equity's renewed efforts to organize the area's actors, and the question of Equity and the Midwest rep field appears to have been permanently laid to rest.

Even though Actors' Equity retreated from the rep field in the early

1930s, controversy about the organization persisted throughout the remaining history of circle stock. Generally opinions concerning the union remained negative, yet the reasons for this opposition varied. Many suggest that economic matters formed the basis of the industry's low estimation of Equity. As Don Weage views the relationship:

> I think secretly we all would like to have been Equity, but that would have placed a financial burden on the managers. And so the managers always talked Equity down. And we went along with it.... By and large we looked down upon it, but there was a certain amount of jealousy, and a bit of longing in this attitude.

Some veteran troupers acknowledge the admiration they held for Actors' Equity during their careers, and when comparing themselves to its membership they freely place rep a rung or two lower on an imaginary ladder of show business prestige. At the same time, these individuals express pride in their own accomplishments and the part they played in the total popular entertainment industry. Some even suggest that union affiliation, at least early in the history of circle stock, helped the self-image of performers suffering from an inferiority complex. But perhaps Maude Gentry speaks for the majority of rep performers:

> We felt we were more versatile and clever than people who did only one part for months. You had to be able to learn fast, jump quickly to different characters, no in-depth soul searching. And we knew only a small percentage of Equity made their living in show biz, but *we did*.... We yearned for more money, and dreamed of great success, but it was so easy on rep (by easy I mean no deception, no politics), the countryside was lovely, and the farmers loved us.

Governmental Involvement

The debate over "fare on and off" payments did not stand alone in creating controversy concerning outside intervention in the rep field. The steady intrusion of federal and state involvement in the business of circle stock caused many to long for a simpler era. In the earliest years of the circle industry, managers worked relatively free of governmental control and restraints. Yet during the First World War the collection of war taxes became the patriotic duty of management. Many managers collected this tax by simply adding a surcharge to their regular admissions, thereby creating odd-sounding ticket prices, such as 44 cents for adults. During the Second World War a like tax met with similar cooperative responses from management—for example, 28 cents charged for adults.

Beginning in the depths of the Depression era, however, greater governmental regulation increasingly affected the circle stock industry. The creation of a system of unemployment compensation during the 1930s, funded in part by employees, clearly benefited troupers during the off-season as designed to do. Yet this additional financial responsibility for management met with extensive opposition.

> We are receiving reports early this season of managers who are sidestepping the payment of the unemployment compensation by adopting various means of evasion. Some have even gone so far as to threaten closing their shows (with salaries in arrears, of course) if the actors insisted on having reports and dues sent in.
> This is just about the lowest form of chiseling that has come to our notice. The manager who will deliberately ignore the compensation, in the face of the small salaries paid, and thus take from his actors surety for three or four months of the winter is rather small in his business methods. There have been a number of cases reported where during the past two years managers collected from the actors and then made no report to the government. In each of these reported cases the actor had every evidence of the evasion, but was without courage to go through with the matter, although howling his head off about the injustice done him. The *Bulletin* was asked to bring the case to the attention of the authorities; but we want no part of it.
> Just one example made of a chiseling manager would put a stop to all this. [*BBB,* 27 June 1940, 1]

The initial concern over unemployment compensation came to the forefront with the signing of the Social Security Act on 14 August 1935 by President Franklin Roosevelt. This act created not only a federally administered Social Security program but also state-operated systems of unemployment insurance. Such historic legislation unquestionably made a lasting impact upon the business of circle stock and tent rep.

As originally drafted, the law applied only to firms with eight or more employees. In 1956, however, an amended Social Security Act expanded coverage of unemployment compensation to firms of four or more employees (Schottland, 83). During the Depression and through the 1940s, therefore, many circle stock companies were not affected by unemployment compensation, because the number of performers in the troupe did not exceed the limits established in the initial regulations.

From 1935 onward, though, many circle stock and tent rep managers who exceeded the maximum employee limitations found ways to sidestep the law. Because the original statute also required a minimum of 20 weeks of continuous work for an employee to qualify for benefits, some managers purposely divided up their season so that any one period of employment did not surpass established requirements. For example, instead of running a circle season lasting 22 or 24 weeks, troupes were known to perform for only 17–19 weeks and then "break" company—frequently for major holidays such as Christmas and Easter. By disbanding for a period of two weeks or so, continuous work ceased and the manager avoided unemployment compensation payments altogether. Afterward managers reformed their companies (usually employing the identical cast) and once more began to count the weeks of touring.

Although a significant number of circle stock and tent rep managers apparently sought to avoid unemployment payments, in early 1940 Bill Bruno attested to the value of the compensation program and criticized managers unwilling to follow federal and state legislation:

> There is no denying the fact that unemployment compensation is proving a godsend to quite a number of troupers during this tough winter. So many write us to that effect. Without it they'd have been unable to pull through. Consequently the manager paying the present low salaries who chisels his people out of this safeguard for the winter is just ten points lower than a louse. [*BBB*, 1 Feb., 3]

Eventually some advertising emphasized a management's adherence to the regulations of unemployment insurance. A Christy Obrecht ad in 1942 reads in part, "Long, sure season. Unemployment insurance after closing. Make salaries in keeping with long season" (*BFB*, 4 Feb., 4).

Concern over the nonpayment of Social Security taxes to the federal government dominated Bill Bruno's advice to the industry in early 1939. Declaring that his warnings applied to "managers of circle companies as well," Bruno stressed:

> This social security tax, if you have not yet informed yourself, has no connection with state or other tax measures such as unemployment, old age pension and like taxes. It is a government tax and differs from the unemployment measure in that there is no exemption as regards number of employees. Even though you have had but one employee, you are required to make a return.

Bruno concludes this warning with some recent events concerning the federal government's enforcement of the Social Security law, incidents possibly not widely known in the industry:

> Remember that while the state agents are inclined to leniency at times, government men appear to forget the meaning of the word. As was proven late last fall when the checkup started in Texas, one show being tied up for two weeks until payment of tax was made. There were several other cases, an Illinois manager narrowly escaping a prison sentence. This and other cases were kept quiet in order not to warn other shows which had failed in reporting. [*BBB*, 2 Mar. 1939, 1]

The interpretation of one governmental regulation–the mandatory withholding of income tax–developed to where astute managers could use the statute to benefit their companies. Theater historian Russell Kittle reports that beginning in the fall of 1943 manager Neil Schaffner, following the guidance of government officials, began dividing the salaries earned by his tent rep and house stock companies into two parts. One amount was designated "salary" (i.e., $25), and an identical amount ($25) labeled "employee expenses." Company members benefited from this bookkeeping technique because withholding taxes applied only to salaries, not an actor's expenses (243). Although no records have been found to verify this practice on circle stock, the use of this tactic (after once entering into the rep field) surely spread to those companies performing circle stock during the closing years of its history.

Chiseling

The union and governmental regulations that management sometimes flouted ultimately were intended to benefit actors. Managers hard pressed to make ends meet, however, frequently felt they had no choice other than to skimp in their dealings with their employees (and ultimately their audiences)–what Bill Bruno called the "chisel complex." An ongoing concern of Bruno, "chiseling" represented a continual financial retrenchment during the Depression which he deemed unnecessary and damaging to the health of the rep system. Acting as a commentator for the entire industry, Bruno frequently expressed his belief that managers had allowed many of the legitimate financial worries of the Depression era indiscriminately to color their entire outlook. This perspective caused them to compensate their companies unfairly and to hold back on proper expenditures so that the public received an inferior product. In Bruno's view, a "chiseler" accepted second best, or even worse, as the proper standard for the profession. In 1938 Bruno discussed the problem as he viewed it:

> For a manager who can be rated as a REAL manager doesn't resort to the prevailing chiseling which has been proven the worst kind of business practice. Just plain cheating–and the sad part of it is that the cheater cheats nobody but himself. To be sure, he can usually cheat the people on his opening nights, and can cheat his actors for a time; but in the long run he is the loser. And the damphool in his blind egotism can't or won't realize what he is doing. He is continuing the killing of the goose which at one time not so long ago laid golden eggs for him. [*BBB,* 24 Feb., 3]

On another occasion, Bruno lamented that chiseling had been elevated to an "art form" during the lean years of the 1930s, citing it as a "canker ... eating the heart out of what was once a dignified profession" (*BBB,* 27 Jan. [1938], 3).

Rehearsal Methods

A good manager oversaw the efficient rehearsal of the ensemble's productions. Rehearsal methods and techniques used on circle stock varied according to the needs and experience of each particular company. Some preparation periods involved only a few practice sessions, while other schedules stretched longer.

Jay Bee Flesner maintains that only three rehearsals were required on circle stock because typically a clear majority of a professional circle cast had performed the specific play before. According to Flesner, the first meeting consisted of a read-through of the script, following which the actors learned their parts. A second gathering roughed out the physical movement for the show. The third and final rehearsal took place on the day the show opened, on stage with the set.

Dick Wolever recalls a compact rehearsal period covering three days which shares some similarities with the procedure described by Flesner:

> At the end of the week, Friday, as I recall, we would have a rehearsal after our performance at night. Just a read-through rehearsal to get an idea what our next week's show was going to be about. On Saturday afternoon we would have a half-way walk through and get our stage directions. On Sunday afternoon, not a dress rehearsal, but a reading rehearsal. And Sunday night another reading rehearsal; supposedly everybody knew their part by then. We would open a new show on Monday.

Iris Hollingsworth recollects a longer period of study and that the first rehearsal—the read-through of the upcoming production—occurred on Tuesday, so as not to interfere with the memorization and mental process for the show that opened Monday evening. According to her experience, preparations for the next bill took place each afternoon on the stage where the play would be performed a week later during their return to the community. If nothing prevented following through with this system, the company could practice its stage business on every stage of the circuit and also plan how scenery might need to be adapted to each performance site.

Given differences in skill and patience, preparation methods varied widely according to the composition of each circle company. Obviously ensembles with less-experienced performers generally rehearsed more. Waunetta Rosier Oleferchik entered show business through her marriage to manager and performer Harold Rosier, and she willingly admits that her inexperience caused the Rosier Players to rehearse each play an entire week: "I think some of the older troupers on our show probably could have easily done it in three days but I was new; every play was new to me, I had to rehearse them." Although a great number of companies followed an afternoon rehearsal schedule, many chose instead to practice every morning during the week. By rehearsing an upcoming production at this time, if a review of lines for the evening's performance was deemed necessary it could take place as the company traveled on the way to the performance site. If an additional run-through of the scheduled show was necessary, it usually took place late in the afternoon after erecting the set.

Unusual "At Liberty" ad promoting a "capable director," from *Bill Bruno's Bulletin*, 24 Apr. 1930 (courtesy of the Museum of Repertoire Americana).

Because circle stock existed primarily as a business proposition and only secondly as an artistic endeavor, stage direction always remained highly expedient and businesslike. As is the tradition of the theater, one individual oversaw the control and rehearsal of the play. This task normally fell to management; however, on occasion, a company member earned extra income by assuming these responsibilities.

In most instances, the designated stage director held script during rehearsals and coordinated entrances and exits. As one veteran performer suggested, these individuals operated largely as "traffic cops" by maintaining efficient and controlled movement on the stage. In general it was the director's job to identify in which "line of business" a character to be portrayed fell, suggesting, perhaps, "Now this role is like Simon Slade," or "He should be played as a G-string." As professionals who prided themselves on their ability to "get up" quickly in a part, little more than this was required of a director. Although such duties suggest minimal value to a company, one should not overlook an important resource entrusted to the director. Because performers normally studied from only fragments of the entire play (known as "parts"), in virtually all instances a master script provided the only complete text available.

In rare instances, a circle ensemble might even find themselves led by the author of the script under scrutiny. *Billboard* reported in 1924 that the highly successful rep playwright Robert J. Sherman of Chicago "motored" to Ionia, Michigan, to rehearse the Gould Players in one of Sherman's new plays for presentation on their circle (8 Nov., 28).

Transportation

Reliable transportation always remained a key consideration for a well-functioning circle operation. Because of the limited size of the majority of circle stock companies, large passenger automobiles were normally used–Cadillacs a frequent choice–in an attempt to accommodate an entire ensemble in one vehicle. An apocryphal rep tradition has it that managers routinely sought slender cast members for circle touring, using ads such as "Wanted–People in all lines for a circle stock. Thin people preferred." Such legends suggest the dilemma theoretically faced by managers in hiring a cast while at the same time trying not to strain the capabilities of the company's modest Model A Ford. Larger groups either relied on two or more automobiles or pressed into service one of a variety of small passenger buses increasingly used on the circuits during the 1920s.

The amount of mileage traveled by a company provided a convenient way for actors to summarize the rigors experienced on a particular circuit. For instance, in 1929 the Edgar Jones Players reported covering 18,000 miles on a two-week circle in southwestern Kansas during 36 weeks of trouping. These figures compute to reveal a circle covering 1,000 miles in possibly 14 workdays, or approximately 70–85 miles round-trip per performance (*BBB*, 23 May, 4).[2]

In 1930 the Ted North Players reported slightly less mileage on their two-week Kansas circuit, with 900 miles covered in 12 or more performances (*BBB*, 6 Mar., 2). The Ben Gray Players, running a seven-day circle in Iowa during 1930, averaged 600 miles per week, with headquarters at Clarion. As such their daily round-trip jump averaged slightly over 85 miles (*BBB*, 17 Apr., 4). On occasion efforts were made to reduce a company's weekly mileage, as when the Caylor Players moved the headquarters of their southern Minnesota circle "from Fairmont to Madelia, making a 150 mile savings in driving distance" (*BBB*, 5 Nov. 1936, 2).

From an actor's point of view, the less travel the better, and in recruiting prospective performers to fill the ranks advertisements boasted about short "jumps." In promoting the Marshall Players, while performing circle stock in Iowa in late 1929, manager H. B. Marshall emphasized "only one jump over 25 miles" (*BBB*, 19 Sept., 4).[3] Ralph Moody, manager of the Hazel McOwen Players, once advertised "home every night at midnight" (*BBB*, 24 Sept. 1936, 2). The simpler assurance of "Short jumps–home every night" came from the Clark and Adkins circle in Missouri during the mid–1930s (*BBB*, 17 Dec. 1936, 8).

Whatever the assurances, performers spent a considerable amount of time traveling the many rotations of a circuit. Many troupes passed the time studying lines individually or running lines as a group. If not rehearsing the show, company members often occupied themselves in friendly

A 1934 Plymouth used for circle stock touring by Sid Kingdon (courtesy of the Museum of Repertoire Americana).

conversation, singing, or numerous word games. On other occasions, listening to the radio filled the journey to and from the evening's performance. Wendell Poe especially remembers the radio in Mid Tilton's large DeSoto automobile. According to Poe, a favorite broadcast of the company came on late Sunday afternoons, when Tallula Bankhead hosted "The Big Show" on the NBC network. Some troupes, however, were forced to log far more total travel hours than others. The cast of an Ohio circle once run by Warren Hanscom included 11 adults and one child, with only one car among them. According to Hanscom, meager resources dictated double trips each day to performance sites (99).

Although jumps in circle stock typically involved some combination of cars, trailers, light trucks, or passenger buses (often referred to as "auto buses"), a few records mention the use of trains for circle transportation. Various sources cryptically mention Benjamin Vernon's and Al Trahern's use of trains on Long Island, occasionally citing basic information but more frequently relating amusing tales of rehearsals on trains and depot platforms. For instance, in 1914 Trahern announced his ensemble would "travel and live in its own special car" (this being a railroad sleeper car) and therefore the company would spend only the weekends in their home base of Sayville (*Suffolk County News,* 22 May, 1). Yet it remains unclear as to how extensively Trahern utilized this form of transportation. In early 1917, however, *Billboard* describes in greater detail the train travel by Murphy's Comedians performing circle stock on the West Coast:

Murphy's Comedians, after playing for several weeks in Bakersfield, Cal., terminated their engagement there and established a circuit of six towns in California, Santa Cruz, Monterey, Salinas, Watsonville, Gilroy and Hollister. The actors and musicians will travel by train and the scenery will be transported by large auto trucks. Mr. and Mrs. Murphy will travel in their own automobile. [10 Feb., 74]

Veteran rep actor Al Pitcaithley, whose voluminous scrapbook collection is housed at the Museum of Repertoire Americana, cites similar train usage in the Midwest. Pitcaithley records that in 1927-28 manager Elwin Strong—whose real name was Roy Savidge, brother of showman Walter Savidge—used train travel for his circle season in eastern Nebraska, a circuit that included the communities of Beatrice and Fremont. Undoubtedly more instances of circle stock train travel took place, but the records of such use have largely been lost.

A *Billboard* account on the Carroll Players in Maine, under the management of F. James Carroll, reports perhaps some of the most unusual transportation ever used on circle stock:

> The choice of Bucksport [Maine] as the base made it possible for Carroll to move his group by water as well as land. There was not a stand on the list that could not be reached from Bucksport by motorboat as well as by car. It would have been impossible to play the towns on different nights and be back at the base the same nights if the trips were made by rail.
>
> Considerable time could be saved by replacing the cars with a big motorboat. The distance from Bucksport to Belfast is about three miles by water, and about forty-eight miles by land, being just across upper Penobscot Bay. The distance between Bucksport and Bar Harbor on the water is also much shorter than by car. [7 Dec. 1929, 86]

Because the transportation used on circle stock frequently proved unreliable, it could not escape an occasional jab of humor. *Bill Bruno's Bulletin*, with a false tone of seriousness covering its humorous intent, once announced, "A certain circle show is reported to have closed last week because of a punctured tire" (7 Oct. 1937, 3). But as often is the case, humor strikes closer to the truth than first realized. Circle stock performer and manager Dick Wolever relates the following experience concerning his own travel practices which nearly resulted in the same outcome:

> We bought a Pierce-Arrow just to transport our circle stock actors and actresses. A big, old Pierce-Arrow that had been chauffeur driven in Kansas City; even had a telephone in the back seat. Five could ride in the back and three in front. And I'll never forget, we had to buy tires for it. Tires at that time cost about $15 for Sears's best. The tires on a Pierce-Arrow cost about $60 a piece. It almost broke the show. We thought the show was going to have to close because we couldn't buy tires for the Pierce-Arrow.

Whereas circles once relied almost exclusively on passenger cars of ample size for transportation, with the passage of time vehicles of even

Special touring vehicle used by the Chick Boyes Players for circle stock (courtesy of the Otoe County [Nebraska] Museum of Memories).

more substantial dimensions came into use. During the late 1920s in his traditional territory of Nebraska and Colorado, Chick Boyes employed a "15-passenger Studebaker bus" (*BBB,* 22 Aug. 1929, 8). In 1928 owner and manager Paul Brown of Brownie's Comedians, in an effort to accommodate further his pair of circle stock companies, provided them with "two new housecars and a new truck" in addition to a "new bus for the No. 2 rotary company" (*Billboard,* 29 Sept., 31). Later that same season *Billboard* reported both of the buses in Brown's organization had been wrecked during a winter snowstorm (16 Mar. 1929, 32).

As Paul Brown's purchases indicate, "housecars" (now commonly referred to as travel homes) began to make their mark in the late 1920s and reached widespread usage by the end of the following decade. The early homemade units, which were constructed by attaching simple living quarters onto a truck bed, demonstrated popularity among performers through rapidly increasing numbers. Although primitive when compared to the luxury of today's models, these improvised trailers invariably provided clean, consistent, and affordable housing, which was not always available in rural communities. By the beginning of the 1940s, transportation methods had evolved sufficiently that "At Liberty" ads placed by performers reflected the change; Ralph and Jessie Nicol once deemed it important to state: "Have factory-built trailer and car" (*BFB,* 16 Apr. 1941, 4).

One aspect of circle stock transportation that created controversy involved reimbursements to actors who drove their own vehicles to performance sites. This money was most welcome and very likely helped meet monthly payments—a vital goal of these car owners. In the minds of many small-time rep performers, having one's own means of travel provided considerable status and prestige. Bill Bruno, however, begged to differ:

> We have always doubted the argument that automobiles were looked upon by the town people as a sign of the actor's prosperity. It certainly is not when the actors have to make the plea that they are "poor actors who don't make much money" when they drive all over town in their new car looking for a $1.50-a-week-double room so that they may be able to pay for the dodgasted thing before it's worn out. Signs of prosperity! Don't kid yourselves.... Since the coming of the automobile the profession has retrogressed from actors to gypsies. And with the advent of the house car, conditions are becoming worse. [*BBB,* 6 Feb. 1936, 5]

Furthermore Bruno repeatedly voiced the concern that a great number of performers had, in effect, become enslaved to managers who knew that one missed installment to the bank meant that an actor's cherished automobile would be repossessed. Knowing this, Bruno argued, some unscrupulous managers "chiseled" the performers by slowly reducing their salaries, believing that they would always accept a smaller salary rather than none at all.

Occasional letters to Bruno from managers expressed displeasure over an actor's habit of spending money for car payments instead of maintaining and building the performer's wardrobe, as demanded in the old rep dictum of "look good on and off [stage]." Yet some managers were known to encourage automobiles in their companies to help hold down transportation expenses borne by management. On the whole, car ownership among performers continually increased, as did gas and mileage reimbursements, eventually becoming important enough to be mentioned in company advertisements. An ad for the 1929-30 circle season of the Hazel Hurd Players emphasized, "If you drive your own car mileage allowed" (*BBB,* 4 July 1929, 9). On the other hand, a letter to Bill Bruno from a concerned manager shows that actors sometimes may have taken advantage of travel allowances:

> May I say a word in defense of the manager who does furnish oil and gas to people who own their cars? Last winter I had on my show a team who owned a car of 1924 vintage. Each Saturday I would put five gallons of gas and sometimes two or three quarts of oil in that ancient bus, although the jumps on my circle were very short—not to exceed seventy-five miles on the week. But there were protests because I didn't put in more gas, so they could drive to the nearest key city on Sunday to visit a movie. And while on the subject, are managers supposed to furnish oil and gas for the

> transporting of some of these ten-ton convert railroad box cars which the owners thereof proudly refer to as their "house trailer home?" [*BBB*, 27 May 1937, 3]

How much these payments amounted to obviously varied from one manager and company to another. *Bill Bruno's Bulletin* reveals that a one-week circle in Minnesota covering 500 miles on its circuit paid $18 per week for "gas only"–a payment considered "ample" so long as the car was considered light in weight (15 Oct. 1936, 3).

Weather Conditions

Because the majority of circles operated during the winter months, travel (especially in the Midwest) frequently turned treacherous because of ice, snow, and high winds. In the estimation of numerous circle veterans, inclement weather produced the greatest hardships encountered, and their vivid struggles stand as testimony to this belief. Still, wintry blasts were not the only troublesome weather with which performers contended. Circles operating in the spring and summer often dealt with heavy rains and, at times, flooding. And following hard on the heels of excessive spring rains, the oppressive heat of summer frequently caused the abandoning of circle operations, especially during the months of July and August. Indeed, bad weather was the nemesis of circle stock.

Numerous tales about circle performers pitted against the wintry forces of nature survive. An account concerning the Edgar Jones Company during a blizzard in early 1929 is representative of many such hardship stories:

> It is the custom of the company to leave Larned [Kansas] after the show Saturday night in order to reach Abilene [Kansas], the Monday stand, on Sunday in time to repaint scenery and get the next show ready for opening the following night. The blizzard came on Saturday night, however, and it was decided to wait until Sunday morning to make the long trip to Abilene, but we were held up because of the impassable roads. Started out Monday morning, fought the blockaded roads all day and arrived at Abilene at 7:30 Monday night to find the theatre half filled with customers. At 8:30 we rang up on time to a packed house, using the old scenery, though most of the effects for *The Vulture* had been built during the week previous while we were on the road. [*BBB*, 17 Jan., 2]

Dick Wolever, circling with Ray Bash out of Salina, Kansas, in the 1930s, provides the following as a testimony to the ferocity of a Midwest winter storm:

> Our Saturday night date was a little town just west of Salina, right down a big broad highway. So we drove out that evening to do our Saturday night show and just as the show started, it started to snow. And by the time the performance was over, there was two feet of snow on the ground and drifts

up to twelve feet. As there was no way we could get out of this little town, the cast checked into the hotel–a very small hotel–and spent the night.

The next morning it was even worse–the snow was deeper, nothing was moving, telephone wires were down; you couldn't contact anybody anywhere. So we spent a quiet Sunday. Monday was the same thing. Everything was closed and with no deliveries into the town the hotel was running out of food and the grocery store was also running out of food. But we got through Monday.

Tuesday morning it had cleared and the highway crews were trying to cut through the highway so traffic could move and so Tuesday afternoon we got started back to Salina. We drove through snow drifts eight, ten, and twelve feet tall, sometimes for a mile or two. Traffic was just one-way, just wide enough for one car; and then every 200 or 300 yards, they had made an opening at the side of the roadway so that if you met a car, one of you could back up and back off the side and let the other car pass. We finally got back into Salina about 7 o'clock that night. Of course we had lost our Monday and Tuesday night shows.

Wolever concludes by attesting, "It was conditions like these that made circle stock tough."

Sometimes the dangerous roads during a blizzard were challenged by performers determined to make it back to their base community. Laura Guthrie relates a gripping story about one such attempt. While on a circle in north-central Iowa during the early years of the Depression, the Tilton-Guthrie Players regularly performed at the Goodell, Iowa, Opera House. During one visit weather conditions swiftly changed and it started to snow just as the house was opened to the public. By the conclusion of the standing-room-only performance the snowfall had intensified into a raging blizzard. Local authorities ordered that no one should attempt to leave town.

Disregarding the warning, Mid Tilton decided he would return the scenery truck to the company's base in Mason City, Iowa. His partner, Bill Guthrie, decided that if Tilton was willing to try to make it through the storm, he would also. The front seat of the passenger car driven by Guthrie included Tillie Tilton (wife of Mid) in the passenger position and his wife, Laura Guthrie, sandwiched in between.

With poor visibility and slick road conditions, Mrs. Tilton looked out the side window to help keep the car on the highway and Mrs. Guthrie carefully watched the tail lights of the scenery truck in front of them to prevent a collision. On occasion Tillie found it necessary to snap her head back from peering out the window to avoid striking it against a roadside mailbox.

Finally Laura refused to allow her husband to drive any farther under the life-threatening conditions. Knowing that Garner, Iowa, lay approximately halfway between Goodell and Mason City, she demanded, "If we make it to Garner I absolutely will not go one step farther. This is crazy–only actors and morons are out in weather like this. We have a daughter to think about and I want to see her grow up. I don't want to end up in a ditch frozen to death."

She prevailed over her husband with such sentiments, and the entire group stopped and spent the night in a hotel in Garner. A telephone call to the Guthrie's landlady explained the situation and set up care for the young Guthrie girl until crews cleared the roads and her parents could return to Mason City.

Trouper Ruby Wren remembers that while circling with the Ben Gray Stock Company in Iowa during 1933, icy roads created a similar life-threatening situation. She recalls, "Coming home one night we slid off the road into a snow bank, with it 18 degrees below zero. We thought we would freeze to death before the show truck finally missed us and came back to the rescue" (MRA Collection).

Although not required in the situations cited above, the countless one-room schools that once dotted this nation frequently provided life-saving shelter for circle companies caught in the fury of a winter storm. Mercedes Brunk recalls that, while she was a member of the Chick Boyes No. 2 circle in northern Kansas during the winter of 1929-30, the unit became snow-bound due to blocked roads. Realizing they could not get through, the company "broke into a little country schoolhouse and built a fire and stayed there until morning." From the perspective of over 50 years, she reflects, "This was real trouping. Since I was so young—with stars in my eyes—it was all very glamorous to me." Barbara Brooks Emory relates a similar story concerning the Dick Dickson Show in Minnesota during the winter of 1937-38. Caught in a monstrous blizzard, the company battled its way to a faint, distant school building and found it an adequate but simply furnished lodging for the night.

> No electricity, but a lamp, and a pot belly stove with plenty of wood in the building. The boys made a fire and we spent the night, until the snow plough got us out the next day. Of course, we were all starved, but the whole thing was really fun—at least it seemed so at the time. Ah! Youth!

The toll of adverse conditions on the performance schedule of circle companies could quickly mount during the long winter season. In 1937, thinking they had avoided the worst of winter by waiting to open until late March, Harvey Twyman's circle in South Dakota lost ten nights in only six weeks due to heavy snow and blocked roads (*BBB*, 6 May, 1). Many managers simply accepted lost performances due to inclement weather as a reality of performing circle stock, especially in the winter.

Yet some managers did not routinely submit to unfavorable weather. Actors who worked for Mid Tilton remember his insistence that a circle company should emulate the famous motto of the U.S. Postal Department. The rationale for his "show must get through" attitude did not develop merely out of duty and dedication, however. Having failed to make an appearance only once, a company could expect the public in that particular town to equate undesirable weather, however marginal, with no performance by the ensemble. This being the case, even a slight snowfall might greatly reduce the size of the audience. By maintaining a consistent record through all weather extremes, Tilton felt the public would also go to similar lengths to attend performances. A steady income for a circle company always remained a primary objective for a successful manager, and units under Tilton's control relentlessly traveled through a gamut of adverse weather conditions to meet their commitments, as did many other organizations.

Besides the harsh realities of precipitation and wind, intense cold presented a sizable obstacle to circle performers. A report entitled "Extreme Cold Hits Circles" summarizes conditions from a period of the winter of 1935-36, yet the account could describe many similar periods from other winters:

> The sub-zero weather of the last two weeks has been unusually hard on a majority of circle companies, resulting in a number of definite closings and many lost nights. The Minnesota and North Dakota stocks suffered most, there being a number of permanent closings. The temperature in both states ranged between 30 and 40 below all of last week, ending with a heavy snow fall and blizzard last Saturday which effectually blocked all roads. The same conditions prevailed throughout the Nebraska-Kansas territory where companies lost three and four nights of the week. The present week opened equally as bad, but with a promise of more favorable weather before its close. [*BBB,* 20 Feb. 1936, 1][4]

Such extreme circumstances presented a variety of challenges to performers, foremost among them being the comfort of travel vehicles, along with the heating of the performance sites.

Travel in extremely frigid conditions called for concerted efforts by the performers to keep warm, all the while remaining mindful of emergencies. For some, stuffing old newspapers around the car door openings helped considerably. Other troupers heated bricks and wrapped them in newsprint to use as foot warmers, or simply bundled themselves in blankets. Still others went so far as to carry kerosene heaters in their transportation units. Family members of the Lew Henderson Players recall a time when extra efforts were demanded because of the extreme cold of winter. Since the company automobile lacked antifreeze, the end of each day required the draining of the radiator. The following day sufficient time needed to be set aside to fill the radiator, start the vehicle, and allow the engine to warm up before leaving for that evening's performance. As for emergency preparations, Maude Gentry admits always to carrying an apple and a candy bar during winter travel in case of being stranded on the road overnight, but she thankfully never found herself in a situation where she needed them. However, Gentry does confess to "lots of practice praying on dark, cold nights."

Managers who claimed victory in the battle against fierce winter weather frequently bragged of their methods in the trade publications. Such boasting can be found in early 1930 when Ben Gray wrote to *Bill Bruno's Bulletin* claiming to be the "hottest show on the road" during the winter months. Gray proudly reported that all cars with his show were equipped with "high-grade heaters" and that he also carried "oil stoves for the dressing rooms" (13 Mar., 4). Certainly seeing to the comfort and well-being of the company marked a wise and conscientious manager.

But the heating of performance sites during frigid cold spells typically presented far greater problems. It was not uncommon for a company to cancel a performance after discovering that the temperature in the hall or theater could not be raised sufficiently to accommodate an audience comfortably. In 1936 reports surfaced that the Nig Allen circle (headquartered in Dodge City, Kansas) lost the first two Monday performances in their base community after finding it impossible to warm the large municipal auditorium adequately (*BBB,* 20 Feb., 1).

One heroic effort to continue performing during an extended cold snap involved the Tilton-Guthrie Players operating out of Mason City, Iowa, during the late winter of 1935-36. At one point in this harsh winter the state of Iowa found itself suffering from a coal shortage, due in part to a recent heavy snowfall.

> The situation became so severe that the governor was obliged to ration coal to several districts, and the circle in which the Players operated was particularly short of fuel. There was no way of getting an adequate supply to the towns in which they played.
> But that didn't stop the Tilton-Guthrie circle. Finding that the managers of the theatres were unable to secure coal with which to adequately heat their houses, the show each night of playing took with them out of Mason City enough coal to heat the theatre, whenever it was possible to get through the snow blockaded roads. Which is the first instance in the history of western show business that this has been found necessary. [*BBB,* 5 Mar. 1936, 1]

Such reports of gripping cold, however, do not necessarily mean that all areas were equally affected at the same time because Midwest weather tends to vary dramatically between locations. Thus Wallace Bruce once crowed during the devastatingly cold winter of 1935-36 that his circle (in an undisclosed territory) "basked in 40 above weather" with a resulting highly successful week while other circles languished in "below zero" weather nearby (*BBB,* 30 Jan. 1936, 7).

Besides threatening the well-being of the actors, poor weather adversely affected attendance and income for a company. Comments and figures recorded by Chick Boyes in his business ledgers show drastic weather induced decreases in income. Once, following a week filled with heavy snow, cold, and blizzardlike conditions, Boyes's terse entry "loss plenty" emphasizes the economic impact of such weather. Even before subtracting various transportation and management expenses, the ledger already indicates a deficit for the week. When compared to the typical income for the circuit, it becomes obvious that Boyes absorbed a significant loss. In many instances, the simple ledger notation of "bad roads" or "cold" during the winter months helps explain the diminished returns for an evening. At other times ledger entries for a performance reveal no income but only the word *blizzard* or the succinct entry "No sho sno."

A good sense of humor proved to be one inexpensive weapon with which to battle such extreme weather conditions. Fortunately comic perspectives seemed abundant among the circle performers:

> I love to be an actor
> > And travel with a show,
> But I do not crave a circle
> > When it's thirty-four below!
> > > [*BBB*, 27 Feb. 1936, 5]

Another performer once wrote to editor Bruno stating, "Just finished a week of below zero trouping. Now ready to join next Arctic expedition" (*BBB*, 30 Jan. 1936, 5). On one occasion Bruno wryly observed that "during the recent extreme cold, a lot of circle actors discovered that radio artists are not the only ones who can work without audiences" (*BBB*, 27 Feb. 1936, 5).

In the South winter weather also frequently produced poor travel conditions, including rain, muddy roads, and occasional flooding. A case in point took place in January 1936 when high water and impassable roads caused a temporary closing of both Kelly Brothers circle companies in Alabama, throwing all involved out of work. Suddenly finding themselves jobless, performers obtained employment as best they could. Some played nightclub dates in Southern cities, while others worked with a nearby theater company until their original circles resumed operation (*BBB*, 16 Jan., 2). Even mildly inclement weather could play havoc to those circles operating in open airdomes. With only a protecting roof over the performers, rain and unseasonable cold proved to be disastrous for business.

With the arrival of warmer weather, conditions rarely improved as quickly as the performers desired. Even when seasonal rains did not cause flooding, the roads of the rural countryside were normally reduced to a quagmire. Of course poor road conditions in the spring were expected and were largely out of the hands of circle management. Still, an astute manager attempted to make decisions to further a troupe's cause. Specific knowledge of better road conditions in another region could well influence the establishment of a new circuit. Lew Henderson, according to his daughter

A simple airdome setup by Chick Boyes in Hebron, Nebraska, during the 1920s (courtesy of the Thayer County [Nebraska] Museum).

Billie Schuller, expanded his tent and circle stock territory from northern Iowa into Minnesota in the early 1920s, in large part because of reports that road conditions held up better in Minnesota since the northern roads were better maintained and graveled.

A different challenge faced those companies that attempted circle stock during the summer months. Because of the intense heat that could build up inside the theaters or halls used for performances, the failure rate for midyear circuits always remained high. This was the case in 1929 when the Nigel Pelham circle, playing the Warner-controlled houses in St. Louis, closed after only one week due to "excessive" summer heat (*BBB*, 1 Aug., 2). Entries in Chick Boyes's ledgers remind one that an abundance of rain or heat or wind during spring and summer months affected travel by both the circle companies and the general public. Ledger entries of "bad roads" during the months of late spring obviously indicate excessive rain. On the other hand, the simple entry "dirt" in lieu of income clearly denotes the choking and blinding dust storms that plagued the Midwest during the dry summers of the 1930s.

Harsh weather could play havoc not only with theatrical troupes but also with the agricultural prospects of an area, and, hence, could make it difficult to attract audiences. Ralph Masters confronted such a weather-induced economic recession in 1940 when he abandoned the opening of a

Depression-era dust storm captured by Henry Brunk's Comedians (courtesy of the Museum of Repertoire Americana).

circle in southern Alabama "owing to late freezes having ruined all crops." Realizing all too well the impact the freezes would have on the local economy and the public's purchasing power, he dropped plans for ten weeks of performances with a five-member company. Masters instead moved the show westward to a new territory (*BBB,* 25 Apr., 1).

Yet when winter storms brought considerable hardships upon the circle companies (especially in the form of snow) but did not damage the growth of crops, Bill Bruno repeatedly reminded his readers to remain calm and philosophical about the weather since the public would still likely pay for entertainment then and in the future. In reporting on severe seasonal conditions hitting Texas in early 1930, Bruno emphasized, "There is, however, the satisfaction of knowing that those shows able to pull through the winter are facing a summer season as unusually good as the winter conditions are bad" (*BBB,* 30 Jan., 7). The basis for such reasoning remained the firm belief that a heavy snowcover added to the ground moisture level during the spring thaw and helped ensure good crops and happy farmers, which in turn was likely to produce a successful tent or circle season the following summer and fall.

Performance Sites

A major managerial challenge involved securing satisfactory performance sites for a company's circuit. Because circle stock reached a wide variety of communities, including many of the smallest rural hamlets, places to perform varied greatly. Managers found possible venues in conventional theaters, community buildings, fraternal meeting rooms, school facilities, labor halls, taverns, and even empty storefronts. According to Dale Madden, Sr., the Madden and Stillian Players "played any kind of hall." He elaborates:

> In the earlier days, most every small town or community did have an Opera House and reasonably good facilities. However, we did not let a poor facility prevent us from playing the town. We would contract a Lodge Meeting Room, or School Gymnasium, etc., etc.

In many instances, especially during the 1930s and thereafter, the best performance site in a small community had been unused for some time. The first exploration of such a site undoubtedly found it cold, grimy, and musty smelling. Dick Wolever remembers:

> Some of the theatres you would go into hadn't been open in two or three years. You would have to practically rebuild them. I've seen front curtains let down that split right in the middle because they hadn't been down in twenty years. And the theatres were usually dirty.

Although educational facilities provided spaces for many circle companies, performers under Mid Tilton's charge tell us he avoided playing circle stock in schools, if at all possible. Tilton thought that for many farmers attending a performance at school evoked negative connotations of learning, teachers, and authority figures, and he further contended that most farmers felt they had to dress up to attend such an event. Yet a circle performance in a public structure or commercial building meant that individuals could come dressed in work clothes and were therefore able to feel comfortable in their "own hall."

In many instances a performance site remained plain and simple. Noreen Depenbrink recalls playing circle stock in a town that did not have any appropriate space, so the company cleaned out an "old storage room" to perform in. According to Depenbrink, "The audience had 'box' seats, and by that, I mean they really sat on old boxes and nail kegs. There was no stage, so we had to perform on the flat floor." The size of venues also could present challenges. Billie Schuller recalls appearances with her family's company (the Lew Henderson Players) in places that were so small "that if you went off left and had to come in right, you went out the door, ran around the back of the building, and came in the other side."

The hall used by the Collier Players in their base community of Goff, Kansas, in the mid–1930s was, according to Jay Bee Flesner, "an old garage" with "the stage and chairs from the tent put into it." The decided advantage in using this setting was that instead of having to pay for both storage and performance spaces in Goff, one site served both purposes, essentially allowing for the free maintenance of the summer equipment, including the tent. Some of these large bare halls even served as community roller skating centers at various times during the month. Performing in these sites became a favorite of the children of Lew Henderson, who could entertain themselves by skating around the chairs as the adults loaded up the scenery truck.

Citing his circle stock experience as not being a pleasant one, R. Norton Walther recalls many hardships connected with the performance sites he appeared in:

> The halls we played were not theatres, they were town halls with no rest room facilities or [central] heating facilities. When you got into town you would have to build a fire after shaking down the ashes and hauling them out. Then dust the seats and try to set up some scenery. Hopefully you got the place warm enough to where you could dress and put on some make-up.

In many instances during the winter months, soon after arriving at a performance site troupers placed their makeup kits near to the heat source in the building in order to thaw out the various supplies, which had frozen during the trip from their home base.

Jay Bee Flesner remembers the cleaning routinely required in many of these halls prior to setting up for a performance:

> The one thing that bothered more than anything else was they would have dances during the week in these halls and very often we had to sweep up all the wax and the dust and the empty beer bottles and things before we got going.

A number of troupes budgeted (not without some sacrifices) to hire help from each community to heat the performance site, straighten chairs, and clean the premises prior to the company's arrival.

Circling in the mid–1950s, Dave Koch especially recalls "dirty, dusty, dark, small theatres" and dressing rooms that were even worse. Sometimes these dressing rooms were used for the storage of food or old farm equipment, or served as the building's rest rooms. Even so, a great number of these halls lacked indoor rest room facilities; some even failed to provide outdoor facilities. In these cases, the performers relied on two chamber pots—one for the men and one for the women—trying not to forget to empty them upon leaving. Because the audiences were familiar with the facilities, they presumably had prepared themselves beforehand.

Although the backstage areas of these performance sites were often cramped and unkempt, stories do emerge to suggest occasional pleasant surprises, as Maude Gentry relates from her circle experience:

> In one tiny town, I think it was Bristol [Illinois], we worked in the town hall and made up in the kitchen. It was the time of ration stamps, but a butcher

there was kind to us and sold us steaks, liver, etc. So before the show we cooked dinner on a big old iron stove in the kitchen and when the customers came in, the place smelled like a café, rather than a theater.

Such a variety of performance areas brought with it a wide array of acting challenges, which required ingenuity and resourcefulness on behalf of the circle companies. Dale Madden, Sr., recalls an interesting performance area in Barada, Nebraska, played during the winter months of 1931:

> This town ... had simply a loft over the general store. Entrance to the loft or so called opera house was gained by an almost perpendicular staircase in the back of the store, past the potatoes, vegetables, canned goods and dry goods, and on up to the show. The manager usually announced when entry could be gained, and the audience which was usually loafing around the store would hastily climb the stairs, pay their ten cents, and go into the hall to sit on planks supported by nail kegs. The planks had been pushed up through the outside window; the stairs were too narrow to carry anything up.
>
> The only heat in the hall was provided by a big wood burning stove, which was installed directly in center stage. There was only about a two foot clearance on the apron of the stage to cross right or left, so on a cold night and with the stove a cherry red from heat, if during the play it was necessary to make a right cross, or left, whichever, one had to run the so-called gauntlet in FRONT of this massive stove. I can assure you that many of those crosses made in front of the stove were done very quickly.

Dick Elsenpeter describes one town in Iowa where "a quarter electric meter" controlled the community hall's power, requiring the cast members periodically to play the part of an "electrician":

> [Manager] Tilton would give every actor like a dollar's worth of quarters and you'd have them in your pocket. You had to keep feeding the meter which was back stage to keep the lights on. Sometimes you wouldn't catch it in time. The lights would go off and you'd feel around for that damn meter. It was dark back there ... [but soon someone would] put another quarter in.

Because of the cost and difficulties in transportation and maintenance, elaborate lighting systems were avoided. While various records show that some circle companies toured with their own lighting equipment, most troupes relied on the available furnishings on location. Either way, the performers likely relied on flat white light produced by some combination of footlights and floodlights, with the possible addition of one or two overhead strip lights. In some settings, the performers made do with only the nontheatrical illumination available above the performance area.

Although the reliance on a backstage electric meter obviously caused problems, events could be worse. Sometimes severe weather brought down electrical lines and threw a performance into darkness. Yet the show still went on. Veteran circle performer Gus Neuhaus fondly remembers being forced to perform during stormy nights by only kerosene lamp light.

Scenery

The typical scenery used on circle stock was designed to adapt to varying performance sites, in addition to satisfying the need for ease in transportation. For the most part these requirements were met by the use of dyed scenery and adjustable battens or frames. With the use of dye, rather than dry pigment paint, scenic drops could be folded or rolled without fear of chipping, cracking, or flaking. In addition, the dyed colors resisted running when they became wet. Advertisements for dyed scenery claimed that upon becoming soiled, such drops could be easily cleaned with gasoline.

If not relying upon dyed muslin for scenic drops, a circle company likely used printed cotton broadcloth, common flannel, or possibly even muslin painted with specially treated oil-based paints. At any rate, because these drops were intended to be rolled or folded they acquired the nickname of "rag" scenery. Adjustable battens and frames were important because performance sites varied greatly in size and shape. Stage widths might range from only 15 feet to well over 30; one night the ceiling above the stage might measure only seven feet, while the following evening a 12-foot ceiling or higher could be encountered.

Although the majority of circles relied upon the convenience of rag scenery, some companies did travel with conventional wooden-frame flats. Tilton's Comedians usually carried a production's complete needs, including both scenic flats and furniture, in their own scenery truck. And although more cumbersome than rag scenery, Tilton's flats could be erected more quickly than setting up a rag set, or so we are told. On one of his circles in the early 1930s, Neil Schaffner boasted of carrying a wide variety of scenic items, including "practical doors, a trouping ceiling, bracket lights, [and] extra footlights and dimmers" (134). At the opposite end of the spectrum, at one time J. B. Rotnour allegedly carried all of his performance supplies—including rag scenery and the obligatory telephone prop—in a large candy box that could fit into the trunk of his Buick. Normally furniture or large props needed for a particular production could be obtained from local businesses. In return merchants likely received a few complimentary tickets or possibly some verbal thanks delivered from the stage during a scene break of the production.

The initial set up of rag scenery was actually quite simple. The first step involved anchoring a number of screw hooks in the ceiling directly above the performance area. From each hook was attached a small pulley, thus the screw hooks needed to be solidly anchored to a rafter support. Next, ropes were run from off stage through the pulleys and were attached to a batten onto which the top of the muslin or other material was fastened. The technique used to give the walls an appearance of being smooth and solid required either tacking down the bottom of the material to the stage floor or placing weights on the bottom of the material and then raising the entire unit with the rope and pulley system until the material became taut.

Most companies included individuals talented enough to paint credibly their own rag drops. Dick Elsenpeter describes the following procedures in preparing scenery from conventional muslin using the popular "diamond dye" method, a scenic painting process using dyes attributed to Jesse Cox of Estherville, Iowa. First, unbleached muslin (ranging in width from 48 inches to 54 inches or even 72 inches) was sewn together (normally with the seams running vertically) to form the desired width and height of the back wall and two side walls for a conventional box setting. Door and window openings within a wall unit were simply formed by inserting shortened vertical strips of muslin.

After sewing together the muslin to form the preferred setting, the application of an animal glue mixture "sized" the muslin. Applying a size coat helped fill the pores of the fabric and tighten it, producing a smoother surface to accept the dyes. To facilitate sizing, the muslin needed to be stretched by either hanging it from a batten and weighting down the bottom of the drop, or placing it on a paint frame. The glue mixture could then be brushed on and allowed to dry.

With the material properly prepared, the application of the dye could begin. According to Elsenpeter, the chosen dye mixture would be dissolved and placed in an apparatus commonly called a "flit gun." Such devices were originally used as hand-pumped sprayers for insecticides, often found in an agricultural setting. After spraying a covering of dye onto the material—referred to as "flitting" the dye on—a sponge or rag would be used to smooth out the distribution of the color. Once this first color had been allowed to dry, a contrasting color could then be flitted on to provide texture.

Pinning six-inch-wide strips of brown or black cloth around an opening left for a window or a door helped frame the opening and suggest woodwork. Because of the need to use scenery more than once, wall units were frequently dyed a pale, neutral color. Then the appearance of the set could easily be altered through the hanging of different draperies or using distinctive props and furnishings. Because these cloth wall units did not have any framing behind them, a painting or portrait could be hung with the aid of a straightened clothes hanger with one end looped over the top batten of the wall and the other end supporting the object. Such "dressing" of the stage became an essential way to alter the appearance of generic drops and therefore stretch a scenery budget.

In contrast to the widely used dye process, Jay Bee Flesner practiced a painting method that, although not based on dyes, also allowed for finished drops to be rolled or folded. This system used oil-based paints, dangerously thinned with gasoline and some glycerin. The glycerin provided

**Scenery truck used by Tilton's Comedians on circle stock based out of Chilli-
cothe, Missouri, in 1957 (courtesy of the Museum of Repertoire Americana).**

the special ingredient that helped the drop to remain relatively flexible and
not crack when prepared for storage or transit. As an alternative to dyeing
or painting muslin, some companies used cloth directly from commercial
dry goods stores, selecting material with a pattern subtle enough to resemble wallpaper. Of the various common cloths used for such scenery, flannel proved a popular choice because of its reputation for failing to retain
wrinkles. Companies hung flannel in largely the identical manner used for
dyed muslin, although the flannel remained in individual units of varying
lengths while muslin was normally sewn together. Flannel pieces were simply straight-pinned together to form the desired combination of doors and
windows.

If a company found itself unable to prepare its own scenic elements,
ads in the trade publications frequently offered scenery for sale. For instance, in 1929 the Hillman Stock Company advertised diamond dye
scenery–"All Drops uniform size, 12 x 28 feet"–from the Jesse Cox Studios,
which had been used the past two seasons on circle stock. No prices, however, were included (*BBB*, 26 Sept., 9). In 1939 Christy Obrecht offered the
following scenery items for "cash" sale only: "Drapes and chair covers,

$3.50 per set; 1 set of Flats, 10 ft high, and 2 slam doors in new crates, $15.00 for set and doors" (*BBB*, 16 Nov., 2). Moreover, the company offered diamond dye "Tack ons" at $5.00 per set, these being common dyed drops capable of either hanging or being attached to a surface. As late as 1941 Bob Feagin claimed that most scenic studios would custom create a basic dyed drop for as little as 20 dollars, which he thought infinitely better than using some type of "calico" setting, an obvious reference to the practice of using printed cloth purchased directly off the bolt from a local store (*BFB*, 5 Nov., 3).

Some scenic methods used on circle stock were more complex. The Sun Players traveled with a free-standing, adjustable frame unit from which a working front curtain and drops were hung; therefore it could be set up in the middle of a gymnasium floor and would operate much like a stage surrounded with a proscenium arch. Built with graduated widths of metal pipe, the unit's dimensions quickly adjusted with the aid of simple thumb screws. Some companies followed a similar plan when appearing in large, open spaces, but lacking a frame unit like the Sun Players, personnel merely hung stage drapes from the ceiling to frame the performance area.

At various times circle performances would be given without the benefit of any scenic effects. While the lack of scenery might well have bothered performers on occasion or caused them to be amused at the absurdity of a bare stage, rarely did it seem to lessen the audience's appreciation. Dick Elsenpeter recalls an incident when working for Bernie Collier, manager and Toby comedian of the Collier Players, which highlights this apparent difference between the perceptions of performers and audience:

> Collier would do the plays as written. As such, one time we did a play in which a line really impressed me. A female character entered and said, "Oh, what a beautiful home. Look at these beautiful tapestries and paintings." And there we were in a beer hall and the only tapestries and paintings were neon beer signs on the walls and crepe paper streamers hanging down from the ceiling, which is really ugly. But this didn't bother you. The audience completely accepted it because you came every week. And I think the secret here is the audience was made to feel a part of the company; they got to know you.

Concerning the dearth—or nonexistence—of polished scenery and lighting, Frank Wiziarde insists,

> The public accepted this. I mean, this was before sophistication became the thing. It is kind of an old cliché, but in those days the play was the thing. I mean we could do the play on a bare stage and as long as it was entertaining, people accepted it and went along with it.

Perhaps director George Cleaver's legendary admonition to circle actors speaks well to this concern: "If you can't act good enough that the audience will forget the scenery, I want you to go home."

Competition

Astute managers attempted to stay abreast of the forms of entertainment that might affect or seriously damage a company's ability to win a share of an area's business. Competition for circle stock chiefly took the form of other touring theater and entertainment units such as rep companies, medicine shows, and vaudeville troupes, in addition to various types of local events. Most of this competition could be considered entirely fair and appropriate, and if the rival unit maintained an above-board policy in its dealings with the public, circle stock managers had no legitimate complaint. Sometimes a circle simply found the going too rough and realized it was best to move on, as related by Neil Schaffner concerning a circle operating in early 1924:

> On our opening week the Wednesday night town was Oquawka, Illinois, and we had about two hundred people in the house, which was not bad considering what we had been doing in rep, but when we came back the following week we did not sell a single ticket. A new dance hall was opened that night and just about everybody in town went there. We skipped Oquawka after that but the town that replaced it was not much better. [82]

Noreen Depenbrink recalls a time when the challenge confronting the Harry Dunbar circuit in Missouri proved too great:

> We opened the box office, but nary a soul put in an appearance, so the manager of the show ambled down to the town square to see what was happening. Well, a *free* medicine show blew into town, so people came down from the hills in wagons, cars and on foot to take in the medicine show. Our audience consisted of an old cow who wandered by the hall, and as we didn't think she would appreciate our thespian efforts, we packed up our wardrobe and scenery and stole away like thieves in the night.

Yet on occasion circle managers had reason to charge other touring units with unfair practices. For example, as a matter of policy, well-established circle companies maintained an identifiable geographic territory into which other reputable groups did not encroach. Because of the long-term commitment the company had made to the area, the troupers thought of it as their own. However, some circle companies—almost always smaller and not established in one area—ignored the industry's acceptance of the "ownership" of these areas and attempted to infringe on an established territory, or, as one trouper put it, a company's "sphere of influence." An interesting map drawn by Mac MacDonald, circa 1934, while touring with the Budd Todd circle in Nebraska demonstrates this thinking. According to his wife, Maree MacDonald, the map displays "Mac's way of indicating the competition for business at that time." In explaining that the bottom center of the map shows Toby Riebel's area completely enclosed within Joe Marion's sphere of influence, MacDonald notes,

It was not unusual for two companies to play simultaneously in the same areas, particularly if business was good and the companies were well known in the area. But it certainly contributed to drying up and burning out the areas, particularly if two companies in the same circle area were using the same bills.... It must have been that the two had an agreement about overlapping into each other's territory.

However, while a challenge to an established company's sphere of influence was one thing (indeed some considered it an example of free enterprise), unabashed fraud remained another. Clearly troupes did exist that were less than honest in their dealings with the public–both financially and artistically–thus giving a black eye to an industry that largely met with outstanding public support. If the disruptions caused by such unprincipled groups were serious enough, they were said to "burn up" a territory, very likely damaging the public's trust in any theater company, reputable or not.

Of the various types of unscrupulous (and often clearly illegal) actions undertaken in the name of circle stock, the one found most distasteful by competitors involved the manager who solicited merchants for support of a circle, collected money in advance, and then disappeared without a single performance, never to be seen again. Persons running this scam–usually under a number of aliases–would strike one region, lay low for a period of time, and then hit an area some distance from the first. Concerning one such event in Cedar Bluffs, Nebraska, in 1936, the *Omaha* (Nebraska) *World-Herald* recorded:

> Strangely enough, the Wm. A. Strange Players did not show up for an engagement here last night, and merchants of the town are out about $25. A smooth stranger was here a week ago with a proposal involving the players, some tickets, and some cash for him as promoter. Last night a crowd gathered at the auditorium to see the show, but no players appeared. After an hour of waiting some one produced an accordion and the crowd danced until late in the evening. [qtd. in *BBB*, 15 Oct. 1936, 1]

Strange, according to this report, had already operated this scam for nearly three years.

In 1941 Bob Feagin addressed the ongoing problem of "burned up" territory, reiterating the sad conclusion that such damage was long-lasting:

> Summing up all our experience, and information, we are forced to the reluctant conclusion that there is something wrong with the circle business.... We all KNOW what caused it. Thank heaven the ones that burned up territory are growing smaller every season. We know of at least five that have been forced to quit in the last two years. The pity of it is that they have left the people in the localities in which they operated with such a disgust and contempt for stage shows that it will be years before a good show can win them back again. [*BFB*, 26 Feb., 3]

Even though the competition from other varieties of touring entertainment could be sizable in itself, the motion picture industry represented circle stock's most challenging foe. Following the introduction of sound motion pictures in 1927, the reaction to its impact on rep theater in general and on circle stock in particular appears to have taken two forms. One response maintained that sound movies posed only a temporary obstacle that would be overcome by a superior product in live drama. Another faction viewed the movie industry as a far more serious threat.

Supporting the position that the sound movies would constitute only an "incidental issue," the primary editorial from the 3 November 1928 issue of *Billboard* reads in part,

> More talk is being heard about rotary stock troupes, and the opening of doors to dramatic companies gradually is becoming a financial necessity for many houses that have tried their darnedest to hold to films or nothing.
>
> The talkies are going to put up a big fight, backed by millions of dollars spent in advertising, exploitation and propaganda, but somehow the feeling is becoming more widespread that the sound screen will have its introductory splurge and then settle down as an incidental issue in the entertainment program.
>
> Dramatic stock appears to have the brightest outlook in the theatrical field. [51]

In the summer of 1929 Bill Bruno preached the philosophy that talkies would not supplant live theater:

> Neale Helvey writes us that he will this summer play only towns that have had the talking pictures for four months or more. Because he has in three weeks found that the public is already tired of the new pictures. He insists that after four months of the infliction of them, the public is ready to take on the spoken drama with open arms.

Further on in this editorial, Bruno once again voiced his frequently articulated position concerning the superiority of live performances:

> When people laugh at supposed pathetic scenes in pictures, with the hokum smeared on thick, there is nothing to fear from the still brutally imperfect talking pictures. The continued boosting of them by the press and magazines of the country—all of them looking for more advertising at better rates—should frighten no one. The interests can make picture[s] but they can't make audiences to like them. As Ted North recently said: "Who's afraid of the squawkies?" Let's not be frightened at shadows, but give the public what it *wants* in the way it wants it and there isn't a chance for the talking pictures. [*BBB*, 27 June 1929, 6]

Shortly thereafter, *Bill Bruno's Bulletin* reported that a "substantial cut in squawkie film charges" would soon take place. The reduction reportedly would save "11,000 small town [movie] theatres" from impending financial ruin brought on by high rental fees charged by motion picture companies. Editor Bruno responded to this by asserting:

> Nothing is going to save the showmen in towns under 2,000 population, unless it is the spoken drama. Many managers are beginning to thoroughly realize this.... There now seems no alternative other than the spoken drama. [*BBB,* 1 Aug. 1929, 7]

As history shows, however, Bruno's optimism could not stand up to reality. Many observers have pointed out that in direct head-to-head competition between motion pictures and circle stock, the live theater was destined to lose out, in large part, because movies could charge a lower admission fee. This viewpoint appears supported by a poll conducted early in 1928 by Chester B. Bahn, dramatic critic of the *Syracuse* (New York) *Herald,* which provides some insight into the cause of what Bahn labeled "the decline of the spoken drama and the ascendancy of movies." Bahn found the "preponderance of opinions held that (1) movies are cheaper, (2) picture houses are more attractive, and (3) the average film is better played than the average road show" (*Billboard,* 19 May, 42). While Bahn's survey reflects the opinions of residents of the state of New York, his results certainly could be projected to the general public as well.

In the minds of many, the taking over of independent theaters by various movie conglomerates stood as the major threat of sound pictures against circle stock. By November 1929 an alarmed Bill Bruno proclaimed, "There can now be no doubt that these [movie] interests have reached some agreement and formed a widespread plan to kill the spoken drama in the interests of their latest infliction, the sound pictures." As evidence Bruno presented the case of a successful circle company that had recently been forced to close:

> Starting its season with two theatres booked in the best towns on its route—one to be played two nights and a matinee, the other on Sundays—the company manager depended upon these towns to keep the show out, even though not counting upon making a fortune with it. But those two towns were necessary to make the show a success. Business in them was all that had been counted upon—and four weeks after the opening of the circle both houses were taken over by one of the chains and the show immediately kicked out. Two other towns of good size were placed in the route to be played on the nights lost by the new turn of things—and two weeks after these houses were also taken over by another chain. Unable to secure further right bookings, the company was obliged to close. [*BBB,* 28 Nov., 6]

Bruno further reported that these four theaters as motion picture venues had been and still were "consistent losing propositions." With this insight brought to light, editor Bruno sarcastically concluded, "Either they [the chain interests] are determined to bring the spoken drama to its lowest ebb or the heads of these companies are intent on dying poor." In the estimation of many involved in circle stock the first contention remained undeniably the truer.

A key consideration to remember is that these two entertainment systems contested each other for both audiences and for performance sites. This dual competition delivered a deadly blow to many circle operations, especially when sound motion pictures were still largely new and had the aura of a fad. The following news concerning one of Sid Kingdon's many circles from over the years became a grimly typical story throughout the late 1920s and early 1930s:

> News is received that the Sid Kingdon Players, who have been on a circle in central Illinois since the ending of the tent season in October, will close December 7th. Kingdon had a good show and worked hard to put it over, but the talkies were evidently too much for him. [*BBB*, 28 Nov. 1929, 3]

Yet some observers believed they saw a positive impact that sound motion pictures could exert on circle stock. The reasoning went thus: First the sound movies would rid the theaters of the silent films, because "talkies" were technologically and esthetically superior. As a consequence, a great number of theater owners would be compelled to please their clientele by converting their projection systems to incorporate sound. But the considerable expense of such conversions plus the high rental fees of sound motion pictures would force many owners out of business, thus freeing the theaters once again for circle performances. Hence the sentiment expressed by the manager of the Fontinelle Stock Company in early 1930, as quoted in *Bill Bruno's Bulletin*:

> I think the "squawkies" were a needed blessing for the small town showman. They have ousted the silent pictures and when the theatre managers get overly ambitious and put in the noisy pictures, they go busted. I have seen this proven in a number of cases and find that it is easier to get house bookings than at any time since the picture shows started. Managers who a few seasons back turned the shows down cold when they wrote for a date, are now writing me asking that I play their houses. The repertoire shows have had pretty hard sledding for the past several years, but I see a brighter future starting for them this spring. [30 Jan., 2]

The attitude of rep theater toward the movie industry during the decade of the 1930s continued to be widely varied. Some consistently charged the picture industry with unfair business practices. Others maintained that the popularity of movies would shortly collapse. Still others suggested that rep theater and sound motion pictures would be best off if they found a way to coexist. In the early 1940s Bob Feagin even suggested that the use of merchant-sponsored circles could be given a much-needed boost by teaming up with the picture operators of rural America:

> We believe that, with improved conditions, there are plenty of independent movie houses in towns of from five to twenty thousand that will be glad to get flesh entertainment one night a week. In fact, we know of one case, last winter, where a theater manager built and equipped a stage in order to get a unit to play it. We would like to see this field opened enough to tempt real

managers into operating in winter. There are folks who can act and there
are folks who can run a show. But the number of those who can do BOTH,
successfully, is pitifully few. [*BFB,* 25 June 1941, 3]

Yet, little cooperation of this sort ever emerged. In the final analysis, even
though motion picture competition brought an end to many individual circle companies and adversely affected scores more, on the whole the industry weathered the storm of the "talkies" as well as, or better than, many had
expected. Two main factors favored the interests of circle stock in this con-
frontation: the circles generally played small, rural communities, namely,
the very last area impacted by the movie industry; and the rural public's
loyalty to the circle companies and their familiarity with both the performers and their product helped maintain attendance at performances.

In addition to motion pictures, challenges for circle stock came from
various forms of local entertainment and public events produced in the territory. The miniature golf craze generated particular concern early in the
Depression era. With some predicting from the very beginning that miniature golf would be only a momentary fancy, its impact produced widespread discussion in the trade journals. During the summer of 1930 when
the following editorial in *Bill Bruno's Bulletin* appeared, the miniature golf
fad had apparently reached its height:

> Some authorities claim it to be more than a passing fad, as miniature
> courses are being installed in the smaller towns which have been unable to
> support regulation golf courses. As the new game can be played both night
> and day, the night business being the largest, it has already shown its effect
> on show business, being claimed as greatly responsible for the tremendous
> drop in theatre attendance in Kansas City during the past month. Almost
> every small town now has one of the toy courses and it is claimed that they
> are being installed at the rate of 100 per day in Kansas and Oklahoma
> alone. The cost of equipment has been cut in half since the start of the new
> amusement and the manufacturers are now building portable outfits which
> can be set up in one day, making them available to even the smallest towns.
> [3 July, 7]

A news brief published a short time later asserts that the tide of miniature golf's popularity had turned—at least according to the frequently optimistic view of Bill Bruno:

> The miniature golf craze is quite evidently fading very fast. If one is to judge
> by the number of courses offered for sale in last Sunday's Kansas City
> papers, the end is in sight. The fad was a quick passing one, although a
> number of tent managers became enthused to such extent that they con-
> templated putting the miniature courses under canvas this winter. They
> have undoubtedly seen the light and several of them have already an-
> nounced they had given up the idea.[*BBB,* 28 Aug. 1930, 2]

Although miniature golf ultimately failed to produce the dire conse-
quences predicted for the industry, the intense fear it generated illustrates

a profession more than mildly concerned about competing entertainment forms. This concern was obviously aggravated by the signs appearing throughout 1930 of the economic disaster slowly engulfing the country.

Various public events presented by local school districts certainly provided circle stock with a more consistent source of competition than did the miniature golf fad. High school basketball games received the barb of several attacks from editor Bruno, including:

> Higher education in the towns of medium size is this winter an unusually big handicap to many of the circle companies who find tough opposition at least two nights in the week in the form of basketball. Some of the towns get hysterical about the dodgasted game which has been making the Friday nights a total loss for the circles. [*BBB*, 27 Feb. 1936, 5]

A few weeks later *Bill Bruno's Bulletin* cited a recent news item that stated that 5 million games of basketball took place at that time in the nation every winter. To this Bruno quipped, "It is safe to say that 4,999,982 of those games are played in circle towns on Friday nights" (5 Mar., 5).

While local sporting events could, in fact, cause a troublesome drain on circle stock revenue, complaints also mounted against other traditional high school events. In 1940 a circle manager from Texas wrote Bill Bruno, "I think that you have to have something different than a dramatic show down here for the schools put on a play almost every week and have proven the biggest opposition we have" (*BBB*, 23 May, 1). Bruno agreed with this assessment and warned managers about the approaching season of annual commencement exercises.

Closely connected to the problems of competition were the managerial adjustments made to maintain a profitable circle in the face of operational and economic difficulties, in addition to widely shifting weather conditions. Circle management could not afford to be static; on the contrary, it needed to be alert to an ever present and ever changing set of challenges, any one of which could spell ruin for a company. For example, the outbreak of a contagious disease in one or more communities of a circuit forced a manager to decide whether the company could afford to eliminate a portion of its circle (and perhaps schedule some replacement performances) or whether it would be necessary to abandon the entire circuit and move on to a completely new area. Companies abandoning a circle due to an outbreak of infantile paralysis or scarlet fever or influenza were not rare.

> The present widespread epidemic of influenza is hurting business for the midwest circle shows to a great extent, particularly in Kansas and Nebraska. In the former state small pox has made its appearance with a number of towns in the quarantine. In Nebraska the flu is so prevalent that public gatherings are prohibited in many towns, causing the shows to lose nights. [*BBB*, 28 Jan. 1937, 1]

In contrast to illness in the general public which occasionally forced circle companies to alter or abandon their touring plans, the economic necessity of performing rarely allowed sickness within a troupe to bring a halt to performances. As Barbara Brooks Emory recalls, "If you were ill, you kept right on going; there were no understudies."

Altering the size of a circuit regularly helped managers to maintain profitability in a competitive marketplace. Taking steps to increase a circle's length (usually from one week to two weeks) or decrease it (usually from two weeks to one) normally mirrored the company's box office condition. Often poor weather and road conditions leading to a decline in business were reasons for trimming back a circle. Reports such as the following—which records alterations made by Ted North in his two-week Kansas circle—are typical of the changes necessary to maintain a healthy circuit:

> The Ted North Players start over their Kansas circle for the third time next Monday and three new towns will be played, Arkansas City having been dropped because of uncertain business conditions in the town, although the receipts made a nice increase on the two nights played the second time in. Howard, Kansas, also has been eliminated as being too small and Ted has leased the City auditorium in Eldorado, which will be played for the first time next week. Goff, Osage City, Holton and Madison are giving the company turnaway business, while Emporia showed a strong increase the second time played. [*BBB,* 6 Mar. 1930, 2]

When good business returned, the mood for expansion frequently seemed difficult to suppress, as seen in this highly optimistic report on a company under the management of Raleigh Wilson:

> The Wilson Players ... who opened on a weeks circle in western Nebraska early in the month, are this week changing to a two week route which takes the company well into Colorado. Business continues excellent with the show clicking nicely in all the towns. [*BBB,* 31 Oct. 1929, 3]

An additional area requiring managerial knowledge and sensitivity was that of local religious practices, especially concerning the question of whether a company would perform on Sundays. From available records it is clear that in the earliest years of circle stock companies did not perform on Sundays largely because it was thought that the religious standards of communities opposed such appearances. Not only did Al Trahern adhere to a taboo on Sunday performances in his circuit area, but he also demonstrated a responsiveness to other religious practices. During his second season of circle stock the *Suffolk County News* used the headline of "Special Note" to record,

> Owing to the generally expressed desire of Trahern patrons in Sayville that the Trahern Stock Company appear here on some evening other than Thursday, which is largely a church night in this village, Manager Trahern will hereafter ... present his popular organization on Monday evening. [17 July 1908, 7]

One might think, however, that such concerns gradually lost their relevance during the 1920s as various other traditional moralistic standards eroded. Yet in any given town such a model is likely to be overly simple. In fact, the inclusion of Sunday performances in circle stock occurred randomly, not centered in any one place or time. Full seven-day circles date from the early 1920s in various parts of this country but in other areas never became popular. Indeed, performances on Sunday appear to have been controlled not so much by societal influence and pressure as by an individual manager's choice.

When confronted with the question of Sunday performances, a manager carefully balanced the pros and cons of such a venture. Was a seventh day of performances necessary for the income it could provide? Could profits overcome the expenses incurred? Was it important to allow the company a day of rest, keeping in mind the hectic schedule of circle stock? Could one community of a circle of seven be found to accept playing on the Sabbath? Would the area being played accept this change or could attendance throughout the circuit be affected as a result?

Caroline Schaffner suggests that predominantly Roman Catholic towns were typically receptive to Sunday performances. Knowing this tendency could help a manager plot out a full seven-day circle. Noreen Depenbrink recalls that communities in the state of Iowa typically remained nonreceptive to performances on Sundays. This being true, a manager plotting out a circle in Iowa might well have avoided performances on the first day of the week. Still, many circle veterans who did play on Sundays remember that this day normally produced their best attendance of the week. Some companies even chose to open their new plays on Sunday in their base communities. Yet a perusal of existing performance schedules shows that the vast majority of circle ensembles played only six days a week, both during and after the 1920s. All things considered, it is apparent that the hectic schedule of circle touring normally demanded a day of rest.

In all, running a circle stock company confronted a manager with a considerable array of problems and challenges. From the initial steps of organizing a troupe to controlling it, from transporting the cast and equipment to running rehearsals, the manager faced continual decisions. If these tasks were not difficult enough, they were compounded by factors such as adverse weather conditions and widespread competition. Of course the ultimate test for any manager was whether his actions brought about a profit. Such financial considerations of circle stock are investigated at length in the next chapter. As one performer aptly reminds us, "We never had subsidies. You either made it or you didn't make it. You had to do things right and you depended on your admission."

6

Real Dollars and Sense

U LTIMATELY THE SUCCESS OR FAILURE of a circle stock organization rested squarely upon the bottom-line figures found in a manager's ledger books. With no subsidies and in a highly competitive marketplace, a circle company normally operated on the slimmest of profit margins. The challenge throughout the history of circle stock involved sustaining a circle's income, while devising ways to minimize costs.

We turn, then, to the financial dealings of circle stock, considered by the standard divisions of income and expenditures. Under income, one must include not only admission prices and the influences on them, but also several methods of increasing a company's income through enticements and the sale of items to the audience. In addition, the types of company organization that did not follow the traditional methods of admission and salary must be considered, such as the merchant circle and the commonwealth plan. On the other hand, the expenses encountered by a circle stock company requiring discussion include such items as salaries, transportation, performance site rental, and advertising.

Admission

Existing records of circle stock—chiefly heralds, handbills, and newspaper coverage—reveal that admission charges for a circle stock performance normally remained within a narrow price range for any specific era. Especially during the decade of the 1920s and again in the Depression-era decade of the 1930s, admission prices fell within a uniform range. Before and after these two periods, however, admission patterns were less constant.

The examples of admission prices for circle stock prior to the 1920s are relatively few and do not suggest any standard range. Apparently the limited (yet growing) numbers of companies practicing circle stock at that time remained isolated enough from each other to preclude standardization of prices based on the influence of competition. For instance, an announcement for Al Trahern's production of *Stop Thief* in 1914 notes prices of "35, 50 and 75 cents" (*Long Islander,* 19 June, 4). Another account of admission prices from Trahern's initial years of circle stock notes that his Long Island audiences were "quick to lend their support at prices from 35 cents to $1.00" (*Clipper,* 1 May 1915, 23). In the Midwest, records of admission charges on the various circles run by the Trousdale brothers are more plentiful, and so a general pricing policy for the Trousdale companies can be observed: 25 cents for adults and ten cents for children, with an occasional price advance for special performances.

During the decade of the 1920s circle stock admission clearly rose and generally stabilized. Throughout this period, for instance, admission charged by the Chick Boyes Players remained nearly constant at 50 cents for adults and 25 cents for children—the standard for the decade. Judging by the careful decision making exhibited in other areas by Boyes and his fellow managers, it is reasonable to believe that management remained highly attuned to the admission prices of other types of entertainment offered in the immediate area. Consequently, one might well take a moment to consider Boyes's competition in his traditional Nebraska territory and the prices these units charged.[1]

In determining admission costs, an obvious starting point for a manager like Boyes was the comparison of prices against those of other circle companies performing in the area. Companies performing under the Hazel McOwen banner presented strong competition to Boyes in central Nebraska during the 1920s and for years to come. In 1921, when playing circle stock in Hebron, Nebraska, the Hazel McOwen Stock Company followed the admission policy of 55 cents for adults and 15 cents for children. Years later in 1929 the No. 2 McOwen circle company charged prices that differed little from the beginning of the decade: 50 cents for adults and 25 cents for children.

Touring theater companies that appeared in formats other than circle stock must also have attracted the attention of Boyes. The North Brothers Stock Company played tent rep on the Hebron Chautauqua grounds in 1920 at prices of 50 and 10 cents. The following year the company returned to Hebron, performing with adult prices lowered to 45 cents. During 1920 and 1921 the Hebron Lecture Course presented a special series of cultural events for the benefit of the city library, including a traveling road show. This production of *Fine Feathers* presented by a "New York cast" carried a $1.00 admission fee for adults and 75 cents for children.

The Nebraska-based Wm. F. Lewis Stock Company, which played central Nebraska under canvas in the fall of 1921, charged nightly general admission prices of 40 and 25 cents. Admittance to the performance with "preferential" seating cost 55 cents. In 1924 Hillman's Ideal Stock Company, apparently touring in one-night stands, performed *The Ghost Between* at prices of 50 and 25 cents. The following year the popular Hazel McOwen Stock Company appeared in a three-night-stand format in Edgar, Nebraska, employing a 50 and ten cents policy.

But Boyes faced competition from nonprofessional theater as well. Numerous amateur groups produced "home talent plays" as fundraisers during this decade. Public organizations such as the Knights of Pythias, the American Legion Auxiliary, and volunteer fire departments found the presentation of plays highly enjoyable and also a successful way to raise money. An organization calling itself the Pennant Club in Sutton, Nebraska, presented a full-scale production of the comic opera *Yokohama Maid* in 1925 with sufficient success to add to the group's treasury. Some organizations even took shows on the road to neighboring communities. The Carleton High School Alumni Club charged 35 cents and ten cents to view its production of *The Road to the City* in 1925. Shortly thereafter the group traveled to nearby Shickley to perform the play for that community.

Various school play presentations were an annual rite of spring and signaled the approaching end of another academic year. The Junior Class of Alexandria High School in 1925 presented *Yimmy Yonson's Yob*, charging 35 and 25 cents. Also in 1925 the Hebron High School Juniors presented *Take My Advice* as its class play, a three-act comedy-drama complete with specialty numbers between acts. Admission charges were 50 cents for adults and 35 cents for students.

The prices charged by nondramatic entertainment also had to be taken into account. With its strong public support, motion pictures represented powerful competition throughout Nebraska during the 1920s. On the whole, movie prices tended to be lower than theater prices. Commonly, adult prices ranged from 25 to 40 cents, with children's admission from ten to 15 cents. For instance, early in 1925 the showing of *Blood and Sand* (starring Rudolph Valentino) in Alexandria, Nebraska, demanded 25 and ten cents. Only a few months later a viewing in Hebron of *The Hunchback of Notre Dame*, featuring Lon Chaney, used a scale of 40 and 20 cents.

Prices charged for less typical forms of entertainment in central Nebraska during the 1920s help to complete an overview of admission costs from the era. Live wrestling in the Hebron Opera House in July 1920 commanded a premium price. The scheduled bout featured Nebraskan Adam Krieger, advertised as the "World's Champion Welterweight Wrestler," facing Ted Andersen of Billings, Montana, with ringside seats valued at $1.50, main floor at $1.00, and the balcony at 50 cents. Whereas at the opposite end of the entertainment spectrum, an admission scale of $2.50, $2.00, and $1.50 was charged for the appearance of the Minneapolis Symphony Orchestra in Hastings in the late spring of 1925.

Such evidence suggests, therefore, that although circle stock operated within a widespread array of entertainment events the industry nevertheless followed a cardinal principle of charging prices in relationship to competing offerings. This principle generally guided management throughout the industry's history, but the difficult and unique conditions of the Depression era required new approaches to both admission pricing and financial considerations in order to keep circle stock operating. Innovators responded, and methods enabling circle stock to adapt to the challenges of the times soon followed.

Under the economic hardships of the Depression era, circle stock decidedly lowered admission prices. For example, in late 1935 the Frank and Eleanor Williams circle out of Clayton, Illinois, played successfully at prices of 20 and ten cents (*BBB*, 2 Jan. 1936, 2). Harry Dunbar in the fall of 1936 reported good business at a straight 25-cent admission. In light of this success, Bill Bruno emphasized, "It CAN be done if you've got a show worth the higher admission" (*BBB*, 1 Oct., 3).

One response to the Depression took form in the creation of circles sponsored by local businesses, which underwrote part of a group's touring expenses. Under this system the admission price of 25 cents for adults would normally be reduced to ten cents, if accompanied by a special ticket. Bill Bruno does mention a circle playing under sponsorship that required a coupon plus only a nickel for admission. When confronted with the urge to reveal the name of this company he declined, adding sarcastically, "If they asked more they'd all be in jail for obtaining money under false pretenses" (*BBB*, 3 Dec. 1936, 3). Bruno even makes mention of rep admissions, without sponsorship, as low as five cents and one cent during this era (*BBB*, 16 May 1940, 1). Because such admission prices provided for extremely slim profit margins, Bill Bruno once queried, "Where does the embryo manager get the idea that there is a heap of money to be made in playing a circle of houses with a capacity of 142 at a ten cent admission?" (*BBB*, 1 Oct. 1936, 3).

How individuals came up with a dime for admission can provide a glimpse of Depression-era finances. Sid Kingdon relates with glee his experience of observing young boys acquire 24 eggs on credit (five cents per dozen) against their parents' account at one grocery store and then selling the eggs for the ten cents needed for the show at another business. Such admission prices certainly appear so minuscule now that it is important to understand the true value of ten cents during the Great Depression. Information supplied by *Historical Statistics of the United States* (I, 326, 468) helps place these prices in perspective.[2] For example, in 1935–36 an average farm laborer (that is, a sole wage earner for a household of four) spent 5–10 percent of his weekly income for his family's outing to a circle stock performance (including a few candy and popcorn purchases). Since, on the average, such a family usually spent only 1.8 percent of its total yearly income on "recreation," it is clear that many families in a great number of provincial communities made considerable sacrifices to attend circle performances.

From the Second World War until the end of the circle stock era, admission prices for the majority of companies slowly advanced from the merchant-plan level of the Depression era until adult prices returned to the 50-cent top prevalent in the 1920s. For example, in late 1940 the Chick Boyes Players played Ogallala, Nebraska, every two weeks at 28 cents and ten cents. By 1949, however, Chick had advanced his circle stock prices to 50 and 20 cents. During the following year Jack Collier's circle company, playing show-and-dance, also charged adults 50 cents, while asking only 14 cents for children.

At any given time, though, the price of admission charged on circle stock depended upon numerous factors, including the size of the company, the location of the circle, the performance site, the overhead expenses of the company, and the type of circle format used (i.e., whether or not the organization followed a show-and-dance format). Even so, the admission charged for a circle performance invariably fell within an affordable range, with the general public's pocketbook well in mind. Addison Aulger of the successful Aulger Brothers tent rep organization once professed an easy method to establish the price of admission. According to Aulger, one needed to know the price of dinner at a café in town, for "if a dinner could be bought in a local restaurant for thirty-five cents then the admission to the show would be the same" (Mickel, 104).

Depression-Era Merchant Circles

As briefly mentioned above, one development of the Depression era that widely altered the traditional pricing structure of circle stock involved the enlisting of financial support directly from the merchants found on a company's circuit. These payments from businesses, in effect, underwrote a company's appearances and helped ensure its continued existence. For this financial support—usually ranging between 50 cents and a dollar, and possibly upward to two dollars for every rotation of the circle—a business owner received special reduced-price tickets, which he distributed to customers or civic and charity groups.[3] During the Depression years, one merchant ticket plus ten cents normally gained admission into a performance. Without a merchant ticket the admission price typically reverted to the full price of 25 cents. How closely companies followed this two-tier price system apparently differed from one troupe to another. Some veteran performers report rigid adherence to the system, while others indicate that if patrons arrived without merchant tickets they were also charged the lower amount. Under such difficult conditions, many managers felt disinclined to quibble over technicalities because ten cents always remained better than nothing. Whether or not the announced pricing procedures were followed, income clearly came from two primary sources: the collection of merchant fees and reduced admissions at the door.

Very little is recorded concerning the origin of the merchant ticket plan, although the practice unquestionably arose during the Depression. In late 1936 Bill Bruno recorded what he knew of the beginning of merchant circles:

> With the drop off in show business [following 1929] being felt as in no other line, somebody conceived the idea of a circle under the sponsorship of the merchants in each town played. We are not at all certain, but we believe the Jack and June Alfred show in Texas to have been the first to try the experiment. We may be wrong again, as we are far from being a historian, but the credit for originating the idea was with Chas. McCollister, then agent on the show. [*BBB*, 17 Dec., 27]

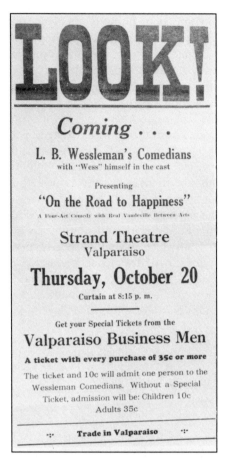

Handbill for L. B. Wessleman's Comedians reminds one that a merchant ticket requires a purchase worth 35 cents or more from a local business (courtesy of the Museum of Repertoire Americana).

What percentage of circle companies operated under merchant auspices during the Depression is difficult to determine. Although it is clear that some groups did operate under the older "straight-admission" policy, the merchant technique became so prevalent that many veteran performers claim that no other type of company structure and admission policy existed at the time.

For most merchant plan companies the importance of the collection of the support payments can hardly be overestimated, since in many instances the immediate future of the circle rested squarely upon the regular and frequent infusion of funds. In some instances money obtained during the initial collection from merchants provided the very capital to form the company. "Making the rounds" for fee collection during each rotation of the circle most often fell upon the shoulders of the manager or, if one existed, an advance agent.

For many managers the use of a company member as an advance agent constituted a wise managerial decision. Although such agents usually received no direct salary, they normally pocketed a portion of the money collected from the merchants (sometimes as much as 50–60 percent). This amount almost assuredly surpassed the salary the performer could receive for acting (yet it still brought money into the hands of the manager); freed the manager from the frequently tedious task of collecting from the merchants; and paid for a combined advance agent and performer.

Advance agents were a luxury for most companies, however, and rounds made by management required no commission or splitting of the income. Thus most managers usually collected their own funds or left the duty to their wives. Waunetta Rosier Oleferchik once exercised this responsibility for the Rosier Players.

> It was my job to sell the merchant tickets. I would go in to each one individually and talk to them about the show; how were they enjoying it and so on. I was probably 18 or 19 years old then and Harold always said I could do it better than anyone else because I was young and pretty and the merchants liked a young and pretty girl.

Although normally paid in cash, on occasion merchant fees received in exchange for discount tickets included items or services of like value. Known in the business as "trade outs," these payments might range from groceries and gasoline to hair care for female cast members.

The actual merchant tickets distributed often possessed special features. Some circles used consecutively numbered tickets with the number marked on both halves. In this method, when torn in two the ticket immediately provided a convenient mechanism for a prize drawing. Other companies changed the color of the ticket on each rotation of the circle, so tickets supplied to businesses on earlier trips could not be used. In so doing, managers made sure that merchants purchased new tickets on a regular basis. During rounds managers (or a designated individual) asked not only what comments customers had made concerning the show but also what was of current interest in the community. In addition to providing useful information about audience response, this regular contact helped strengthen the connection between the company and area business leaders.

The number of merchant sponsors from a particular community supporting a circle varied, due largely to the size and vitality of the area's business district. In 1937 Sid Kingdon maintained 49 sponsors in the combined communities of a circle based in Hamilton, Missouri—a feat Bill Bruno believed to be a record (*BBB,* 21 Jan., 2). More often the total number of sponsors averaged from 20 to 25 businesses in the six communities of a typical circle. In many merchant circles the names of all sponsors and a short advertisement for each were read at every performance from the stage. On other circles the tent rep tradition of hanging small advertising banners prevailed—one for each sponsor around the proscenium arch. Banners put up at the beginning of the season remained in place so long as the payment of the sponsorship fee continued.

Messages encouraging the audience to patronize the local sponsoring establishments normally held a prominent position in programs or handbills distributed by the troupe, although many companies did without such items. A typical example of such encouragement is found in material prepared for the Sid Kingdon Players performing in Hamilton, Missouri, complete with the long list of merchant sponsors mentioned previously:

> Co-operate with your local merchants, make it worth while for them in bringing to the community a show of this wholesome type. Those who live in the country should remember that the shows are for them as much as any one and that they will assist greatly if they will bring their produce to town when coming to the show and then trade with our merchants before going home. [MRA Collection]

In countless instances, the creation of a merchant circle during the harsh reality of the Depression meant the difference between productively working in one's chosen profession or going on relief. Yet the relationship between the business community and the circle stock company did not exist only to aid the actors. Through the drawing power of an ensemble's regularly scheduled performances, merchants believed that they witnessed increased activity in their businesses and the community. And with the cost of support kept low by spreading it among many, both performers and merchants profited from the arrangement.

Commonwealth Companies

Going "commonwealth" provided an alternative organizational method for circle companies lacking sufficient operational funds or experiencing financial problems. As the name implies, a commonwealth arrangement meant that all members of a company shared equally in the income and expenses of running the organization.

Reasons for adopting a commonwealth structure varied. Even the normally small costs associated with starting a circle troupe sometimes presented a barrier to the conventional technique of the company's owner providing the necessary capital. Also, the uncertainty of meeting set salaries caused many groups to adopt this sharing plan. In still other cases, the desire of a group of performers to continue on together following the planned end of an engagement or the financial collapse of an organization often suggested a commonwealth arrangement. In many instances, commonwealth companies chose not to rely solely on admission receipts but also formed under merchant sponsorship.

No matter how much determination a group of performers operating a commonwealth circle could muster, the task remained no easy proposition. Indeed, commonwealth enterprises experienced a high failure rate. As Bill Bruno once remarked,

> One must give credit to those of the folks who take chances with the commonwealth shows. These companies, no matter how well organized, are in the majority of cases, just that—a chance. But managers take these same chances every spring. Credit must be given all these folks for the evident desire to be doing something rather than to be listed among the unemployed.

Because of such inherent problems, Bruno continued by urging those associated with commonwealth shows to help ensure success by placing one individual of the company in a position of top authority:

> No business can function successfully without a head and if the folks with these commonwealth shows will place the management in the hands of one person and abide by this management the chances of success are much greater. [*BBB*, 9 Jan. 1930, 7]

In early 1930 Bill Bruno singled out for attention the seven members of Billy's Comedians, highlighting their recent completion of five successful months of commonwealth trouping in Kansas, led by Billy Morse and Fred Garwood. Bruno praised their accomplishments, maintaining that the difficulties of working commonwealth could be overcome, chiefly through "loyalty and a desire to keep working."

> The managers insist that there was not an argument during the season, that everybody connected with the show put forth every effort at all times, and that no complaint was made even when business was occasionally terrifically bad. It was then that the folks smiled most, if one is to believe Billy Morse. And while none of them succeeded in making their usual salaries, all are satisfied to have pulled safely through the winter. At least they have succeeded in proving that a commonwealth show can go out AND STAY OUT if the right sort of folks are with the company. [*BBB*, 20 Mar., 6]

Although Bruno is probably guilty of painting too rosy a picture of Billy's Comedians, his point about the need for careful cooperation is well taken. A successful commonwealth company relied upon considerable effort and willing teamwork within the group. When cooperation waned, as it certainly could, the number of failed commonwealth companies easily out-distanced those that succeeded.

Of the multitude of tales recounting the hardships of circle stock, few rival those tracing the exploits of commonwealth companies. Some troupers report that operating on commonwealth during the Depression made them feel as if precariously perched on an edge. Robert La-They, while on a commonwealth company located in western Louisiana and eastern Texas during the Depression, once experienced the emotional highs and lows of boom to bust in only one day.

> When Franklin D. Roosevelt declared a bank holiday and closed the banks, the night before we had played Springhill, Louisiana, and had a packed house. And I guess we made around $10 or $12 a team, which was good money in those days during the Depression and everyone was happy. The next morning we got the news that the banks had been closed; but we were booked into the theatre in Jefferson, Texas, for that night. However the bottom had dropped out. When we checked up, took out for the gas and oil, we received the huge sum of 25 cents per each person. Boy, that's going from one extreme to the other in 24 hours.

When operating a commonwealth company under merchant support, the collection of money from sponsors often ranked as the most eagerly awaited event for these groups, especially if the income at the door the previous week had been slight. Noreen Depenbrink vividly recalls that while on the Nig Allen Show in Oklahoma, she and Dot McClure sold ads to local merchants to be read from the stage before the show. On one occasion their return from collecting payments caused considerable commotion, as "the actors descended on us like vultures, wanting to know how much money we had gotten from the merchants so we could all eat that night." Eventually this commonwealth company closed, unable to continue after too many solicitations went unrewarded. Depenbrink recalls that following the end of this circle, her husband "had to 'hock' 7 suits to get enough money for gas to get us out of town."

Maude Gentry relates the story of another commonwealth company in dire circumstances. Her tale concerns the Model Players, a company she and her newly married first husband joined in the fall of 1935. This six-person merchant-sponsored show based in Carrollton, Missouri, adopted the commonwealth plan soon after forming because of low receipts. Labeling the Model Players "the saddest show" she ever experienced, Gentry remembers that a swift end to the venture loomed as a possibility from the very beginning and eventually did happen, as the players were forced to abscond under cover of night.

> One night after Mr. Atkins [the company manager] had collected from the merchants, and we were ready to give the show, no one came. So we gathered our belongings, kept the merchant money, and sneaked out of town by

back roads, hoping the sheriff didn't come after us! Hubert and I were young and just married; it did not bother us much. We were doing what we wanted to do and were happy.

In most instances a commonwealth company could expend few resources for advertising and promoting the circle. Such advertising as could be employed remained, out of necessity, simple and straightforward, with few of the flourishes that more affluent organizations could afford. To compensate, commonwealth troupes relied heavily on traditional word-of-mouth advertising and a solid reputation. Companies sometimes even used names that, in appealing to the spectator's imagination, could carry the lion's share of their marketing efforts. Don Weage recalls that the naming of a commonwealth unit as the "California Comedy Company" involved some simple yet creative logic. California helped the venture "sound large," Comedy made the group "sound amusing," and Company wrapped the "whole thing together as a legitimate show."

While the merchant and commonwealth formats provided appropriate methods for many circle stock companies to continue during the Depression era, some troupes resorted to even more innovative techniques to continue operating. In 1940 the Exchange Players based at Millville in eastern Minnesota received considerable attention because they accepted produce for admission. According to the company's herald,

> You have produce—we have entertainment. Let's get together! Bring your eggs, potatoes, live poultry, canned meats, canned vegetables, canned fruits, etc. All non-perishable products accepted!

Bill Bruno's Bulletin further reports that the company employed this exchange system only in their home base; spectators in all other towns on the circle continued to pay 35 and ten cents. Manager William Jule explained the rationale behind the policy of accepting produce for admission:

> I am personally acquainted with a good many farmers who have told me that they couldn't come to the show because they simply did not have the ready cash. They all have extra produce, however, at all times, and it simplifies matters for them to gather up a few dozen eggs or a sack of potatoes and bring them in. The local produce man is on the door and takes everything off the company's hands immediately at market prices. To save possible embarrassment to those who could not come to the show without the produce, the wealthier farmers hereabouts are co-operating and the first one to start the ball rolling was a gentleman who could well afford to buy out the show, opery house and all, and pay cash. [30 May, 1]

In additional defense of his actions Jule claimed that the Barter Theatre in Abingdon, Virginia, followed a similar practice, noting that *Life* magazine had found the Abingdon payment system "worthy of several pages" in a recent issue.

DEAR FRIENDS:

THE CALIFORNIA COMEDY COMPANY

will be at the

REEVE HALL
Monday, February 14

—Presenting—

THE THREE-ACT STAGE PLAY

"NO WEDDING BELLS"

Singing and Dancing between the acts featuring RICHARD ELLIS of Hollywood; DON WEAGE of the Broadway Stage; GEORGE and GOLDENE of the Harry O. Brown Show and NINA, the Singing and Dancing Lady.

ASK YOUR LOCAL MERCHANT ABOUT TICKETS

Real live entertainment and not a Motion Picture!

REMEMBER THE DATE!

Postcard promoting the California Comedy Company emphasizes the composition of the troupe (courtesy of the Museum of Repertoire Americana).

True to Jule's word, *Life* recorded the efforts of this innovative and pioneering theater ensemble in a story entitled, "Barter Theatre Trades Drama for Ham and Eggs." While not clearly a circle stock operation, this enterprise, founded by native Virginian Robert Porterfield, performed each of its 11 productions during the summer for three nights in Abingdon, then the company traveled "on a ten-day tour of mountain towns and resorts in an ancient bus widely known as 'Bessie.'" Concerning their unusual admission policy, *Life* recorded:

> In June, Porterfield arranges for a supply of staples like milk, cornmeal and greens, in exchange for season tickets. Other items come by themselves. One lady bakes a celebrated marble cake which she delivers weekly. Others bring cucumber pickles, lard, jelly, smoked hams, honey, gooseberries, ducks and even flowers for the table. One farmer dragged his cow to the box office, asked how much milk was required for two good seats, and extracted the price of admission on the spot. About 50% of the audience bring produce, the rest pay the 40 cents admission. Weekly cash gross is about $450. [31 July 1939, 54]

Established during the Depression in 1933, Porterfield's company totaled 38 members in 1939. Although he paid no salaries he clearly fed the company well and housed them in dormitories of the disbanded Stonewall

Jackson College for Women. Porterfield even paid playwrights in produce rather than cash: we are told that he sent a smoked ham to vegetarian George Bernard Shaw to cover royalties.

While the admission policies of the Exchange Players and the Barter Theatre received prominent attention during the Depression, many other circle companies in those days quietly accepted produce or home-baked items in lieu of established admission charges. Waunetta Rosier Oleferchik relates a touching instance of such barter when, new to show business, she first experienced the offer of produce at the box office:

> In Gregory [Michigan] we had a lovely little family that never missed our show—a widow lady with three small children, ranging in age from four to eight years. She raised a few chickens and always kept a part of her egg money to buy tickets for the show. This particular week the chickens were not laying and she didn't know what to do. She completed her usual weekly baking, although the entire time worrying about the children because she knew how disappointed they would be. She finally had to tell them there just wasn't any money for tickets. Then one of the youngsters said, "Mom, maybe Mrs. Rosier would like a loaf of homemade bread." She thought about it, then wrapped up a nice big loaf in a clean towel and went down to the basement and brought up a jar of strawberry jam; then they got ready and came to the show. I was selling tickets and I noticed them when they came in. They stood over to one side until everyone had bought their tickets and sat down, then they very timidly came over to the ticket booth and explained the situation. I looked over to Fannie Henderson who was taking tickets and eyeing that lovely loaf of homemade bread. She nodded "yes" and I told the lady we would be happy to accept the goodies for the admission price.

In the years that followed, the Rosier Players periodically received produce for admission—chickens, eggs, even freshly butchered meat. Because the company worked at this time under the commonwealth plan, the items were shared by all, with some concern that bartering did not become a regular habit of spectators: "We had to be careful and not let it get out of hand as we had expenses to pay, rent for the opera house, advertising and etcetera, and of course our actors had personal expenses." It is clear that in order to survive the Depression era, circle stock management required an especially wide range of attributes, including hard-nosed realism, empathy, drive, and resourcefulness.

To ensure regular income successful managers might even bend the law a bit, as seen in a policy followed by the Lew Henderson Players. When individuals on relief in What Cheer, Iowa, received instructions not to spend any money on traveling shows, Henderson created two methods to get around the regulation. Henderson's children recall that because audiences tended to arrive in town well before performance time to chat with their father outside the theater, arrangements could be made at that time for individuals forbidden to attend the show to do so. Some individuals on relief gave Henderson money to cover their admission but received a "complimentary pass" instead of a regular ticket. Or after taking their dime admissions well ahead of the performance, Henderson greeted the individuals on public aid outside the theater near to curtain time and ushered them into the theater to attend the show "on the house." While the practice clearly circumvented local authority, one Henderson family member places the practice in perspective: "We needed the dime too. We had to eat; there were a lot of us."

Even though ten or so cents seems of minor importance today, rep playwright Al Clark once suggested that the hard social and economic times of the Depression created a challenging audience, one not so easily pleased because entertainment to many had become a luxury:

> People must buy bread and shoes, but they do not have to go to shows. They look at their fifteen cents a long time before laying it down for a ticket. They want their amusement, but they expect just as much and more for their fifteen cents than they did for fifty cents twenty years ago. [*BBB*, 19 Dec. 1935, 23–24]

It is an old adage in show business that spectators measure the quality of an entertainment in part by how much they have to pay for it. To characterize circle stock audiences of this era as uncritically accepting any entertainment offered to them is without basis, and lowered admission prices may well have made the audience more difficult to win over at times.

Show-and-Dance

Even though circle stock and various rep formats shared many identical practices for increasing income, the policy of show-and-dance remained largely unique to circle touring. The system of show-and-dance operated as the title implies: following the presentation of a play (interspersed with specialty acts), a dance band—normally composed of performers within the company—took the stage as soon as possible and provided music for a dance, perhaps two hours in length. Because the "show" portion itself might last anywhere from 75 minutes to two hours, the delivery of nearly four hours of continuous entertainment required considerable effort and stamina on the part of the company members. In some locations, the evening's activities lasted even longer. Billie Schuller (of the Lew Henderson Players) notes,

> On show-and-dance the local people often had a pot-luck dinner before the show that they had arranged for themselves. They had their dinner, then the show, and then the dance. The townspeople would make a whole day of it.

DANCE!

The Chick Boyes Orchestra and Entertainers

Will Play a Dance Immediately
After the Show

Herald promoting dance following performance by the Chick Boyes Players (courtesy of the Otoe County [Nebraska] Museum of Memories).

Schuller adds that often the company was invited to join in the preperformance meal.

While the practice of show-and-dance on circle stock developed and flourished during the 1930s, the method's beginnings appear to predate this period considerably. Although no definite date of origin has been established, various accounts of show-and-dance usage over the years record its popularity with theater companies and audiences alike. In 1907 the George B. Zeis Company, presenting the play *Marriage* in Sag Harbor on Long Island, followed the performance with a dance that "kept up until 1 a.m."

(*Corrector,* 8 June, 5). A few years later the Hill-Donaldson Stock Company, a professional organization touring Long Island, traditionally reminded their audiences, "DON'T FORGET–Dance will follow the play" (*East Hampton Star,* 31 May 1912, 3).

Al Trahern's ninth summer tour witnessed at the Sayville Opera House the "novel idea" of "dancing between the acts and after the show, all for the price of one admission." Promotional material further outlines the process:

> Mr. Trahern has sacrificed 100 seats on the lower floor under the balcony to make a dancing floor 30 feet wide and 65 feet long which is ample space to accommodate 50 couples making it possible for those in the audience to dance during the waits between acts. After the performance, if more space is required, other chairs will be removed. [*Suffolk County News,* 23 Apr. 1915, 2]

Whereas this dance feature eventually gained the approval of the Sayville audience, the first attempt to induce the locals to dance between the acts "was not a huge success but dancing after the performance was thoroughly enjoyed and our young people will no doubt soon get accustomed to the innovation" (*Suffolk County News,* 21 May 1915, 1).[4]

The Otis Oliver Stock Company, while playing permanent stock in Dubuque, Iowa, combined a performance with dancing to follow during the summer of 1916:

> Otis Oliver ... has created quite a bit of interest by inviting his audience upon the stage after a performance to participate in an informal dance. The new venture was a decided success last Friday night, when the members of the company and a large number of the audience spent a pleasant half hour. It has been decided to stage this feature every Friday night throughout the stock season. Box seats, as prizes, are offered to the best dancers. Needless to say, the innovation is increasing the attendance at the Majestic. [*Billboard,* 17 June, 16]

Perhaps reports of these successes or the successes of others provided the model for similar formats to follow.

Show-and-dance on circle stock developed as a method to broaden the appeal of a company and hence increase attendance. With the performance of a play and specialties already constituting a full evening's entertainment in itself, appending a dance to the events at a small additional fee provided added incentive for many to attend each and every appearance of the company. For others, the addition of a dance enticed them to a performance for the first time. The price scale for show-and-dance typically used by the Chick Boyes Players when touring Nebraska in the 1940s set adult admission to the show at 25 cents; admission exclusively to the dance segment also cost 25 cents. But if one desired to attend both the show and dance, admission totaled 35 cents. Thus the addition of a dance could increase income significantly, not only from those in faithful attendance but also from a new clientele primarily interested in dancing.

Records from the Boyes ledgers on show-and-dance performances at Haswell, Colorado, during the winter circle season of 1936-37 demonstrate the money-making capabilities of the later portion of the program. On the average, the amount entered under "dance" represents a full 85 percent of the amount recorded for the take at the "door." On some occasions, however, the dance revenue represents 125 to over 175 percent of ticket income for the performance of the evening. Various admission practices for show-and-dance were attempted by Chick Boyes and others over the years. Some companies stressed that they performed both the show and the dance for a single admission, while other groups claimed they presented "free" dances without any advance in prices following each performance. Despite such claims, both methods normally employed some hidden advance in prices.

Dance bands formed from the members of a small circle company were little indeed. A typical five-piece band consisted of such basics as piano, drums, accordion, guitar or fiddle, and perhaps a brass instrument. In some larger organizations, a vocalist or two might be added to the band. Numbers performed by such bands might well include polkas, waltzes, schottisches, fox trots, quadrilles, and two-steps, along with any number of audience requests. Obviously show-and-dance performances required a venue other than a traditional theater with permanent seating. This posed few problems in the 1930s and later because a large proportion of circle stock performances took place in open-floored halls, gymnasiums, taverns, and community centers.

The change-over time from the end of the play presentation to the beginning of the dance most certainly took less time than the actors doubling in the band desired, typically due to the audience members eagerly clearing away chairs in anticipation of the dance. With the chairs placed around the edges of the performance space, a liberal sprinkling of wax on the floor followed to aid the dancer's movements. In many instances, the application of wax propelled the youngest in attendance into action as they energetically worked the wax into the floor by sliding to and fro.

If company members did not perform in the dance band, they normally completed the dismantling and loading of the set in preparation for leaving as soon as possible following the conclusion of the dance. With the strike of scenery and technical equipment accomplished, some company members took time to study lines. Many troupes allowed members to mix with the audience during the dance. As townspeople traditionally loved interacting with the company personnel, this proved an enjoyable time for the performers. In some uncommon instances a show-and-dance company was divided between those involved only in the performance and a separate group of musicians to play for the dance. A report on Val's Radio Players once emphasized:

DANCING AFTER SHOW FOR YOUNG AND OLD

All Instruments Fully Amplified

PLAYING — Fox Trots, Polkas, Waltzes, Quadrilles, Schottisches, Two Steps and Requests

COMMENTS

The Mayor of Summerfield Says: | A Nebraska Manager Says: | An Illinois Manager Says:

Detail from brochure promoting dances to follow circle performances by the Collier Players (courtesy of the Museum of Repertoire Americana).

> A four piece hillbilly band is featured. Two cars are run so that the actors go back to headquarters immediately after the play and do not have to wait around for the dance which the band plays after the show. [*BFB*, 22 Apr. 1942, 2]

With the great popularity of this kind of circle, by 1939 Bill Bruno reported, "The circles appearing to be the most successful are the show-and-dance shows, which do not solicit merchant sponsorship, but play at 40 cents admission, making the dance the feature" (*BBB*, 19 Oct., 1). By 1950 the dance portion of an evening's entertainment presented by the Jack Collier Players centered on square dancing, the current rage at the time. The *Champaign-Urbana* (Illinois) *Courier* captured the atmosphere of one such dance on a Saturday night in Sidney, Illinois, through the observant eye of the newspaper's reporter Lynn Ruester and the comments of Herb Wilson, the doorman at the town hall:

> Before the square dancing started the chairs were arranged in order around the edge of the dance floor. The parents sat in the chairs visiting with their neighbors while the kids swarmed over the floor. The family atmosphere was complete even to the extent of a few swains who went about visiting with mothers and fathers in laying the groundwork for dances with daughters that would come later.

"It's all a family gathering," Wilson told us. "Almost everyone who's got children bring them right along. The admission is 14 cents for them. For adults it's 50 cents."

"That's why there's never any trouble," he went on. "We don't even have a town marshall for the dance nights. There'd be nothing for him to do. We had one little fight last year, but it didn't amount to anything." [12 Feb., 33]

Without question, the demands of show-and-dance created a hectic and tiring lifestyle because of the long hours and the strenuous effort involved. In a personal letter from Jack Collier to fellow performers L. Vern and Ora Slout, dated 13 April 1948, Collier speaks of their demanding schedule, noting that his company was "always riding or showing or playing a dance." He continues:

We jumped from the house show to Happy Bills show. We jumped from there to Topeka and put out our own show and dance unit through the old towns that we used to play around Holton, Ks. and it has really kept us busy. Seems like we are on the jump all the time. We were playing seven nights and five dances. We dropped one town so we could live longer. We expect to play Illinois with the tent, then Nebr. for winter and back into Holton for the spring.

The letter continues, with Collier outlining recent changes and additions to improve the dance segment of the show. Yet he found that such efforts left too little time to better other elements of the show:

It has been a mighty busy winter but we have a swell little band along with the show. Lucille taught Don to play the drums last winter. He plays a nice rhythm now. Bought Margaret a new 120 base accordion and a new electric steel guitar. She makes both of them talk. I learned to play the bull fiddle this winter. Taught Don to do the magic. He does it swell. Put a lot of money into sound system, instrument pickups, amplifiers, etc. Also costumed the band. But didn't get up in any new plays, that's the rub. [MRA Collection]

Candy and Popcorn Sales

The old tent rep adage that "candy moved the show" indeed had some truth. The added income from the sale of candy packages frequently provided the very funds necessary to move a company and its canvas theater to the next engagement on the schedule. Candy sales in touring rep are said to date back to around 1915 (Kittle, 195).

The sale of candy on circle stock also made a significant addition to a company's income. The extent to which tent rep and circle stock relied upon the sale of candy is reflected in a poll conducted in 1935 by one of the major candy suppliers. Results (obviously favorable to the candy industry) revealed that at least seventy-five per cent of the managers, especially those of the smaller and the medicine shows in particular, answered that they would be unable to operate without their candy revenue. [*BBB,* 17 Dec. 1936, 3]

For selling the candy, individual performers traditionally received a 10 percent commission from the company manager, or one penny for every dime box of candy sold.

As generally practiced, the candy sale on circle stock differed little from the methods used on the tent shows. Occurring during a scene- or act-break, the candy segment started with a curtain speech normally given by the manager (or possibly the lead comic) to explain the sale. Tradition dictated that the sales pitch make great fun of the quality and quantity of the candy, such as when Harry Hugo warned his customers that the product he sold rated as a "splendid candy" if only one had the "endurance to chew it" (*Omaha* [Nebraska] *World-Herald Magazine,* 11 July 1948, 14). Then company members passed through the audience selling the small ten-cent boxes of candy. To encourage sales, the person delivering the "bally speech" announced that coupons had been placed within select boxes of candy and that these coupons could be exchanged for a wide variety of prizes displayed on stage: table lamps, blankets, wall hangings, serving trays, small Kewpie dolls, the popular large French dolls, and the like. Some companies used coupons that identified specific prizes, while others used coupons indicating only that a prize had been won, thus leaving it to the sale leader's discretion to determine the appropriate prize. The success of the candy sale relied upon the pitchman's ability to arouse the public's deep-seated desire to obtain something of value for next to nothing. Some companies packaged a cheap trinket in addition to the candy in each package, while most were filled only with five to seven candy kisses of notoriously poor quality.

According to R. Norton Walther, the candy sale required deft audience manipulation, with great importance placed on timing:

You always knew where the coupon was in your candy tray which you used to sell candy. They marked it, maybe with a little hole punched in the top of the box or something like that. So you waited until you got out in the front, sold two or three boxes, then you put out the one with the best prize in it. That stirred up the rest of the audience because they saw this person get a nice prize and they all then bought like crazy.

The system employed here and others similar to it involved knowing which candy packages contained valuable coupons and using them to spur sales.

A slightly different method followed by some candy suppliers and circle companies used only numbered coupons in the packages. Apparently the individual controlling the candy sale from the stage announced a few winning numbers before the sale began and then manipulated the event by distributing prizes of varying value to encourage purchases as needed. G. H. Taylor, manager of the Glendora Players, found favor in this system:

We like the numerical system—that is coupons 1 to 30, as we can dispose of whatever items we deem fit. If the sales are slow we can put out a few big flashes to stimulate the sales and not wait for the coupons calling for specified articles to be brought to the stage. This is the best system that we have ever tried with our candy sales, and the results have been gratifying. [MRA Collectio][5]

With some troupes the candy sale provided an opportune time to have fun with an unsuspecting individual, such as awarding a blushing young bachelor with some rubber baby pants. Or, since only male company members typically sold candy, a young actor might slip a note of admiration to an attractive female spectator in a specially prepared box of sweets.[6]

Major candy suppliers in the Midwest typically sold not just candy but a complete sales "unit" to the rep companies, including the candy packages, coupons, and an appealing group of "flash" pieces—the eye-catching premiums offered during the candy sale. For example, in 1930 the Union Concession Company of Chicago offered a "Cloth of Gold Special" for $15 C.O.D. which consisted of

330 packages of Jockey Club with THIRTY-THREE brilliantly colored outside flashes including an Oriental Shimmering Cloth of Gold, Silver Plated Bread Tray, Silver Plated Cake Tray, Console Set, Perfume and Atomizer Set, etc., plus three Colorful Coolie Coats. [*BBB*, 27 Mar., 12]

A major setback for candy sales occurred in June 1935 when the Federal Trade Commission issued a final cease and desist order on the interstate shipping of candy units sold to companies. The commission charged that candy sales and the chance distribution of prizes as found in the rep shows contained the elements of a lottery not permissible in interstate shipping. The commission also accused the three major suppliers of candy—the Gordon-Howard Company of Kansas City, the Universal Theatres Concession Company of Minneapolis, and the Union Concession Company of Chicago—with unfair competition practices. Efforts to create a packaging method that met with Federal Trade Commission approval immediately followed, and soon the industry was operating again with a revised system.

The new method was to sell the managers packages containing candy only as one sale, and to sell them the merchandise units as they ordered them. The candy companies would give the managers no use instructions. The show managers found no difficulty in combining the candy and the merchandise and continued business as usual. [Mickel, 82]

In addition to the ever-popular candy sales, some circle companies sold popcorn for additional income, although these sales were not connected with prize offerings. Even though it often meant hauling a heavy popcorn machine up to a second-story performance site, the steady financial reward of popcorn sales compensated the effort. Popcorn sometimes created

$15 Candy Shipments

Cash in on these New and Sensational Assortments of THREE HUNDRED AND THIRTY Packages of Jockey Club with 33 Outside Flashes

In the Following Combinations:

1—Blanket Assortment
2—DeLuxe Blanket Special
3—Jungle Robes Combination
4—Aluminum Assortment
5—Household Assortment
6—Linen Shower
7—Bridal Shower
8—Nebraska A Combination
9—Nebraska B Combination
10—Wisconsin Combination
11—Mexican Show Special

12—Beach Coat Combination
13—Merchandise Assortment
14—Cotton Pickers Special
15—Italian Spread Special
16—Golden Bed Spread Special
17—Indian Assortment
18—Cloth of Gold Special
19—18th Amendment Special
20—Scotch Motor Robe Special
21—Algerian Assortment
22—Matinee Combination

"Nightly Changes of Flash Make Sales"

Best Wishes for a Banner Year to All

Union Concession Co.
456 S. State St.   Chicago, Illinois

Candy sales advertisement employed by the Union Concession Company is typical of the period, from *Bill Bruno's Bulletin*, 17 Apr. 1930 (courtesy of the Museum of Repertoire Americana).

disruptions during the performance, however, especially when younger audience members insisted on popping the empty sacks. It did not take long to solve the problem, though: the corners of the sacks were clipped before being filled to avert any troublesome situations.

Candy and popcorn sales normally enlisted the aid of the majority of the company, or at least most of the males. In some instances, however, a single company member controlled the sale of a concession item. When Dick Elsenpeter assumed the role of Toby on Tilton's Comedians in the 1940s, he received the privilege and added income of selling popcorn. To help run the concession a local boy was obtained to walk through the audience hawking the popcorn prior to the performance, for which the young salesman received free popcorn and the privilege of remaining to view the show. Elsenpeter recalls both the frustrations and joys of running the concession:

> The sanitary conditions really alarm me now. But you popped your popcorn and then sent your youngster out into the crowd to sell your popcorn. Then you had to run back and put your make-up on and get ready for the show. As soon as the show was over, you packed your kettle and so on. There was no time to clean it before or after. I think under other circumstances, you could have taken it home and cleaned it. I'm sure every four or five years these things had to be sand blasted. But it was added income and I rather enjoyed it. You got to talk with the customers to the show this way. You learned their reactions to the plays, to what you were doing, and you became more visible.

Whereas candy sales usually netted Elsenpeter five dollars a week, income from his popcorn concession could total between ten and $15 in the same period of time. In comparison, Elsenpeter's added payments for assuming the feature comedy roles on Tilton's Comedians totaled only five dollars a week. Elsenpeter distinctly remembers that the five dollars in candy income alone normally paid his rent for the week.

The added income from concession sales for the owner/manager could be considerable. Dale Madden, Sr., estimates that when vending "Toby's Popcorn"–so named because Madden appeared in makeup "(the red wig, etc.) while working the popcorn"–he often sold to "about 90 percent of the audience." If one considers that during the Depression the Madden and Stillian Players took in ten cents for each admission and then sold ten-cent popcorn to nearly the entire audience, the impact of the popcorn sales on the gross take for the performance was considerable.

Other evidence suggests more modest success with candy and popcorn concessions, yet the income from such sales appears relatively consistent. For example, according to information found in the Boyes business ledger covering the 1936-37 winter circle season, average sales of candy and popcorn typically totaled between 10 and 12 percent of the admission take for the evening.

Despite the importance of the income for both management and performers that these added sales provided, it should be remembered that not all circle stock companies sold candy or popcorn. Some considered such sales too cumbersome and time consuming. Waunetta Rosier Oleferchik notes that the Rosier Players did not conduct such sales, stating, "We were lucky if they had enough money to buy a ticket."

Radio Connections

At the same time as the rise in popularity of show-and-dance units, many circle stock companies established connections with radio stations within their circuit area. At first performing gratis in exchange for air time (later often paying a small fee), numerous circle companies availed themselves of the powerful advertising medium that these fledgling radio stations offered.

Russel Nye, a noted popular-culture historian, classifies the decade of the 1930s as "radio's own," a time when "everybody listened to radio and few criticized" (393). During this decade the young, energetic, and rapidly growing radio industry brought the news and entertainment of this nation and world to an estimated minimum of 60 million Americans (Nye, 393).

In the 1930s radio programming existed on two distinct levels. Broadcasting to the highly visible national market were the growing–and soon to be powerful–radio networks, while literally hundreds of local radio stations (whether existing as independents or connected with the networks) serviced their small market areas as best they could. Unaffiliated stations found the task of filling air time during this era an ongoing challenge, and even stations affiliated with the networks were still in want of local programming.

To fill this need, local station managers placed area and transient talent before the microphone. And of the various sources of entertainment available in the rural setting, the circle stock and tent troupes were rated among the best. In fact, in many respects the radio broadcasts by circle companies mirrored on a local level the tremendous popularity of comedians, vaudevillians, and musicians dominating the network broadcasts.

Obviously the structure and content of such radio broadcasts varied according to the talents within a company, but these performances were chiefly composed of variety acts and promotion for scheduled circuit appearances. The entertainment mainly included instrumental music selections by individuals or by the company band, solo or group singing, recitations, monologues, duet comic banter, and even comic or dramatic skits. Spread throughout were liberal doses of publicity concerning upcoming plays to be performed by the company and other information concerning the ensemble. The broadcast might even include commercials for sponsors underwriting the company's broadcasts.

Because of the full schedule already faced by circle stock performers, little preparation or rehearsal time could be given over to these broadcasts. Hence, performers naturally turned to their already prepared specialty act material. Few companies found it difficult to fill air time, and their radio

The Town Hall Players (a circle stock company) ready for a radio broadcast sponsored by Mayr's Seed and Feed (courtesy of the Museum of Repertoire Americana).

performances had a lively, spontaneous feeling. To involve the audience, frequently a company's small band performed requests called in to the radio station or requests that had been left with the troupe during the previous evening's performance.

Reports concerning the success of circle units using radio surfaced in the early to mid–1930s and spurred other companies to create similar connections. In 1935 *Bill Bruno's Bulletin* recorded the prosperity of such companies:

> Evidently taking their cue from the success of the radio broadcasts of several amateur hours and dramatic programs, an increasing number of the western shows are making daily or occasional broadcasts. All of them appear to be finding the idea a profitable one, especially the circle stocks, and the stations seem to welcome the broadcasts made gratis by the companies. It's good advertising and the idea of a few professionals doing dramatic plays should become more and more popular. [31 Oct., 1]

Existing receipts show that the Chick Boyes Players purchased air time on a bimonthly basis in 1941 over radio station KGEK in Sterling, Colorado. Boyes's broadcast pattern involved purchasing 15-minute time slots on two consecutive days at $3.75 per quarter hour. The schedule of

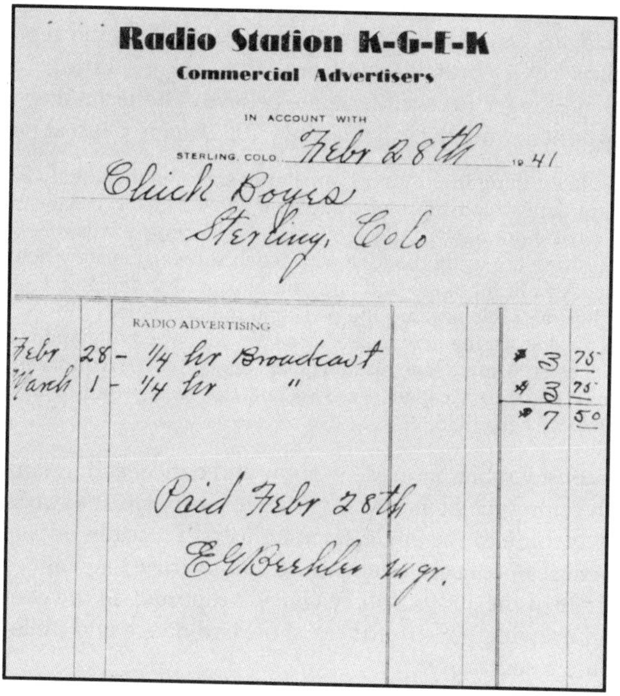

Radio Station K-G-I-K
Commercial Advertisers

IN ACCOUNT WITH

STERLING, COLO. Febr 28th 19 41

Chick Boyes
Sterling, Colo

RADIO ADVERTISING

Febr 28 - ¼ hr Broadcast	$ 3	75
March 1 - ¼ hr "	3	75
	$ 7	50

Paid Febr 28th
E G Buehler Mgr.

Receipt for radio air time purchased by the Chick Boyes Players (courtesy of the Museum of Repertoire Americana).

broadcasts on consecutive days indicates that Sterling likely acted as the home base for the circle at that time.

The broadcast times for circle units using radio hookups varied greatly. While some companies obtained air time in the early morning hours, in 1930 the Hazel McOwen Stock Company broadcast every Monday afternoon from Clay Center, Kansas (*BBB,* 13 Feb., 2). In roughly the identical area at the same time, Joe Marion's circle company broadcast over station KGBZ in York, Nebraska (their headquarters town), but this troupe's weekly broadcast took place after its circle performance "every Saturday night, going on the air at midnight and continuing until four o'clock Sunday morning." Often during the odd hours of the Marion company's radio performances they dedicated musical numbers to rep companies in Kansas and Nebraska, and even on occasion a special number went out in honor of *Bill Bruno's Bulletin* (*BBB,* 20 Feb. 1930, 2).

Interest in radio sometimes spilled over into a company's live performances. While the William Balthazor circle in South Dakota did make daily broadcasts in 1937 over KWTN in Watertown, it also was in the habit of presenting the dance portion of an evening with "mock broadcasts from the stage" (*BBB*, 28 Oct., 1). By the following year Bill Bruno reported that in some cases live broadcasts from the stage during a performance were no longer necessarily make-believe. The technology of portable radio transmitters, widely available since 1921, made this feat possible.

> The latest thing in the circle game appears to be the weekly Saturday night "barn dance" consisting of a one hour show which is broadcasted, followed by a two-hour dance. All at a 25 cents or 35 cents admission. Several northern shows are using the idea with much success, capacity houses being the rule. A radio hook-up and large auditorium for dancing, together with an orchestra of fair size, are the principal requirements.
> Latest to try the new idea is Cecil Vernon, operating on his circle around Rochester, Minn. Gave his first "barn dance" at the Armory in that city Saturday night to a capacity crowd and the idea promises to be a success. [*BBB*, 24 Feb. 1938, 2]

The considerable success of show-and-dance and radio broadcasts, along with numerous blends and variations, brought renewed energy and some new income to the circle stock industry. Probably because of the resounding success, concern over misuse and overuse inevitably arose. Early in the decade of the 1940s Bob Feagin still reported on the continued popularity and drawing power of these show-and-dance and radio circles, but voiced some reservations:

> We haven't had a single show of this type to report bad business. We wonder if this idea will gradually replace the Merchant Circle? Also we wonder will it be ruined by carelessness as the Merchant Circle was ruined in certain areas? We sincerely hope not. But we know several lads that we hope DON'T TAKE OUT ONE. [*BFB*, 23 Jan. (1941), 3]

Despite Feagin's concerns, the highly successful alliance of circle stock and radio created during the 1930s continued to benefit each partner of the union for years to come—even after many of the circle companies were forced to purchase their air time instead of receiving it gratis. This change assuredly came about because of the significant rise in available network programming and the greater abundance of prerecorded material which helped local and regional stations fill their programming schedules.

Although one cannot place a direct monetary value on its impact, the use of radio proved to be an important and effective advertising medium for circle stock. During the period when companies promoted their interests by performing for free air time, this use of radio might well be considered an "added bonus" attendance incentive used to build the clientele within the company's territory. Indeed, the transmitting signal of many of these radio stations often could reach only to the geographic limits of a one-week circle. Yet as companies increasingly were required to purchase desired air time, the use of radio might be better classified as a necessary advertising expense.

The Ballyhoo

Theater historian Jere Mickel defines *ballyhoo* as "a synonym for any kind of show business advertising gimmick" (212). Under this broad definition the following discussion explores some of the techniques employed by circle stock management in their attempts to increase attendance at performances.

Confronted with formidable opponents, especially the motion picture industry, the circle manager turned to an abundant collection of inducements and ploys to stay in business. As Jay Bee Flesner asserts, you always "figured out some way to improve business," drawing upon "a million tricks" if need be. The various inducements used on behalf of circle stock (and in some cases against it) can be divided into three major categories: contests of chance or giveaways; direct audience involvement in the performance or events based upon audience participation; and additional entertainment of a unique nature during the performance.

When investigating the first category of inducements used on circle stock, one finds that a variety of games of chance and free gifts found a comfortable home on the circuits. Al Trahern utilized his connection with the music industry to award those purchasing advance tickets with souvenir sheet music "retailing at fifty cents a copy"—much of it his own composition.

On one occasion in 1908 he announced that a copy of his popular ballad entitled "Just a Picture of You" would be a bonus, reminding his audience, "A different song will be given away each week, and if this week's song is missed, it will spoil a beautiful collection of famous songs" (*Corrector,* 16 May, 5). Drawings held for food proved highly popular during the Depression. Sometimes labeled "Grocery Night" by those in the profession, the announcement by various companies of a "Complete Christmas Dinner Given Away Free" provided incentive for a large segment of the population during hard economic times. If not food, a drawing for an attractive door prize—perhaps an especially large candy sale premium—might be tried. For a performance of *Little Miss Lightfingers,* the Chick Boyes Players once ran a men's "lightfoot" contest, giving away a ticket to the first man to arrive at the ticket office (MRA Collection).

Presenting a free performance when appearing in a community for the first time also should be construed as a giveaway technique. Such gratis performances were intended to "hook" spectators into the habit of attending, in addition to allowing any skeptical patrons to judge at no cost the quality of the show. Whereas in tent rep the policy of admitting one lady free for each paid adult admission largely developed into an opening night tradition, similar practices on circle stock clearly remained less frequent. Yet a 1934 herald advertising the Lew Henderson Players, in addition to stating admission prices of 15 and ten cents, also notes, "ONE LADY FREE with A Paid Adult Ticket / ONE CHILD FREE If Under Twelve Years–With A Paid Child Ticket" (Collection of the Author).

One game known as "bank nights" (perhaps the movie industry's most serious weapon against circle stock) eventually was added to the arsenal of tactics utilized by the rep industry. What constituted a true bank night remained quite simple–a drawing for a cash prize, the winner needing to be present to collect the money. If a winning individual could not come forward at the drawing, the cash prize increased each time, and continued to do so until someone claimed the jackpot. During the depths of the Depression, the possibility of winning a hefty cash prize created a nearly irresistible attracting force.

Bank nights at the movies, however, developed a reputation far from spotless. Questions arose when those holding winning tickets rarely, if ever, could be found among the typically large audiences assembled for drawings. But when a jackpot winner happened to be present in the audience, even more pointed questions could arise. The following event illustrates one such situation when a movie manager "refused to make payment of a $150 'bank' and was sued in a local court":

> The case had a peculiar angle in that the winner had just purchased her ticket and entered the theatre when her number was called. The manager refused to pay, claiming that the purchaser should have been in the theatre at the time the drawing started. As duplicate number roll tickets were being used, one wonders how the duplicate number happened to get in the box for the drawing fifteen minutes before the ticket was sold at the box office. [*BBB*, 30 Jan. 1936, 1]

Yet trouper R. Norton Walther believes that the design of bank nights did not require underhanded manipulations to prevent people from winning. Walther emphasizes that because names for drawings continually increased week after week and that only a certain number of patrons could fit into a movie theater on the night of a drawing, as the jackpot grew the chances of being present at the same time one's ticket was drawn decreased significantly. Simply put, according to Walther, overwhelming odds made unfair practices pointless.

Whether or not the movie bank nights were rigged, great numbers of individuals came to believe that no real possibility of a major payoff existed. Eventually the lure of bank nights at the movies waned. Yet this development came too late to benefit the competitors of the motion pictures. In many instances the negative impact of bank nights simply proved overwhelming for even successful circle stock companies, let alone struggling ones. An account of the demise of the Neal Players while circling in 1936 stands as a testament of other similar happenings:

The Henry and Ruby Neal Players are reported to have closed at Cheyenne, Wyo., last Saturday night after almost continuous playing for four years. After a prosperous summer in Colorado, the company moved to a new location, playing four nights in a Cheyenne theatre and the remaining three nights in nearby towns. The experiment in the city proved unsuccessful, largely because of heavy picture theatre opposition. A continuous "bank night" and other give-away program[s] was carried out by the movie managers. The closing resulted after a four weeks' battle. [*BBB,* 12 Nov., 1]

While many troupes were adversely affected by the practice of bank nights, other companies met the challenge head on. Of the various methods used to battle this ploy of the movie interests, advertising aimed at exposing the fraudulent techniques of bank nights proved most effective. One notable campaign launched by Fred Brunk when playing under canvas in western Colorado in the mid–1930s benefited all of rep theater. In this battle Brunk fought the use of bank nights by extensively advertising his answer to the practice: "Bunk Nights."

His ads are a burlesque of the picture man's, he offering to give away from $500 to $15,000 each night, the prizes doubling. At Glenwood Springs last week the Brunk ad. on Wednesday contained this: "The Third Big Night of Prosperity! Adolph Hitler was not present last night, so he is $1,500 loser. Tonight–$2,500! Try and get it. Not a chance!" On the night previous Al Capone's name was called and he failed to be present to claim $1,000. The bank night swindle was ridiculed so thoroughly that the picture man was finally forced to give away $75 in self-defense. [*BBB,* 2 July 1936, 2]

Following reports of Fred Brunk's efforts and other kindred approaches, Bill Bruno informed his readers that inside information from the motion picture industry confirmed the powerful impact that these burlesques made. News obtained by a former trouper, then operating a motion picture house, told of a change of attitude on the part of the movie interests:

Whereas we were advised in May to "pour it on the tent shows with nightly bank nights while they are in your town," a circular letter received last week from the western brain trust advises against the practice. The closing paragraph is significant. It reads: "DON'T leave your gate open to the wise tent show managers."

In concluding his report, Bruno urged, "Pour it on 'em when they try it on you. For nothing is so deadly as polite ridicule" (*BBB,* 16 July 1936, 1).

Some circle stock managers even chose to adopt the bank night system and operate it in an appropriate manner. Dale Madden, Sr., reports that the Madden and Stillian Players developed their own successful form of bank nights in order to draw audiences:

We deposited in our treasury each day ten dollars, and hoped that it would not be drawn out too soon and be allowed to build up. The ten dollars came high for us but by sacrificing some of our living conditions, and being quite

> prudent in salaries, the Bank Night did build up in a few weeks, and the crowds quite naturally increased accordingly. We had six play dates a week and each night was Bank Night in each town.

Imitation can be not only sincere flattery but key to survival in a competitive marketplace.

A second major area of promotion found on circle stock made prominent use of audience involvement and participation to increase attendance. Involving one individual, a group, or even the entire audience in a performance frequently heightened the already strong tie existing between company and community.

One traditionally successful technique to increase business on a circle, according to Jay Bee Flesner, involved casting a local citizen in a production, especially a child.

> Every circle I was ever on, along about when you were running short of bills after ten or twelve weeks, using *Ten Nights in a Bar Room* with a local girl would give business a shot in the arm.

Flesner describes the necessary steps as follows. Two weeks ahead of performance the company announced the need of a young girl for the part of Little Mary in the production. The following week the manager selected the girl and rehearsed her with the company, instructing her to memorize her lines with the help of her mother during the coming week. On the day of the performance, the young actress rehearsed her scene with the ensemble in the afternoon and performed the role—"she only had about four lines"—that evening. Without fail, Flesner recalls, this technique would "pack the house."

In another format local performers were asked to appear not in the play itself but as a specialty act. Raleigh Wilson, managing the Wilson Players on a circle of Colorado and Nebraska towns, announced in 1930 that the addition of a nightly "Whoopee Party" after the play performance had significantly increased business. Described by Wilson as "nothing more or less than several acts given by local amateurs," the Whoopee Party increased ticket income as friends and relatives of the performers jammed the house. When area talent could not be obtained, Wilson staged "community sings" with similarly good results. The audience sing-along idea, according to Wilson,

> was taken from these cinema palaces where slides are thrown on the screen and the audiences asked to join in the chorus. The idea with this show has proven to be rather informal, an extemporaneous stunt that produces intimate contact with the folks such as the movies can't do. [*BBB*, 6 Mar., 3]

Wilson also reported that when regional interest and talent warranted it, old-time fiddle and harmonica contests helped boost audience attendance.

The allure of monetary awards further boosted audience participation. Whether the first prize consisted of three crisp dollar bills, or an equal number of shiny silver dollars, or even a small government bond, such offerings provided a strong incentive to win for most participants.

An "amateur night" contest used by Joe Marion on his Nebraska circle in 1935 impressed Bill Bruno, and he deemed the practice "well worth passing on to the other shows." Bruno summarized the system in the following fashion:

> Joe is conducting an amateur night each week at each of the towns played. The winners of each week's contest will then at a later date compete and the winners of these eliminations will be given a two week's engagement over the circle on salary. The idea is a good one, in that it stimulates interest from week to week. It is a fact that Joe's business had doubled and tripled in the towns visited since he put on the amateurs. [*BBB*, 7 Nov., 3]

Chick Boyes Players

—*In*—

A Big Double Show

A Three-Act Comedy

"She Couldn't Marry Three"

EXTRA FEATURE

Opportunity Night

With Local Talent

A VAUDEVILLE REVUE

3 - PRIZES - 3

1st. *A Genuine Diamond Ring.*
2nd. *Cash Prize.*
3rd. *Cash Prize.*

NOTE:—*Anyone can enter this contest. Leave your name with the manager of your local theatre or drop a card to* CHICK BOYES PLAYERS, Hebron, Nebr.

Perhaps a local talent show with a genuine diamond ring as first prize was needed to boost attendance following many weeks on the circuit (courtesy of the Otoe County [Nebraska] Museum of Memories).

Soon after the introduction of such uses of audience involvement, reports of amateur contests offering cash prizes each night of a circle became common.

Another idea to increase attendance involved the addition of a popularity contest to the evening's festivities. Often such events determined the most popular girl in a community through an audience vote. Members of the audience normally obtained ballots for the voting by purchasing either candy or popcorn and the winning girl received a prize, perhaps a humble diamond ring valued at only a few dollars. The Gordon-Howard Candy Company even offered a "Miss Popularity" candy and flash assortment with "vote coupons on the box" (*BBB,* 5 Dec. 1935, 8).

Groups of children on stage traditionally drew positive audience response. Parading local infants in a "Tiny Tot Revue" or inviting older youngsters to enter a bubble-gum blowing contest delighted the crowd. Occasionally the same ideas were applied to adults. A "silk stocking revue" seeking the "young lady with the most perfect limbs" might be used to perk up attendance on a circle. When running this contest in Oklahoma during the late 1930s, Henry Brunk sought as many as 20 local girls to participate under the following guidelines:

> Entrants in the contest will appear on the stage and the curtain will be raised only enough to show their limbs below the knees. The audience will be the sole judge of the contest and the young woman who receives the most applause will be awarded a number of premiums. [MRA Collection, unidentified clipping, hand dated 15 Feb. 1938]

Dance contests provided another effective gimmick with which to involve the audience. Henry Brunk, while on the 1938 circle centered in southwestern Oklahoma cited above, offered a "Big Apple" contest. Advertising for the event proclaimed, "You have heard of the 'Big Apple' dance from coast to coast. ... Now is your opportunity to see it done in Mangum." Contestants received free admission to the theater on the night of the competition, and if they arrived at the theater early they also obtained free instructions from the company's dancer on how to do the "Big Apple." A cash prize for the couple judged the best once again provided the major inspiration for competing (MRA Collection, unidentified clipping).

Some companies even used "bingo" as an attendance incentive, finding it combined the elements of a game of chance with audience involvement. Ralph Moody, after seeing competing movie managers in Nebraska promote "Screen-O," reacted in self-defense. Moody presented his game of "Tent-O" first while under canvas, using kernels of corn for markers, later adding it to his winter touring. Bill Bruno reported in 1935, "The novelty of it caught on so well that Ralph now is using it on his circle. The idea is a new one and the [bingo] cards should not be hard to get" (*BBB,* 31 Oct., 8).

While such contests display varying degrees of ingenuity, the staging of an "Auction Night" as an added feature on circle stock ranks among the most ingenious, or possibly the most infamous. In this ploy a lively auction was added to an evening's bill of entertainment, although no direct monetary benefit came to the company. Manager Henry Brunk of Brunk's Comedians, who relied heavily upon added promotions during his single season of circle stock, explained his auction night to the public in this fashion:

> Several articles are selected, mostly ladies' apparel, for the auction. The items are auctioned off to the highest bidder, and after the cash is paid to the auctioneer for the items, the money is in turn given back to someone in the audience. Perhaps someone might receive a five dollar bill for two dollars, and then someone will in turn get the two dollars for a dime and so on down the line until everything on the stage and the proceeds are disposed of. Sometimes the comedian's shoes are auctioned off, or perhaps the leading lady's stockings might be sold, and again it might be the shirt right off of the leading man. The Auction is held just for the fun and amusement that is derived. [MRA Collection, unidentified clipping, hand dated 4 Feb. 1938]

SPECIAL-EXTRA

COMING HERE _____

'Tiny Tot Revue'

See all your stores and business houses represented by tiny tots from 2 to 6 years in parade on our stage. A loving cup awarded to the winner.

The above all in addition to the

CHICK BOYES PLAYERS'

regular dramatic and vaudeville program

A Double Show at Regular Admission!

Don't Miss This Extra Novelty of the

'Tiny Tot Revue'

A "Tiny Tot Revue" offered a performance bonus that was hard to resist (courtesy of the Otoe County [Nebraska] Museum of Memories).

This same idea was taken to a titillating extreme when auctioning a "complete outfit of clothes off a girl." According to Jay Bee Flesner, who remembers participating in such auctions while on circle stock, the procedure involved auctioning clothes piece by piece off an attractive female cast member, the clothing often loaned for the event from a local apparel store. The first item to be auctioned off might be the model's handkerchief was auctioned off, then the master of ceremonies proceeded to auction off the hose, the dress, then she's in a nice slip. Then the panties. She would pull the slip up just enough to get a peak on the side. Auction them off, then the bra. She would loosen it and take it off under the slip. Then auction the slip off. And when she'd take that off, she had on a bathing suit.

As tradition dictated, the company did not keep the money paid for the removal of the clothes, but rather used a reverse auction to return the cash to the audience. Although the first half of the auction employed a unique adult twist, the second half of the event remained similar to Henry Brunk's auction night. During the reverse auction Flesner recalls awarding money to individuals who first signaled the possession of various common items: 50 cents for a yellow lead pencil, a stick of gum, or possibly a bobby pin. A dollar offered for a white button typically stirred a frantic search in the audience. Eager to claim the prize, men often ripped one off their own shirts–so many that Flesner suggests "fifty percent of the men" went home with a missing button. Even so the liberal return of money during the reverse auction normally helped members of the audience cover the expense of repairing or replacing an item, such as sewing a shirt ripped in obtaining a desired object.

Although he freely admits that such an auction was "kind of tacky," Flesner sees little harm done. And while the practice appears rather suggestive for the conservative morals of rural America, it is perhaps no more so than the mildly suggestive titles willingly used by the circle and tent companies. As in the distinction between play titles and the plays themselves, such auctions delivered far less than they seemed to promise. Regardless of what some of the pious thought, such auction nights typically produced heavily attended performances and provided advertising for a local clothing store, all the while costing the circle company nothing.

Still another method used by circle stock companies to boost attendance involved increasing the amount or variety of entertainment offered during a performance, with little or no advance in admission. We have already seen that various circle companies of the Trousdale brothers used motion pictures in place of or in addition to the traditional specialty acts. The Trousdales surely adopted this policy not because they lacked appropriate specialties but because of a desire to tap into the intense interest in silent films at the time. Records also reveal that the Trousdale-Horne circle company once served notice in Anamosa, Iowa, that beginning promptly at eight o'clock, "the entire company will appear on the stage and 'make up' before the audience for the character they are giving in the play" (*Anamosa* [Iowa] *Eureka,* 25 Feb. 1915, 8). During the 1930s, stage magicians, illusionists, and hypnotists proved quite popular as added attractions on the circles. For example, in 1936 the Mal Murray Company used "McKnight the Hypnotist" while on its week-long circle (*BBB,* 26 Mar., 3). A few years later Price Markwell–known professionally as "Curman the Magician"–joined the Ray Cass circle in Illinois as an added attraction (*BBB*, 7 Apr. 1938, 3).

Whereas the Trousdales on occasion used short silent films in place of specialty acts, a trend from the 1930s joined circle companies and movies. The marriage of these two entertainment forms largely took place when troupes could not complete a circuit of performance sites without turning to fully operating motion picture houses.

In this venue once a week or once every two weeks, a circle company performed sandwiched between the showings of popular full-length motion pictures. Troupes typically claimed "No advance in prices," and during the 1930s admission for what usually amounted to two showings of a single film plus a complete stage performance frequently ran as low as 25 cents for adults, ten cents for children. While these performances required the splitting of the "take," such an arrangement obviously remained far better than none at all.

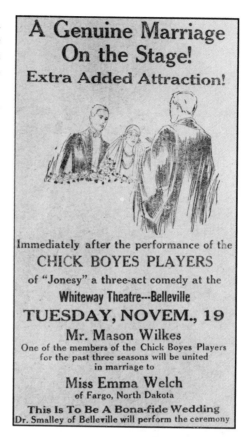

A Genuine Marriage On the Stage!
Extra Added Attraction!

Immediately after the performance of the
CHICK BOYES PLAYERS
of "Jonesy" a three-act comedy at the
Whiteway Theatre---Belleville
TUESDAY, NOVEM., 19
Mr. Mason Wilkes
One of the members of the Chick Boyes Players for the past three seasons will be united in marriage to
Miss Emma Welch
of Fargo, North Dakota
This Is To Be A Bona-fide Wedding
Dr. Smalley of Belleville will perform the ceremony

On occasion the combining of real romance with an evening of entertainment could assure a sellout performance (courtesy of the Otoe County [Nebraska] Museum of Memories).

Advertising for these events likely announced a "Big Double Show," with film selections "on the screen" and a single play performance "on the stage." These combinations could cause problems, however, for as Sid Kingdon recalls, the sound speakers required for motion pictures greatly reduced the stage area to perform in. Yet with adjustments a circle company could enact an entire play in only the three feet of stage area that normally remained in front of the movie screen and speakers. While it might appear that in such situations circle stock took a back seat to film, unless the company played exclusively in movie houses in conjunction with films,

—PREVIEWS— 25c	LaVista Theater				

Detail from February 1938 schedule of the La Vista Theater which reveals Brunk's Comedians sharing the stage with motion pictures (courtesy of the Museum of Repertoire Americana).

rarely did such arrangements constitute more than one or two slots on a circuit.[7] Even so, since times were difficult, forging a relationship between motion pictures and play performances was not dismissed out of principle. In occasionally bedding down with rivals, managers once again demonstrated their ability to adapt the circle stock format to the conditions they found and thereby continue to tour.

Expenses

When a manager surveyed the expenses of operating a circle stock company, the outward flow of money fell in five main areas: salaries; transportation; rental of performance space; advertising; and a wide variety of miscellaneous expenses. With the aid of surviving circle stock financial records—most prominently the Chick Boyes ledgers—one can investigate these expense categories and ascertain several pre– and post–Depression differences. Of the major expenditures in circuit playing, none reveals a more pronounced difference between these two eras than that of salaries.

Reliable records of salaries paid on circle stock throughout its 50-plus years of existence are few. Yet a handful of personal recollections, some salary offers in advertising, a few historical accounts, and the remaining circle business ledgers provide enough information to piece together a narrative on salaries. It is important to note that the base salaries paid to circle stock and tent rep performers remained largely identical during their shared histories. While total salaries on tent shows often exceeded those of circle stock, this difference is because of the extra salary payments available during the canvas season. Additional money could be earned, for example, by driving an equipment truck, helping with tent set-up, or distributing posters.

According to Bill Bruno, the level of salaries prior to the First World War held steady at $25 a week for singles and $45 for doubles (i.e., couples) (*BBB*, 12 Nov. 1936, 3). Following World War I, the 1920s witnessed a general advancement of salaries to the point where a single performer commanded $45–$50 and in

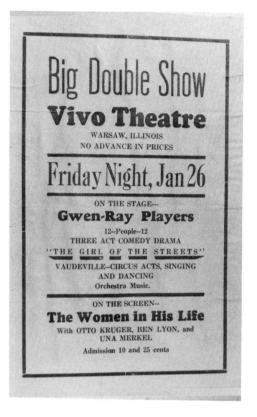

Gwen-Ray Players appearing in conjunction with motion pictures with "NO ADVANCE IN PRICES" (courtesy of the Museum of Repertoire Americana).

a few cases as high as $75 a week (Bernheim, 100; Mickel, 104). With the onset of the Depression, however, these wages were never to be seen again in the industry. In the early to mid–1930s a range from ten dollars to $17.50 a week for singles and $25–$35 a week for doubles predominated, with a general trend of slowly rising salaries throughout the decade. By 1940 Bruno teasingly advised an eastern acting team to request $70 a week for a summer tent engagement and to "try to get anywhere near that figure" (*BBB*, 22 Feb., 3). The simple truth of the matter is that wages had not advanced as quickly as this young couple hoped. Yet some definite advancement in salaries is evident in the waning years of circuit trouping. By the mid–1950s, very near the end of the circle stock era, reports of $75 a week for a two-person circle team were not uncommon.

Figures from the Chick Boyes ledgers generally support the preceding overview. The existing ledger for 1925 reveals that the total cost of salaries averaged over $415 per week. Figures such as this remind one that as a labor-intensive business salaries consistently composed the largest area of expenditure on a circle. Because of highly detailed records in this 1925 ledger we can determine that in playing circle stock at this time an average of 75 percent of all expenses went toward salaries. The 1936-37 ledger shows an astounding drop in the average weekly total of salaries paid out—down to slightly under $90. The 1940-41 ledger demonstrates a modest recovery, with slightly over $100 per week on average spent on salaries. Although the weekly salary averages from the two Depression-era ledgers appear painfully minute these figures appear to reflect wages paid only to actors and not to Mr. and Mrs. Boyes, whereas the 1925 average appears to include regular salary payments to management. Records verify that Chick Boyes consistently maintained a total of seven to eight performers on his circle companies, mostly hired as husband and wife "teams" and paid as teams. This being the case, the ledgers appear to reflect the payment of typical salaries for their respective eras, or perhaps slightly below average.

The level of wages for performers, especially during the economic hardships of the 1930s, provided considerable fuel for controversy and debate. Much dissension centered on managers who increasingly demanded more work of their company without appropriate compensation. Giving voice to the concern, Bill Bruno complained that once upon a time there existed "a limit to what you gave your manager in return for your salary," whereas during the Depression, Bruno claimed, no limit appeared to be the norm. On one occasion Bruno supported his argument with the following example of the grueling daily routine of one manager's several circles during the winter season of 1936-37:

> People must double orchestra and do what are called specialties—if you wish to be polite. Salaries, $15 and $30. Rehearsal every morning at 10 o'clock, daily half-hour radio broadcast at 2, a drive of from 19 to 62 miles in snow, cold and ofttimes blizzards this winter, show at 8, followed by a three to four hour dance played by the actor-musicians and then the drive back to the base—and repeat. All for the munificent salary of $15 per week, provided no nights are lost because of the manager's inability to book or because bad weather denoted a small house. The average of lost nights was two a week during the winter. [*BBB*, 18 Mar. 1937, 3]

Bruno also points out that this same manager had recently taken credit for donating the services of his three companies for a flood relief event. Bruno concludes his description of this benefit with the query "As the actors lost that night's salary and donated their efforts, who deserves the credit?"

As depressed salaries continued through the 1930s, many actors could no longer justify the effort required for the compensation received. Note the sentiment of one performer who after ten years of trouping decided that the rep profession held no future. Especially painful to this performer was the realization that past experience and effort apparently made no difference in calculating salaries.

> I found, Bill, that experience, ability, earnest and conscientious effort don't seem to count in the business any more. Managers want to pay everyone the same salary without regard for capability. Why? Well, as a recent boss of mine said: "They all get the same salary on here. No kick that way—one guy can't crow over somebody else." I suppose that's one way to look at it from the manager's viewpoint. But how about a fellow who has put in several years of effort and has worked hard to make himself an above-the-average performer. Shouldn't he rate a little better than the "First-of-May" who has nothing to offer but a good profile, a wide pair of shoulders and wavy hair? [*BBB*, 20 Jan. (1938), 3]

The performer concluded that it was time to quit show business entirely.

Companies led by parsimonious individuals certainly existed, but not all managers acted in this manner. Letters to *Bill Bruno's Bulletin* frequently carried reports of circle managers who treated performers with respect and fairness, as evidenced by this testimony:

> When we signed we did so on a small salary as we knew it to be sure and that the new circle was an experiment. But were assured that should it prove a winner, the salary would be increased. Which I considered the usual blah. Imagine my entire surprise when at the end of the second week our envelope contained an additional $7.50 with a note stating the new salary would continue so long as present business held up. That's one for the book, isn't it? [3 Feb. (1938), 3]

In the same issue Bruno published an excerpt of a letter that he found unique and encouraging, yet he humorously considered it "even more on the Ripley order" than the letter above. It reads in part:

> The blizzard caused the show to lose three nights last week. But on Saturday night the envelopes were handed out with the full salary and a note saying it was in appreciation of Sunday nights we had played in the past. [3]

On the other hand, one aspect relating to salaries that frequently drew the ire of managers involved what they saw as the unnecessary or extravagant purchase of automobiles by company members.

> The car habit has been a curse to show business. Got a bunch on here who are working year in and year out for Ford and General Motors, and they can't buy wardrobe or clothes as they always have car payments to meet. The fact that we keep them working all year round, with exceptions of three weeks between seasons, means nothing to the once popular "grouch bag." Have this year given them a season of forty-nine weeks and the car owners are grumbling that they can't afford or haven't the money to take the three weeks' layoff. BUT the funny part of the whole thing is that those on the

show who have received the smallest salaries and felt that they couldn't afford to buy a car, are the only ones who are not complaining that they can't afford the layoff. Figure that out. [*BBB*, 2 Jan. 1930, 7]

Bruno on occasion wryly observed that actors frequently purchased new cars in the flush summer season yet paid for them in the less secure winter season. He implied that the consistent work required to pay off an automobile loan created or maintained many circle companies expressly for that purpose, very likely weakening the industry in the meantime.

Expenditures listed for the beginning of Boyes's fall 1940 circle season record typical "organizing" costs faced when a company geared up for the circle season. The majority of such expense is connected with transportation, normally the largest area of circle expenditures after salaries. For example, engine work and a new tire for the company's Dodge totaled over $50. For the company's larger Lincoln automobile costs included: $35 for storage, $12 for a new battery, ten dollars for insurance, six dollars for license fees, and nearly five dollars of assorted expenses incurred when taking the Lincoln out of storage. In addition to these expenses, nine dollars is recorded for a trailer top to protect scenery and properties in transit.

Organizational expenditures for the following year's circle in fall 1941 included many similar expenses. In the area of transportation, $40 worth of new tires, $12 for repairs, and six dollars for a battery are listed for the Dodge. In addition, $18.50 covered the cost and installation of overload springs for the Dodge. Miscellaneous costs for the start of the 1941-42 circle season included over $85 for printing and "billing" (i.e., promotional) expenses, telegraph and telephone costs in excess of $15, and "ropes and battens" for the hanging of rag scenery in the neighborhood of $15. In sum, the ledgers show nearly $320 of startup costs for the circle season commencing in the fall of 1940, while the following year these costs totaled roughly $200. Although insurance is cryptically mentioned in the ledgers, accurate records of its cost for the Chick Boyes Players are not to be found. While of little importance in the early years of rep, accounts of the industry following the Depression era indicate the growing need, and expense, of both personal and property insurance.

The cost of renting a performance site varied considerably, depending upon the type and condition of the space, the size of the community, and typical attendance there. In many cases, especially for communities in Kansas, the Boyes ledgers record rental costs of only three to five dollars a performance. In other areas rental charges ranged as high as $30 for a single visit. The 1940-41 ledger reveals that an increasing number of performance sites based their rental fees upon a percentage of the gross take of the evening. Known as a "sharing contract," this method of determining rental fees seemed especially popular in the communities of western Nebraska and both eastern Colorado and Wyoming where the Chick Boyes Players performed. The percentage charged varied from the low of a 25 percent cut of the gross at Julesburg, Colorado, to the considerable fee of 50 percent of the gross at Scottsbluff, Nebraska. In one Kansas community the required 10 percent of the evening's gross of $6.50 amounted to a rental fee of only 65 cents.

In the area of publicity the most common expenses were advertisements placed in various community newspapers on the circuit. The majority of ads announcing upcoming appearances of the Boyes company cost from one to two dollars, with the range stretching to a high of five dollars. One advertising expense typically found shortly after the addition of a new community to a circuit was that of a mailing list usually costing between three and five dollars. No indication is given, however, as to the source of these lists. Perhaps Boyes purchased them from the local newspaper, the post office, or a civic organization in the area.

The ledgers also reveal that on occasion Boyes used the venerable telephone "line call" to promote his circle company. In such an advertising ploy Boyes delivered a folksy message simultaneously to a number of households through a large party-line hookup. One such promotional call in 1941 involving nine different lines cost 90 cents.

An expense periodically evident in the ledgers deserving of some attention is that of performance permits or licenses. Normally license costs are associated with tent touring and its proverbial necessities of "lot, license, and lights." But whereas tent shows needed a place to erect a canvas theater, the legal right to perform outdoors, and a source of electricity to illuminate the performance, circle stock obviously required far less. Still it is evident that some communities required a license fee for performance rights, normally ranging in cost from three to six dollars.

Additional expenses varied according to the community. Entries for performances in Sterling, Colorado, consistently record $2.50 for "police," while janitorial services required in Seneca, Nebraska, cost one dollar each performance. The floor wax needed for show-and-dance dates routinely cost upward to one dollar. In a number of communities played as a show-and-dance date a required music tax normally amounted to only one dollar. Other miscellaneous expenses include entries for props ranging from 50 cents to five dollars. Entries labeled "furniture," often for only a few dollars, note additional furniture items needed for a particular production. The purchase of a "piano kit" for two dollars obviously indicates the need for repairs or tuning somewhere on the circuit. Other interesting expenditures found in the Boyes ledgers include $6.70 for wigs, while a series of recurring entries in 1936 for drayage ranged as high as two dollars. Yet the records do not reveal where or under what circumstances this additional transportation cost came about.

In similar fashion, various ledger entries are equally difficult to understand because they fail to offer us sufficient explanation for their inclusion in these business records. Taken as a whole, however, these few existing ledgers provide the best evidence we have of the economic dealings of circle stock. But obviously no industrywide standards can be determined for profit and loss. This notwithstanding, examples from the Boyes ledgers can be seen as fairly representing trends. For example, the week of performances beginning on Sunday, 1 March 1925, is highly typical of the relative success of companies under the management of Boyes at that time. With a total gross of $678.20 for seven performances and expenses totaling $566.55 for the week, Boyes showed a profit of $111.65 for this segment of his two-week circuit. Weeks before and following this one demonstrate marked contrasts, though. One particular week the ledgers record a loss of over $200 (probably because of adverse weather conditions in January), while the other three weekly losses during the period of January through April of 1925 average only around $50. Yet during the final rotation of the circuit in late April profits reached nearly $550 for the two-week period. Even so, the total profit for this 18-week season of circle stock averaged only $65 per week.

During the Depression, however, the profits earned by the Chick Boyes Players (as recorded in the 1936-37 ledger) were considerably less for various reasons. Even though often performing show-and-dance for added income, profits normally ranged from five dollars to $60 per week and on only a few occasions reached as high as $90. But because these records are less meticulous than the 1925 ledger, such figures are highly misleading—if for no other reason than that transportation was not figured into the results. Taking into consideration that transportation expenses in 1925 averaged over $90 per week, one can easily see that the weeks showing a slim profit in this 1936-37 ledger likely had none, and those weeks already displaying a loss actually suffered a far greater one.

Special Problems in the Wartime Economy

After the economic straits in which the Great Depression placed circle stock, World War II ranks as having the next greatest effect upon its financial development and practice. The war exercised two different influences, however. At the very time when the need for entertainment in a war-weary country increased, the manpower to meet the demand marched away to active combat or to defense manufacturing jobs.

Prior to America's military involvement in World War II, advice to circle stock troupes centered on remaining clear of the subject:

Perhaps you didn't know that war plays, or any mention of war, is poison on any circle at this time. The public in general wants to forget all about war or its possibility.... So if you want to successfully continue on your circle eliminate the word "war" from your performances. [*BBB*, 13 Jan. 1938, 3][8]

With the entry of the United States into war following the surprise attack on Pearl Harbor, circle stock companies suffered from the general shock and disbelief that gripped the public. As a result, troupes as a whole experienced an alarming drop in business. Many managers expressed concern over the wisdom of attempting to continue in the face of seemingly overwhelming odds. Bob Feagin felt this period of adjustment required patience.

We, just like our armed forces, have to ride the shock of the first impact. Right now, Mr. Average Citizen has his ear glued to his radio. This phase will pass and soon. Then, if past performances are a criterion, they will be more eager than ever for entertainment.

So lets heed the request of our President and remain cool. [*BFB*, Christmas Special, 1941, 10]

The shock of the country's rapid entry into the war and the resulting slump in business is clearly reflected in the ledger entries by Chick Boyes for the week following the attack on Pearl Harbor. Next to the $20 loss for the week Boyes simply penned the note "1 week of war." The loss stands in marked contrast to the company's previous rotation of this section of its circuit when Boyes recorded a profit of over $130.

As the country plunged into combat preparations, the industry found itself faced with growing rationing restrictions at the very time when it sought to expand to fill the entertainment needs of a nation at war. In his personal history *The Fabulous Toby and Me*, tent rep manager Neil Schaffner suggests that the rationing restrictions that affected his operations were a mixed blessing. Schaffner points out that the Office of Defense Transportation declared tent companies essential to the war effort and, therefore, allotted all the gasoline they needed for their operations. Yet tires came under the jurisdiction of the Office of Price Administration, and the tent shows did not receive a favorable classification from that office. Schaffner recalls that his company

would not have been able to operate if it had not been that good friends in our old established towns from time to time gave us spares from wrecked vehicles and others that materialized mysteriously from places I did not bother to find out about. Instead of suffering, we actually prospered in the tire department. By the war's end we had a stock of spares that reached to the ceiling of one of our trucks. [158]

Many of the tires received by the Schaffner Players were said to come from farmers in their territory, as the agriculture industry remained largely exempt from tire restrictions. Very little is recorded about how specific circle stock companies fared in the face of tire and gasoline rationing, but one can safely assume that this branch of rep resorted to the same solutions as Schaffner's tent operation. We do have knowledge of a few fortunate managers' boasting of outfitting their vehicles with new tires only weeks or in some cases only a few days before the imposition of tire restrictions. Yet some admit they purchased tires not because of impending controls but because they foresaw sharp price increases on the horizon (*BFB,* 21 Jan. 1942, 3). These fortunate managers notwithstanding, one response to tire rationing involved scaling back a company's circuit since the considerable mileage covered in circle touring promoted tire replacement. In one instance SeaBee Hayworth reduced his weekly circle mileage by 250 miles to save on tires, accomplished through the switching of three towns on his circuit (*BFB,* 11 Mar. 1942, 2).

Up until May 1942 when it ceased publication, *Feagin's Bulletin* acted as a clearing-house for information on the subject of rationing, with Feagin frequently providing strategies to survive the duration of restrictions. Once, Feagin's warning concerning an important consumable applied equally to circle stock and tent companies:

> Another thing that we must remember is that the tire rationing was but a beginning. Other things will be rationed. One thing in particular we must watch for is ELECTRICITY. We strongly urge that every operator, that is in a position to, see about getting a portable light plant. In that way you will be independent if you are refused lights at any time. Let's don't be caught flat-footed in this as we have so many other things. [*BFB,* 28 Jan. 1942, 3]

Yet only a few months following his warning Feagin reported a definite improvement in the situation, stating, "We have it on good authority that there will be ample electricity for all" (*BFB,* 29 Apr., 3).

In spite of the widespread concern that rationing raised in the circle stock industry during the Second World War, some optimists saw a benefit in the scarcity of tires: a gradual decrease in automobile use by the general public to the benefit of all forms of rep theater.

> The tire situation, which may hamper you in getting into town, will also slow up your customer's jaunts to the county seat on bank night. As the motor traffic slows down more and more, people are going to look for entertainment in their own localities. We can fill that need if we're on our toes. [*BFB,* 28 Jan. 1942, 3]

Feagin even envisioned the wholesale demise of the automobile:

> It would be strange, would it not, if this war, which at first looked like the ruin of our business, should turn out to be its salvation? And it COULD happen. The automobile took our business from us and the passing of the auto COULD give it back to us.... And, mark our prediction, we may again

see the time when the banner agent, instead of high pressuring the filling stations with their gas business, will bear down on the livery man by the threat to take their hay business elsewhere. And the town may again go down to the local train to see the actors come in. Ridiculous? Fantastic? So was the attack on Pearl Harbor—until it happened. [*BFB,* 18 Feb. 1942, 3]

While this fantasy of a return to simpler times never came to fruition, the difficulty of acquiring tires certainly did not spell doom for the industry, or, conversely, become its salvation.

Indeed, the negative impact of World War II took more worrisome effect in the loss of performers from the profession. This drain on personnel took form not only in those called to active duty, but also in the temporary loss of performers to higher-paying defense jobs. As the rep field faced continued dwindling of personnel resources in the spring of 1942, Bob Feagin emphatically voiced the concerns of many:

In all our experience we have never heard the howl for desirable people that we are hearing this spring. Of course there has always been that last minute search by managers who neglect to sign their cast early, but this spring seems to be even worse than usual.

We cannot help but believe that this is caused by so many leaving our ranks for the better paying defense jobs. And that is a condition that repertoire has GOT to recognize—and deal with—if it survives.

There may have been a day when actors hung on and starved and scrimped for the pure love of their art. But if there ever was such a day it has definitely passed. Actors are now looking, as all other professions are looking, for security. And he certainly CANNOT attain it on a twenty week season.... A commander in the field that can't replace his casualties is licked. And it takes quite a while to train OUR replacements. How many of us are TRY-ING to get young folks to select our profession as their life work? If they DO wish to adopt it, what inducement can we offer them? [*BFB,* 25 Mar., 3]

Despite such pleas, the personnel shortage created by World War II did not remain a temporary one; it became a permanent legacy of the conflict. Following the war's conclusion, only a small percentage of performers, having once experienced the high pay and security of employment elsewhere, ever returned to the ranks of rep.

In the study of the financial aspects of circle stock one is clearly reminded that times have changed and both this nation's pay scale and cost of living are now vastly different from those of earlier eras. Sensitive to these differences, veteran trouper Dick Wolever vividly contrasts the present with the past:

I pay a yardman $30 each time he mows my grass and takes care of my yard in the summer. He comes for about four hours once a week. The sum of $30 would have bought you a good leading team—leading man and leading woman—back in circle stock time. You could buy the best dinner in a hotel dining room for $1.50. Now if you don't tip more than that, they don't want you back.

Out of necessity the question of profit and loss has always remained the primary benchmark in the evaluation of a circle stock operation. But the salary earned by a performer frequently did not stand alone in his evaluation of a circle season because such highly intangible factors as comradeship and experience gained influenced the performer's thinking. Reacting to the vast amounts of energy, enthusiasm, and effort expended in circle stock, Dick Elsenpeter once remarked, "You know, if you had worked this hard at any other endeavor, you couldn't help but make millions before you were forty." However, the swift reply—"It's a lifestyle. It's not a job"—caused Elsenpeter to reconsider his thinking. And because few, if any, ever made a truly sizable income from circle stock, the above admonition says a great deal. In a simple way the maxim "It's a lifestyle" pays tribute to the countless circle stock veterans who desired chiefly to continue practicing their craft, while doing whatever necessary to keep the business ledgers in the black.

7

Variety Galore

T HE ABILITY OF THE CIRCLE STOCK format to change in order to meet the specific requirements of a company always proved to be one of its most admired characteristics. While the possible adaptations of the basic one- or two-week circle structures were consider-able indeed, widely used variations can be grouped into three basic cate-gories: circles extending the size of circuits beyond two weeks in length; circles found in locations and environments different from the norm; and circles changing the format and content of traditional circle stock practices.

Variations in Length

Whereas the majority of managers maintained one-week or sometimes two-week circles, a few thought that even larger and longer circuits could be profitable and yet still manageable. However, the difficulty in operating a three-week or longer circle lay in the special housing and transportation provisions required because of the expansive physical territory that these circuits covered.

In order to facilitate transportation in such circles, some managers used two different base communities during a single rotation of the circuit. In this method roughly one half of the circuit lay in close proximity to the first headquarters, while the remaining half surrounded a second base some distance from the first. Using two headquarters required the performers to establish housing arrangements beforehand in each of the communities. Even so, many managers maintained lengthy circuits with only one base community. In this system as many towns as possible would be played out of the home base. When the jumps between the base and the next perform-ance site became so long as to prevent returning each evening, the com-pany then traveled from town to town staying the evening in prearranged hotels or boarding rooms. Following the final performance during the rota-tion of such a circuit, a company was often required to make a mammoth jump back to its headquarters. Veteran trouper Caroline Schaffner reports that with the Chick Boyes Players the performers fared well during that segment of their three-week circuit in which they were unable to return to their base community because all extra lodging expenses were borne by management.

Yet three-week-long circles remained far from the upper limit in the industry. Indeed some large circles rivaled the size and scope of the one-night-stand circuits formed during the early years of the twentieth century, but nevertheless rightfully remained true circle stock operations because they faithfully returned to each community with a new production on a regular schedule. Some managers appear to have been quite adept at operating large circles, and they became widely noted for such efforts.

Of such managers, Peter Borgen stands as one who established a solid reputation for extended circuits. In the summer of 1939, for example, he managed a four-week circle of towns in northwest Minnesota (*BBB*, 15 June, 2). Another specialist in substantial circuits was Cecil Vernon, who maintained a 30-day circle in North Dakota in 1935 (*BBB*, 28 Nov., 3) and a few years later in Minnesota an even larger one.

> Cecil Vernon's new circle idea, favored by unusually good winter weather, continues to be successful in southeastern Minnesota. Vernon is playing a circuit of forty towns, returning to each every six weeks, his orchestra playing short dances after shows, and a daily broadcast is made from station KROC at the base in Rochester. [*BBB*, 13 Jan. (1938), 1]

Since they made daily radio broadcasts from Rochester, this company of 12 seemingly maintained only one base community even while performing regularly in over three dozen communities.

Others maintained still larger circles. William Balthazor is remembered as a manager who routinely thought "big" in his use of the show-and-dance format and connections with radio stations. In 1938 *Bill Bruno's Bulletin* reported "remarkable business" for Balthazor's considerable circle in South Dakota and western Minnesota:

> Company has been enlarged to twelve people which includes a seven-piece orchestra for dances. Now playing a circle of 50 towns and *Ten Nights* was started on the route last week. Watertown is being played every Saturday night to turnaway business with a "barn dance frolic" which is broadcast from the local station. [27 Jan., 1]

Perhaps the largest reported circle is that which the Moroni Olsen Players maintained during late 1928. The circuit wound its way through eight states (Wyoming, Utah, Montana, Idaho, Washington, Oregon, California, and Nevada) and one Canadian province (British Columbia) while visiting 60 cities. But while the company played only one production during a trip through the 60 communities and, hence, should be classified as a circle stock company, each rotation of the circuit clearly took more than 60 days. Such a schedule suggests either more than one performance in some communities or, because of the size of the circle, "dark" travel days without performances–techniques not normally associated with circle stock (*Billboard,* 1 Dec., 30). When circle circuits reached this size, unquestionably many of the typical characteristics of circle stock began to disappear.

Variations in Location and Environment

Although circle stock organizations normally performed in permanent structures, temporary theaters sometimes served the needs of a company when it was deemed impossible to secure enough standard sites to complete a circuit. And because of circle stock's close association with tent rep, canvas structures typically provided a solution. In many such instances managers conveniently pressed into service equipment already owned or controlled by the company. Yet the use of tents required time, labor, and expense well beyond that required in traditional circle touring. While not a widespread practice, its use is documented in several instances when it served as a necessary method to keep a circle operating.

Al Trahern found it necessary in the late 1920s to utilize a tent during every rotation of his Long Island circuit. In 1936 Bill Bruno reported that two different companies in Colorado belonging to Henry and Ruby Neal were to open "under canvas," claiming this action "something rather new for circle companies" (*BBB,* 18 June, 1). Each of these units needed to hire a full-time boss canvasman to head up the care and maintenance of the tent.

Late in the Depression manager Eddie Hart could not secure an appropriate site in his headquarters town of Battle Creek, Nebraska. So he relied upon his own tent show equipment and according to reports played the town "to capacity every week" (*BBB,* 9 Nov. 1939, 2). Evidence is also found that Chick Boyes played his familiar western Nebraska circle territory in a tent. An undated handbill exists that urges citizens of Broken Bow, Nebraska, to "See the Chick Boyes Players in Their Tent Theater / Located back of [the] Penny['s] Store every Tues and Wed / Ask Anybody Who Saw Our Show Last Week" (MRA Collection).

Apparently unaware of previous ventures of playing circle stock exclusively under canvas, editor Bob Feagin praised Choates Comedians in 1941 for their tent circuit in Illinois:

> Seven towns will be played, a set-up of stakes being left in each town and the outfit moved each day. The outfit is being completely repainted white with a red trim.
> Another new feature will be a chorus line of five girls to be used in numbers between acts and to be featured in concerts.

The *Bulletin* will watch this novel idea with much interest. We have screamed ourselves hoarse for somebody to try something different. Maybe this is it. If it IS, just watch the scramble to imitate it. Good luck, Arlie, and let us know how it goes. [*BFB,* 16 Apr., 1]

While the use of a tent for part or all of a circle's performances generally proved successful for those who attempted it, the practice obviously had its challenges and dangers. Expenses might include buying or renting the tent, while the costs of repair, maintenance, and transportation were a certainty. As with any tent company, concerns about high winds and accidental fires must surely have weighed heavily on the management of a circle troupe performing under canvas.

For these reasons some circle stock companies chose to use an abbreviated form of the canvas theater—the airdome. While airdomes were often permanent structures in urban settings, the portable versions of these open-air theaters typically resembled a tent theater with most of its canvas top missing. In airdomes (whether temporary or permanent) the stage normally remained covered in some manner with the audience area open to the sky but enclosed on all sides. It is most likely that circle companies touring as airdome units used the side walls and stage section of a "dramatic-end" tent employed extensively in the industry at that time. The popularity of this tent stemmed from the fact that the "dramatic-end" allowed for the repositioning of support poles and, hence, an unobstructed view of the stage. In actuality this stage area consisted of a separate section, and since it could be removed and set up independently, the "dramatic-end" stage section proved ideal for a touring airdome arrangement.

It is also evident that reports of circles employing an airdome setup were not using the same technique of "airdoming" strictly associated with tent companies.

The "airdome" for the tent companies referred to the practice of taking down the sidewalls of the tent and enlarging the seating capacity by erecting poles along the sides at some distance from the edge of the tent top, then placing the airdome canvas along these poles. [Kittle, 224]

Tent show managers used this version of "airdoming" chiefly to increase the capacity of their canvas theaters in addition to improving air circulation. Even though the possibility of confusion exists because of identical terms being used for very different physical setups, it seems highly unlikely that reports of circles using airdomes refer to a technique of accommodating overflow crowds in a canvas theater.

When confronted with the choice of performing circle stock in either a canvas tent or an airdome arrangement, several reasons favored the selection of the latter. Clearly an airdome required less expense and effort in transporting and erecting the unit. In addition, the cost of an airdome performance license invariably was less than that for a tent. Of the various managers or management teams who operated circle stock using an airdome, Henry and Ruby Neal received considerable attention concerning both their methods and apparent success. The Neals often operated circle stock a full 12 months of the year using a combination of theaters and airdome settings. At the beginning of summer in 1937 *Bill Bruno's Bulletin* reported that the Neal Stock Company had finally closed its winter season on a northern Colorado circle and moved to an airdome circle in the central part of the state:

> The Neal company is said to be the only circle playing under airdome in the west. Seats and stage are temporary in each town and only the sidewall and stage covering are moved, making the daily setup very easy. The idea was tried out for the first time by the Neals last summer and proved very successful. [*BBB*, 3 June, 15]

Although the dangers of bad weather and high winds remained ever present, the Neals maintained a remarkably consistent performance schedule over the years, at least according to accounts in the trade publications. The Neals once claimed that over a three-year span an average of only one airdome performance a year fell victim to inclement weather (*BBB*, 24 June 1937, 1).

A highly unusual arrangement of airdome circles was organized by Cal and Florence Berry out of Maryville, Missouri, in the early 1930s. In the territory surrounding this northwest Missouri county seat, this couple established no fewer than three one-week circuits, each with a separate company. The fact that these performing units rotated through each of the circuits required the troupers to learn a new bill only every three weeks. Robert La-They, who stage directed and performed with Berry's No. 3 show during the mid–1930s, recalls,

> Unlike most circles that played theatres, schools, halls, and empty store buildings, this show operated in the summer time and had three "dramatic ends." The seating capacity out front was board seats and was in the open air with a sidewall around it. In other words, the stage was just the back end of a dramatic-end tent.

La-They also recalls that the Berry airdome units charged an admission of five cents with a merchants' ticket and an additional five cents for "a seat to sit down on."

Normally managers brought the concept of airdomes to established circle companies and circuits, but in at least one instance the opposite took place. In 1924 manager Carl Cookson organized "three rotary dramatic stock companies to replace the former policy of moving pictures" at park airdomes controlled by the trolley company in Lawrence, Massachusetts (*Billboard*, 21 June, 24). While this turning of movie airdomes into dramatic airdomes marks a small victory of circle stock over silent motion pictures, it did not successfully forecast the future outcome of the struggle. Following the introduction of the "talkies" a few years later, the tables turned once again as sound movies largely displaced the few remaining rep companies performing in the airdomes.

Whereas canvas theaters and airdomes provided the most common alternative venues for circle stock performances, just about any space could be pressed into service. A one-week circle organized on behalf of the Strolling Players in Connecticut during the summer of 1919 employed two theaters and four agricultural barns.

> The barns, which are commodious, have been fixed up like theatres, with stages and portable scenery and with camp chairs for seats. Night performances only will be given and after each show the chairs will be removed and then an old-fashioned country barn dance will begin in which the players and all in the audience who desire will take part. [*Clipper,* 11 June, 12]

While most of the variations in performance locations took place in circle stock's accustomed rural setting, records reveal that circle touring could also successfully be maintained in urban locations, especially prior to the onset of the Depression. Because *Billboard,* the dominant show business publication of this era, originated in Cincinnati, Ohio, urban circle stock activity in and around that city is particularly well documented.

Billboard first reported the popularity of circle stock in the smaller, outlying theaters of Cincinnati in the early 1920s. For the winter of 1922 the publication's rep editor predicted good circle stock conditions in Cincinnati for both audience and management alike, but only if a spirit of cooperation among the several companies could be engendered.

> The melodrama fans who patronize the suburban houses in Cincinnati and vicinity will get their fill the coming winter, as there promises to be at least three small circle stock companies operating by the end of September. There will be prosperity for that many organizations, provided the managers all work in harmony instead of outbidding one another for the houses, as seemed to be the trouble last winter. [12 Aug. 1922, 27]

Besides Cincinnati, metropolitan centers such as Chicago, Boston, Detroit, Cleveland, New Orleans, Indianapolis, and even New York City maintained successful circle business in their neighborhood theaters, often called "rotary houses." Circle stock in large cities undoubtedly benefited from substantial numbers of potential spectators and short distances between theaters. Yet such circles faced intense competition and experienced considerable difficulty in overcoming the limitations placed on them by organized labor.

For these reasons attempts to establish circles in Kansas City almost invariably failed, even though Kansas City represented the very heart of the rep kingdom. In 1929 Bill Bruno reported yet another failed attempt, due in large part to excessive labor demands:

The recent report that Bert Howell had booked a circuit of houses in the city for circle stock, while appearing authentic, has evidently gone the way of all attempts to start something of this kind in the village. It is known that five houses had been booked and that the work of organizing the company was started, but it is asserted that the stage hands union, learning of the proposed venture, served notice on all the house managers that their demands would have to be met before a dramatic performance could be given. As stage hands here have a minimum scale of $11.00 per man per night, that ended that attempt. [*BBB,* 10 Oct., 2]

Even though attempts at circle stock in Kansas City had failed for a number of years, an optimistic Bill Bruno still held out hope for it to take its rightful place.

It seems strange that almost all cities of size have circle stocks playing and that Kansas City has none. Nor has it had a circle company in the last several years, with little or no promise of one this winter. Time was when they successfully operated here. Whether it is the fault of the demands of the hoggish stage hands or the fact that none of the company managers have the initiative to form a circuit is a matter of conjecture. Some day some progressive manager will realize the opportunity and then we'll have a mess of city circle stocks of every kind following in his success. [*BBB,* 10 Oct. 1929, 7]

A labor dispute also ended efforts by Ed Williams to re-establish a circuit in St. Louis in 1929, after having played circle stock in that population center for four consecutive years. According to an account of the problems received by Bill Bruno,

"The musicians are out and have been for the past ten weeks," writes Williams, "and have been trying to come to an agreement with the house managers. All negotiations have failed, however, and it is now understood that they are going to call out the operators and stage hands to help them. There is nothing left for the theatre men except the talkies and this is no time in which to try dramatics." [*BBB,* 28 Nov., 5]

Earlier Williams had delayed the proposed opening of his circle season in St. Louis because he found the majority of his theaters of previous years "tied up with talkie contracts." But as soon as these contractual arrangements had expired, the musicians' union dashed all hopes for Williams's fifth season of circle work in that city (*BBB,* 24 Oct. 1929, 3).

Apart from the interest *Billboard* took in local circle activity in Cincinnati, most urban circle stock operations were not well advertised or discussed in trade publications, probably because productions at such theaters were not considered newsworthy in comparison with the dramatic entertainment offered by the more prestigious downtown theaters. Reports of urban circles that did find their way into print remained largely perfunctory announcements of dates and performance times. On occasion, though, a bit of the spirit and vitality of these venues and the performances in them comes through. In late 1922 circle stock audiences in Cincinnati proved to be somewhat unruly, and *Billboard* queried:

> We often wonder when, if ever, the nuisance of unnecessary chatter will cease in some of the Cincinnati suburban theaters booking rotary dramatic shows. Managers should at least try to make patrons understand that others are entitled to full value in the enjoyment they come to find and that it is almost criminal to destroy their pleasure. A little announcement thrown on the screen before the performance or from the manager in person may reduce the evil, for we believe that some people will be conscience-stricken and be impressed with this admonition to such an extent that they will at least try to be more considerate and appreciate the rights of others. [18 Nov., 29]

That same year the Lois Merrill Players playing on the outskirts of Cincinnati were said to make audiences "forget sorrow, toothache, election and financial worries." Furthermore, the rep editor of *Billboard* exclaimed, "We enjoy nothing better than to be swept away for an hour by a cyclone of merriment, and as soon as we have an idle hour we're going to see [director Sam] Reed's company and experience such a delightful thrill" (11 Nov. 1922, 28).

Finally, a consideration of the various locations employed by circle stock should mention the industry's migration—infrequent as it seems—to lands both north and south of the United States. As early as 1919 *Billboard* noted the eager preparations of the Victory Players for a four-week circle in western Canada (21 June, 20). Similarly, Richard Kent—who once warned prospective actors in a casting notice, "If you can't stand the small towns, don't answer. I play them all"—obtained notable success with circle stock in the rural Canadian provinces (*Billboard,* 3 Aug. 1929, 29). *Bill Bruno's Bulletin* reported in 1930:

> Kent opened in September last with one company playing a circle, soon afterward added two more companies and only recently organized the fourth. Strangely enough Kent has the entire territory to himself. [30 Jan., 2]

Records also reveal additional circle stock activity beyond our borders. For instance, a *Billboard* article entitled "Rotary Stock for Bermuda" discloses that a trio of American entrepreneurs in 1925 constructed a 700-seat theater in Hamilton, Bermuda, for the purpose of booking both "moving pictures and rotary stock companies" (17 Oct., 29).

Variations in Format and Content

A final area of circle stock variation is found in the rearrangement or change of the traditional components of the circle format. Such modifications proved popular with managers in their ongoing quest to discover the best product with which to please an audience.

Matinee performances often provided a simple, yet profitable addition to a company's schedule. A Saturday or even a Sunday matinee proved highly successful for many companies. Other managers found that squeezing in extra evening performances suited both their own and their audience's liking. An undated handbill for the North Players, featuring Arthur Kelly, notes that while appearing at the Lyric Theatre in Colby, Kansas, the company regularly performed two complete shows (at 7:15 and 9:15) on the Friday evenings of its circle (MRA Collection). Similarly, manager Fred Twyman reported in 1929 that the Hazel Hurd Players held double performances in a total of five towns on their Texas and Oklahoma circle in order to accommodate the crowds (*BBB*, 19 Dec., 3). As a rule extra performances did not indicate companies in desperate financial straits but rather demonstrated the eagerness of performers and management to capitalize on a company's already established popularity in a community. The six members of the Gus Locktee circle located in Kansas once earned additional income not by presenting a play twice in one evening, yet performing twice just the same. Bill Bruno reported the details of this unique arrangement:

> After playing their Sunday night performance in Louisville, Kansas, the company drives ten miles back on its way to the base and stops at Manhattan to do a short midnight floor show at the Flowers Inn. The innovation is going over good as, believe it or not, nearly a third of the Louisville audience follows the show over. [*BBB*, 16 Jan. 1936, 1]

Other managers rearranged the traditional order of the circle stock performance. Harry Hugo once chose to present the entire play without interspersing specialty acts throughout it. Instead he finished off the evening with a rousing revue of vaudeville routines (*BFB*, 26 Mar. 1941, 1). William Balthazor went a step further by eliminating the play entirely. Known previously for following a standard show-and-dance policy, Balthazor experimented in 1938 with "a vaudeville program with dances following" supported by an enlarged orchestra (*BBB*, 14 Apr., 1). Such juggling of the traditional performance order and content was attempted with some regularity over the years, but it never really caught on with either the companies or the public.

Often managers hit upon a new combination of performance and admission policies uniquely suited to their circumstances. In early 1936 word surfaced of an interesting variation by manager Lew Henderson in which his company performed

> a merchants free matinee daily and combine[d] a show at night with a dance following at an admission charge of thirty-five cents. The idea has caught on so well that Henderson will stay on the circle through the summer, not taking out the tent. [*BBB*, 5 Mar., 2]

Some managers did not rely upon the typical dramatic fare of circle stock (that is, full-length comedies, farces, and mysteries) but turned instead to other types of theatrical offerings. Al Trahern produced light operetta and musical comedies during the early years of his Long Island circuit, and periodically the circle stock managers who followed him adopted the same policy. For instance, the Harry Evans troupe performed musical comedy through a circle of towns in Montana and North Dakota in 1929. This company of ten used no chorus, although within its ranks Evans carried the makings of a singing quartet and six tap dancers (*BBB,* 12 Dec., 2). Doc Gardner, a veteran agent and manager in the Minneapolis theater scene of the 1930s, once developed a two-week circle presenting musical comedies (complete with chorus) through the larger towns of Minnesota (*BBB,* 25 Feb. 1937, 1).

While a few circle companies did employ one-act plays for performances, many others specialized in a genre of condensed plays–the "tabloids" or "tab shows"–which were particularly popular in urban environments. Most frequently associated with the presentation of shortened musical comedies (complete with a female chorus line), tab shows also denote shortened nonmusical dramas and comedies usually lasting less than one hour. In 1920 Bell's Comedians, led by owner and manager Raymond Bell, successfully presented "50-minute comedy-drama tabs" on circle in Washington State (*Billboard,* 21 Aug., 14). In 1936 "Boob" Brasfield entered into his second year on a circle of Lau Amusement Company houses with headquarters in Rome, Georgia. Performances by his company of 12 lasted all of 55 minutes, obviously indicating the performance of tabloid plays in association with motion pictures–hence, the short length of the live show (*BBB,* 3 Sept., 1).

Of the various circle stock managers who concentrated on staging tabloid shows, "Seabee" Hayworth earned a widespread reputation for both his ambitious undertakings and his overall success in the presentation of musical tab shows. Long associated with the Wilby-Kincey chain of motion picture theaters in the South, Hayworth in 1941 described his operation in the following manner:

> I carry a combination Musical Comedy and Vaudeville show with a band and a line of girls. Two novelty vodvil acts are booked each week as added attraction. Show is transported in Buick, Packard and Studebaker Sedans. We do 29 shows per week, change program weekly a[nd] cover a route of 1000 miles PER WEEK. [*BFB,* 23 Jan., 1]

Later that year Hayworth continued boasting of his management of "a combination rep-musical tab and vaudeville revue" playing "circle stock in the finest first-run picture shows in the south" (*BFB,* 24 Sept., 3). Harold Smith (who adopted the stage names of both Lawrence Clark and Alan

Moore) toured with the Hayworth Players in North Carolina during 1939. Smith recalls performing each day a total of four one-hour tab shows—complete with specialties—between feature film showings.

Some enterprises even replaced the play performance of circle stock with motion pictures. Although these efforts cannot be considered true theater events, such "talkie circles" developed an eager following during the late 1930s and into the following decade, especially in the South. The McKay picture circle operating in Kansas in 1940 earned income solely through its ten-cent admission price, while some picture circles even operated under merchant sponsorship (*BBB,* 23 May, 4). At this same time business proved so good for L. H. McDonald's movie circle in eastern Arkansas that management planned to add a second unit as soon as possible (*BBB,* 16 May, 2). A 1941 issue of *Feagin's Bulletin* notes that Jack Hart operated a picture circle out of Foreman, Arkansas, while Jay Bee Flesner headed a similar operation around Henning, Tennessee (Jan. 23, 2). These circles proved very popular with performers or managers in need of income because the capital requirements for running a movie circle were minuscule. Films were relatively inexpensive to obtain and easily transported, and in a darkened setting movie operators essentially needed only an electrical outlet, a projector, and a screen. Some circle companies even chose to maintain a foothold in both the touring theater and the motion picture industries, as when in 1937 Henry and Ruby Neal took control of the movie theater in Lenora, Kansas,

> buying the equipment and leasing the building. [They] will run pictures on Saturday and Sunday and play the company there every Wednesday night. The merchants of the city are behind the move a hundred per cent. [*BBB,* 6 Dec., 4]

Although numerous examples of variations on the basic circle stock system are easily cited, the great majority of circle troupes found that the traditional structure, without major embellishments, met their needs. At the same time circle stock provided an easily malleable format, capable of being shaped to fit the needs of managers and companies in a wide variety of social and economic settings. This malleability, in fact, may have been a two-edged sword. While it allowed circle stock to continue through hard times, some critics saw in such a wide variety of forms the lack of a clear identity, which may gradually have led to the decline of circle stock, a topic to which we now turn.

8

A Quiet Demise

I N LOOKING BACK ON THEIR CAREERS, veteran performers rarely have chosen to dwell upon their experiences relating to the decline of circle stock. Even so, it is clear that a number of factors deleteriously affected the final years of the industry. Chief among these were the general decline of the touring rep theater system as a whole; the loss of experienced personnel to age or other employment and an inability to replace them; the general overuse of the circle stock format; and the increasing competition of radio, motion pictures, and especially television. Even though circle stock continued into at least the late 1950s, the industry experienced a steady decline in quantity and quality following its peak in the mid–1930s.

Decline in Quantity

The apparent high point in the proliferation of the circle stock system occurred during the worst part of the Great Depression. According to information compiled by Bill Bruno, the total number of "road attractions" operating during the final months of 1935 reached levels higher than at any time since 1917.

At the time of his report Bruno tallied 228 tent, house, and circle stock companies, and he claimed that the count was still in progress. Of this preliminary figure Bruno determined that circle stock companies represented over 65 percent, adding:

> The number of circle companies is almost beyond computing. But one is safe in saying that there are at this time at least 150 operating on one and two week routes. There is hardly a spot on the map being missed by the enterprising managers and if this keeps up, some of the towns will be playing two shows per week. In fact, that condition has already arisen. It won't last, however, because it must be a rather large town to stand two a week. And managers are far from wise who will attempt playing a town already

established by another show. One of the two managers must eventually go broke, and it's a safe bet that it will be the interloper.

Added to the dramatic shows out this fall, are an even greater number of medicine, vaudeville, picture and other shows. (*BBB*, 24 Oct., 1)

When Bruno ventured to estimate the extent of the circle stock system in later years, the resulting numbers fell short of the 1935 figure of 150 companies. In late 1936 Bruno estimated 100 circles operating "in the west and south, with more planned after the holidays" [*BBB*, 17 Dec., 35]. Less than three years later Bruno reported that the number had fallen further:

> The present winter season, just getting well under way, witnesses the peak of circle operation. At this writing there are over sixty known companies playing on circles in midwest territory, with what is best termed a congestion about to occur in Iowa. That state had an above normal corn crop, the price is good and slowly rising, and the state is literally covered by the circles. With more shows moving into the northern part. The result is inevitable and we are already hearing rumors of early closings. However, there is a continued demand for people and no hardship will result. [*BBB*, 19 Oct. 1939, 1]

Concurrent with this apparent decline in the number of circle stock companies, the locus of activity moved. On various occasions during the 1920s and 1930s both *Billboard* and *Bill Bruno's Bulletin* had cited the state of Nebraska as home to the greatest number of circle companies.[1] But by early 1938 Bruno noted that "Minnesota heads the list of states in the number of circles this winter" (*BBB*, 13 Jan., 3).

Whereas the estimate of the strength of the circle stock movement in 1935 was approximate and clearly only regional in scope, there is some reason to believe that the figure does not represent the true height of the circle industry. Because of the interconnective relationship between circle stock and tent rep, it may well be that the total number of circle companies related proportionately to the size and strength of the tent industry at any given time. And while in 1935 Bruno tallied a grand total of 228 rep companies of all kinds, traditional figures for the number of tent companies alone a few years earlier are considerably higher.

The most frequently cited figure is from 1927 when Don Carle Gillete (editor of *Billboard*) stated in the *New York Times* that as many as 400 tent theater companies dotted the countryside of this nation (16 Oct., sec. 9, 2). While other estimates are lower (around 300–325 companies), it is clear that figures concerning the total number of tent companies are indeed impressive (Bernheim, 99). Even though circle stock flourished during the Depression, it is possible that at the very height of the tent movement circle stock also experienced a similar peak of development, surpassing the 1935 figures of Bill Bruno. However, accurate records do not exist to test this theory. Moreover, with Bob Feagin ceasing publication of *Feagin's*

Bulletin in May 1942 and with the continual reduction in the number of reports on rep theater in *Billboard* during the 1940s and 1950s, a detailed account of the circle stock industry increasingly failed to be recorded. Consequently, the approaching end of circle stock activity failed to generate notice. For even though "Roadshow Rep" (*Billboard*'s nostalgic and often maudlin review column of the touring theater industry) provides us with glimpses of circle stock activity in the 1950s, it did not survive to record the end of the circle era. In March 1956 *Billboard*'s rep news column obviously fell victim to dwindling reader interest and never again appeared.

Yet evidence supplied by veteran troupers confirms that the practice of circle stock survived at least into the year 1957. So it remains highly probable that some of the final surviving circle companies endured beyond 1957, most likely continuing to depend upon the popular show-and-dance performances that supported various companies as they persevered through the 1950s.

Decline in Artistic and Management Practices

The beginning of the decline, however, had started many years earlier. As early as the late 1930s, Bill Bruno warned that various artistic and management practices of circle stock were undermining the quality of the industry's product. In his many editorials Bruno repeatedly attempted to bring to the forefront the woes and afflictions of the rep system. Of the many problems, Bruno thought that the inability to attract and properly train young performers remained the most devastating. The blame lay, he maintained, at the feet of parsimonious managers who never hired, or hired inadequate, stage directors, thus failing to instruct new performers in the business properly.

> The cry for new blood in show business becomes more insistent as numbers of the youngsters drop out after a trial of two or three years of absolutely fruitless effort. For what have the great majority of managers to offer "youth?" Not even a director to teach the young folks the first rudiments of acting. The call is for pupils—and no school to put them in. The old "repertoire school" died during the last decade. Directing, if you are polite enough to call it that, at this stage of the downfall of the drama is a simple case of "Everybody for himself, the devil take the hindmost—and to hell with the audience."
>
> With the great number of shows the manager himself tries to do the directing. Usually he knows as much about producing a play as we do about balancing the national budget. Or they are too busy with other managerial work to give the direction the attention it should have. So is it any wonder that so few of the youngsters can really act? Who is to teach them how? [*BBB,* 28 Apr. 1938, 3]

In the same issue, Bruno lambasted managers who thought they could do without stage directors:

> Any manager who can't afford to pay a competent director, and we don't mean a "script holder," a salary to put on his shows ought to leave the outfit in the barn. Because the right kind of director can do more for his show than can any other one factor. If he can't realize that fact it wouldn't be a bad idea for him to stay with the outfit–in the barn. Good plays need good direction. As do good actors. But managers will offer an alibi that "a lot of actors resent direction." Which [as an] excuse is very poor. No actor will resent direction if it means better performances. They are all out to learn. All have ambitions. If not, they too should join the manager and outfit in the barn. [3]

By 1940 Bruno argued that rep still lacked an adequate mechanism to replenish its aging ranks:

> Every profession requires new blood to keep it from from [sic] passing into the discard. Lord knows there is little of the drama and acting remaining; but efforts should immediately be made to save what is left. The best way to do this is to take on a certain number of promising aspirants (even though they can't do a trapeze act or double every instrument in a 60-piece symphony orchestra) and teach them how to ACT. [*BBB*, 25 Apr., 3]

As for other methods of obtaining training and performance experience, the industry generally placed little value on preparation outside of itself. In an editorial Bob Feagin once expressed the common attitude among the rank and file of rep personnel concerning academic theater preparation:

> If a young man wishes to enter the field of Law or Medicine he goes to a Law or Medical school. But if he desires to become an Actor, can he go to school? Oh, yes, there are Dramatic Schools, but from what we have seen of some of their graduates, it is more of a hindrance than a help in entering our field. The staff of these places simply have no idea or understanding of Repertoire's requirements. [*BFB*, 19 Mar. 1941, 5]

During the final months of distributing his newsletter catering to the Midwest circle stock and tent industry, Bob Feagin agreed with Bruno's earlier assessments but painted an even drearier picture. Feagin believed that the ability of individuals to operate a circle company on only a limited investment and budget (once regarded as a chief positive characteristic of circle stock) had in latter years caused the system to begin feeding upon itself by allowing too many companies into the field. In the circle troupes of the early 1940s Feagin saw widespread mismanagement and abuse of the system caused primarily by large numbers of actors unable to obtain "a good job in the winter season" and hence starting ill-planned circle stock units. This excess of circle companies and the concomitant drop in quality provoked considerable discussion and consternation, at least from Bob Feagin:

These actors, in their own minds, doubt their ability to successfully manage a show, and, for that reason, hesitate to invest any sizeable amount of their savings in equipment. The result? They organize a show, and take it in the sticks where hall rents are cheap. They are, in the main, hard-working and conscientious. But they are licked before they start. You can't bring in game without ammunition. ...we have watched circle business closely, and each season IT SLIPS DOWN ANOTHER PEG. We know territories that were lush five years ago, that won't even come to see what kind of a show you have. They are simply disgusted and have turned to other entertainment. [*BFB,* 19 Nov. 1941, 3]

Such impassioned editorials by Feagin blame the decline of circle stock during the 1930s and 1940s on managers who thought of it as only a make-shift measure and who therefore lacked a wholehearted commitment to the system. Perhaps Maree MacDonald's experience with the Elmer Gordon Show in 1936 while based in Edmond, Kansas, provides us with a clear portrait of this half-hearted, nonprofessional approach to circle stock. MacDonald describes the manager/owner Gordon as a "western Kansas farmer" who

knew absolutely nothing about show-biz except that he wanted to be in it. He based his ability to finance the show on the fact that he had started getting his Social Security. He had lined up a few towns, but later turned the booking over to anyone in the company who would do it.

On one occasion Feagin argued that his own circle experiences typified those of many uncommitted troupers:

We kept this nightmare going for a full winter season. During that time we owned ONE set of alleged scenery. We rehearsed about twice a week, if everybody felt like it. Our vaudeville consisted of some corny gags and songs. We felt that, at the admission price we charged, that no effort was needed and we wondered why the natives didn't come to see it. Now we wonder why they didn't lynch us.

Feagin then describes an experience that entirely changed his thinking and forced him to take the form seriously:

Later we saw a circle run under real management. To our amazement, they rehearsed like a show. They carried scenery and props like a show. And, what impressed us most, they did BUSINESS like a show. We have never forgotten that lesson.
    The average actor, in using the circle for a stop-gap, loses sight of the fact that a circle is a BUSINESS just the same as a hamburger stand or a garage, and what he gets out of it is going to be in direct ratio to what he puts in it. You can't invest ten dollars and expect to hit the jack-pot. [*BFB,* 5 Nov. 1941, 3]

Not only did circle stock clearly feed on itself, but it also stood accused of feeding on other rep theater forms. For instance, when reflecting on the poor showing of the tent companies during the late spring and summer months of 1939, Bill Bruno places the blame on the flood of circle companies. Bruno reasons that, prior to the large increase in the number of circles during the 1930s,

> there were very few shows touring during the winter months and people were "show hungry" when the summer came. Now one would guess them "fed up" at start of the tent season–in many cases suffering acute indigestion–with no desire to see a show until August. [*BBB*, 4 Jan. 1940, 4]

The disruption of the show business industry and society in general by the Second World War further exacerbated the decline of the rep movement. "Things were different" is a common phrase used by veteran troupers to describe the industry following the end of the war. A number of examples illustrate changes that had taken place. For one thing, few troupers having enjoyed the more substantial wages paid by the defense industry and other similar types of employment returned to the modestly paid forms of rep at the end of the conflict. And of the performers who had continued in the entertainment field during the war, many now blended into the allied mediums of radio and television. Others found employment in the fast-growing nightclub industry of the late 1940s. In addition, the new vogue for drive-in movie theaters severely cut into potential audiences by providing inexpensive family entertainment in many areas. Times had undeniably changed.

Part of what ailed the industry at this time can be labeled backward vision. Some managers clearly failed to adjust their thinking about business and artistic matters from the models established in the heyday of rep in the 1920s. For too many, various aspects of show business had not evolved with changing conditions but remained wedded to the comfortable traditions of a bygone era. In the 1935 Christmas issue of *Bill Bruno's Bulletin*, the Gordon-Howard Candy Company (obviously concerned about prevailing attitudes of the industry) placed a full-page advertisement entitled "A Resolution for 1936." It reads in part:

> We have a suggestion for a real resolution that we wish you would all consider seriously and it is simply this: RESOLVED, That in 1936 we will forget the big business that each of us enjoyed in the peak years under entirely different conditions than those which we are now experiencing. Let us all adapt ourselves to present day circumstances and run our businesses accordingly. [19 Dec., 26]

In 1941 Bob Feagin also admonished the rep industry to be realistic and to distinguish between present-day show business and that of only memories:

> Show business is still here, it's just changed. So has the grocery business. Our advice is to forget last year and try to figure what would smack 'em THIS year. We also remember "the good old days." Yes, there [were] jobs

galore, hundreds of shows and a bond between troupers that we admit doesn't exist now. BUT we also remember that practically every opera house we played had a store-room full of trunks left by stranded companies and we hardly ever played a date that a collection wasn't taken up to help some stranded actor, or team, sometimes a whole company. Yea, brother, there were problems in those days too. [*BFB*, 16 Jan., 3]

With America's entry into World War II, Feagin's plea for rep to change with the times became even more emphatic:

THE WORLD THAT WE KNEW UP TO A YEAR AGO, WE SHALL NEVER SEE AGAIN. From now on, as never before, the public will be intolerant with old-time and obsolete methods. And all of our wishful thinking won't stop this.

The operator that is smart enough to realize this will keep his ear to the ground and change with the trends. This operator will survive. And there will be those that will stubbornly claim that what got money in 1926 will get money in 1942. The graveyard of repertoire is littered with the tombstones of those that believed this. [*BFB*, 28 Jan. 1942, 3]

By the 1950s a lengthy list of problems confronted circle stock, with television posing an especially difficult challenge. Many circle stock veterans point to the readily available "free" entertainment of television as the final knockout blow to an industry already weak at the knees. Yet the response of the remaining touring shows to this latest interloper followed the same tired line taken years earlier in response to the advent of sound motion pictures–that is, "We are not afraid, live drama will survive." Dot Sund's report to *Billboard* at the end of the Sun Players' 1953-54 winter circle certainly follows the tradition of placing the industry's difficult situations in the best light possible:

Circle stock business was good despite the competition from TV, Miss Sun reported, and says that she thinks the medium, sooner or later, will help tent shows by making the people vaudeville-minded again. [5 June 1954, 65]

After years of bravely facing adversity, Pollyanna died hard.

A perusal of the final years of *Billboard*'s "Roadshow Rep" column helps one understand the changes taking place in the industry during the early and mid–1950s. In addition to declining numbers of circle stock and tent companies, one can detect two developments that were direct responses to the general decline of performance opportunities and available actors. First, many performers turned to touring educational shows, often in teams of two, for employment during a good part of the school year. These short variety performances, normally combining both informational and entertainment aspects, included such elements as dramatic readings, acting scenes, musical numbers, or even makeup demonstrations. School assembly programs provided jobs for many who, sometimes appearing at three or more schools each day, very likely would otherwise have had to obtain employment outside the entertainment industry. Second, the rise in small theater companies composed exclusively of one family appeared as a response to the difficulties of fielding a troupe in the conventional manner. By assigning necessary character parts to family members, a manager avoided the trouble of obtaining performers from the dwindling pool of available actors and kept all income in the family.

Amidst these organizational and management woes, one should not lose sight of the individual performers and their frequently difficult circumstances. Of the hardships faced by individuals in circle stock, one veteran performer warned:

> You are dealing with an area of work, existence, and struggle about which its "survivors" (and I use the term deliberately) have mixed emotions. There were a lot of problems and frustrations in it for many people, and some would prefer to forget the whole ghastly business.

R. Norton Walther, in the rep business from 1934 to 1941, willingly admits "circle stock for me was mostly a miserable experience," adding:

> You had nice people to work with but such rough facilities.... The hardships that you put up with because you were bound to be an actor, I sometimes wonder why you did it but at that time jobs were scarce and you wanted to be an actor and you took whatever came up. There were lots of people then out of work; it was the beginning of the end of repertoire and circle stock.

Or as Flo Darling, whose circle stock background dates from 1938, views the experience:

> When some of the others are recalling all the "wonderful" times, I remember the rain, slush, mud, cold rooming houses, studying a part by a 40 watt light bulb and finding a mouse in bed with me!

One must be careful, however, not to allow the financial troubles of the declining years of circle stock to distort one's view of its artistic quality both in its prime and near the end. Although reliable evaluations of the quality of acting and performances are hard to come by, the few that survive provide a generally balanced picture of the industry. On the whole, there are a number of reasons to suggest that in judging the quality of circle stock performances, one may remain generally positive without fear of being charitable. First of all, the majority of these performers took great pride in being seasoned veterans and in mastering their "lines of business" such as leading ladies, juveniles, and the like. While few of these performers ever received formal education in the theater arts, they did acquire considerable on-the-spot training, normally graduating from one line of characters to another as they aged.

On one occasion in 1927 the editors of *Billboard* gave a prominent position on the newspaper's editorial page to praise the virtues of rep acting, as opposed to the level of performances commonly found in urban centers at that time. Despite the newspaper's infrequent editorial comment on the rep industry, the praise expressed rings genuine:

> It seems to be the consensus of opinion among theatrical reviewers in the smaller communities that the acting in the traveling repertoire shows, both in theaters and under canvas, is far more serious, earnest and unselfish than the work of Broadway players.
>
> Whereas in the big town a great many of the actors are out for individual glory and will do almost anything, irrespective of the effect on fellow players, to achieve their end, in the small-town companies there is a conspicuous absence of this self-exploitation, and an equally conspicuous example of genuine coordinated effort for ensemble effect.
>
> On Broadway the acting—or demonstration of personality—frequently is such that the play itself is pushed in the background, whereas among the repertoire shows it is always the play that stands out first. [3 Dec., 46]

Perhaps this editorial in such an influential trade publication as *Billboard* sparked an increased interest in Midwestern actors; two years later Bill Bruno reported:

> Time was when eastern managers refused to sign people from the Kansas City base, but recent developments are most enheartening. Last week a show which had during the past fifteen years refused to employ K.C. actors, engaged five from one of the agents, having discovered that the best people in repertoire are now booking their engagements out of this center.
>
> Even the eastern managers have discovered the fact, for we have a letter from one of the stock managers operating in the east begging us to submit good talent to them for engagements this winter. [*BBB*, 22 Aug. 1929, 7]

In years to follow available evaluations of circle stock performances from the local perspective often appear quite honest, providing an appropriate blend of both praise and criticism. A lengthy article by Arlone Twyman entitled "What's Become of Toby?" focuses on the effect of World War II on circle stock in the state of Nebraska, and provides a sensitive, yet realistic, evaluation of the acting typically found on the circle circuits:

> What kind of actors do you find trouping in Fairfield, Wilbur, Crete, Polk and St. Paul? Many times very good ones, and just as many times, very poor ones. It's only a trouper who can go back year after year and still please.
>
> Hollywood could well have profited in the services of such players as Ralph Moody, Skeets Cross, Dorothy Mills, Jay Coggshall, Lulu Nethaway, Harry Hugo and many other midwest troupers.
>
> Planks used for seats could tumble down, the manager could fill up the stove down front during a dramatic scene, Junior could throw a tantrum, but these seasoned troupers worked a little harder and succeeded in holding the crowd out front. In some cases, where the electric lights failed, kerosene lamps were placed on stage and the show went on.

In spite of the fact that these actors have to be their own electricians and stage hands, as well as musicians, vaudevillians and dramatic actors, they have continued to troupe at very small salaries. And why? Perhaps the innate love of show business or maybe a feeling of loyalty. Maybe they want to stick until the end of a rapidly dying profession. [MRA Collection, clipping from the *Omaha* (Nebraska) *World-Herald*, hand dated 1943]

A few years later a performance review of Tilton's Comedians appearing in the *Bloomington* (Illinois) *Pantagraph* includes both positive and negative comments, while all the time displaying an understanding of the nature of circle stock performances shortly before the onset of the 1950s. The opening paragraph of the story entitled "'Indoor Tent Show' Draws Crowds" finds favor, as the reviewer claims that

Broadway drama critics may deal with a technical excellence seldom achieved by "Tilton's Comedians," but they seldom see performers more versatile or audiences more visibly satisfied.

The commentary concludes, however, with a critical yet understanding tone:

The shows border on the corny side. They play some royalty bills but stick mostly to public domain stuff like this season's revival of *Ten Nights in a Barroom.* The few risque lines they allow are subtle as a sawmill.

Tilton's Comedians overact and mug the footlights to an extent that blase patrons of the legitimate theater might not recognize the art for what it is: making money on rural circuits. [30 Nov. 1949, 20]

Part of the perceived decline in quality of circle stock performances clearly did not result from poorer acting but from the growing sophistication of a new generation of audiences nurtured by watching films and television. One ventures to say that the acting probably became no better or worse, but that the audience—or at least some members of it—could now compare the rep actor with performers on the two coasts.

For their own part, rep actors frequently compared themselves to "city" actors and understandably found themselves better conditioned for the hardships of life on the road. Barbara Brooks Emory's tale of a character actress from New York City joining the Chick Boyes Players during the winter of 1935-36 certainly conforms to many of the distinctions made by the members of the industry between the actors of the Midwest and those of the East. Since this actress "had never been farther west than Jersey City," the methods of circle stock undoubtedly made a lasting impression on her. As Emory recalls,

She was properly horrified at everything connected with the show: our primitive living conditions, the so-called towns, the people in them, and the halls where we performed. In none of these halls did we have running water or bathrooms.... She firmly refused to wear what she called her "good wardrobe" in this outlandish country.

In fairness to the actress, Emory adds that "she was a good scout, always knew her lines to the letter, and I learned considerable stage technique from her."

Whereas it is evident that a few performers ventured westward to the circle stock territory of the Midwest, a considerable number of rep actors successfully moved from the rural circuits to more upscale theaters in the East and westward to the growing film and television industries. In fact, many troupers are capable of reciting by rote a list of performers from the rank and file who attained national prominence. But movement between these two theatrical worlds must be considered the exception and not the rule. Circle stock veterans willing to express regrets about their careers frequently mention their fears of having missed opportunities for additional growth and experience as performers. Having turned down or lost the opportunity to join a larger rep organization, a prominent permanent stock company, or the "big time" in a major metropolitan center, the doubt of "What if..." still lingers on in more than one veteran's mind. Often performers with such misgivings about their past professional choices explain that, of the factors influencing their decisions, the security of circle stock employment and the public response to their efforts weighed too heavily in their thinking.

Dick Elsenpeter, one of the last performers known to assume the Toby character line, sees only one way to view his decision to portray this popular character:

> I curse the day I put the red wig on. The day I put the Toby wig on my head is probably one of the worse days of my career, because from then on I became a Toby and no longer a serious actor.

Admitting that playing Toby became "intoxicating" because the audience "loved you automatically," Elsenpeter concludes, "You'll always wonder, if I hadn't put that wig on, would I have gone someplace else?"

Despite such reservations, most veterans cite the support they received from the audience and from their fellow performers as making the experience professionally rewarding. As for the audience's response, it has proved difficult after all these years to gather first-hand accounts from the spectators of circle stock. This is unfortunate, for evidence suggests that especially within the context of the Depression era the circle stock experience took on great importance in the lives of audiences. But the simple fact remains that the lasting impact of circle stock performances upon the hundreds of thousands in attendance over the years can no longer be measured effectively.

Fortunately some anecdotal accounts survive to provide us with a glimpse of the importance that circle stock had in the lives it touched. One of Gus Neuhaus's chief remembrances from his touring days is when audience members clasped his hands following a performance and earnestly said that they "wouldn't know what to do" if the circle troupers had not performed there once a week. Iris Hollingsworth fondly remembers, "We had the love of the people in the town. You'd come out and get a hand on your first appearance, like in the big city or somewhere." Or as Jay Bee Flesner asserts, "We were glamor to those people, believe it or not. We were glamor. It's the same kids that now pay $15 or $17 to see Bruce Springsteen. They paid a dime to see us." Numerous performers have echoed Flesner's view. As one trouper phrased the thought, "The glamor of theater is the thing we brought to rural America."

While we have difficulty in measuring the impact of circle stock upon its audience, numerous expressions of love and loyalty from audiences made lasting impressions upon circle stock troupers. The following record of Henry and Ruby Neal's twenty-first wedding anniversary, which fell while they were touring a circle in Colorado during the 1930s, clearly demonstrates the genuine support and affection received by performers. In this instance, the Neals were

> surprised by the folks of the little town [Briggsdale], who gave them a farewell party at which a mock wedding ceremony was the high light of the evening, and in which Ruby was made to promise to support Hank for the rest of his life. The ceremony was performed by the editor of the *Briggsdale Banner* and was followed by a sumptuous supper. [*BBB*, 3 June 1937, 15]

Today veteran performers still recall various acts of warmhearted devotion from their audiences, both while actively performing and years after. Waunetta Rosier Oleferchik remembers a time when she and her husband Harold Rosier visited an old circle community for a quick meal some 15–20 years after their regular weekly appearances had ended. Not expecting any special treatment, they were welcomed by a greeting that greatly surprised them.

> One day in the 1950s we stopped in Dansville [Michigan] for lunch, and the lady that ran the restaurant recognized us and sent her daughter down to the barber shop run by the restaurant manager's father to tell him we were there, as she knew he would want to say hello. On the way the young lady stopped at several businesses and stores and it wasn't long before half the town was there to say "Hello" and tell us how much they had enjoyed the shows.

For the performers, time has undoubtedly softened the hard edges of the experience and intensified the memories of enthusiastic audiences. And a special loyalty is known to develop for persons or institutions that provide safe passage through difficult times. Certainly the enthusiastic support given to performers from appreciative audiences endeared circle stock to these entertainers. Mercedes Brunk's experience while circling with Collier's Players out of Beaver Dam, Wisconsin, most assuredly was repeated countless times across this nation:

Dick Elsenpeter (as Toby) and Maude Gentry performing with Tilton's Comedians in the waning years of circle stock (courtesy of the Museum of Repertoire Americana).

> We would drive to a wide spot in the road with a beat-up old tavern. I would look around and say "Where are the people coming from?" They would always say, "Just wait and see." Then we would all dash into the tavern. All the men in the tavern would get up and help our boys set up a stage and dress it with the scenery. Soon you would see lights coming from every direction. The place would soon be full. It was really amazing. Those people were so hungry for entertainment.

Whatever the reason for circle stock's popularity among other performers, Maude Gentry energetically declares, "I really liked circle," and provides a checklist of those aspects of circle touring she found most pleasurable:

> I liked not having to move to a new town each week and hunt for rooms. I liked knowing our home town, for example, where to eat or shop. A person could get more mail, so I started taking the *Christian Science Monitor.* And I could get to church. I liked doing one show at a time, because by the end of the week you felt you were doing a good job. I liked meeting people that liked us. Some of them would invite us to eat now and then, to friendly special dinners of deer and wild game.

Many veteran troupers declare that the sustenance they received from their fellow performers stands out as the greatest strength of the circle stock system. Of all the evidence to demonstrate this viewpoint perhaps one tale exemplifies the mutual support provided by these performers, in addition to ingenuity and stalwart determination. This well-circulated story concerns the sudden death of the spouse of one circle company's character actress. As the event is affectionately recalled by those involved, and even by those who report the incident second-hand, rehearsals during that week had prepared the play *Turn to the Right* for the coming rotation of the circuit. This popular play, simply described by one trouper as a "story of mother love and redemption," obviously relied heavily upon the matriarchal role and, as fate would have it, had been scheduled to be played by the character woman of the company.

But because she had left to accompany her husband's body to the burial site, the situation required fast action to cover for her absence. Without hesitation the company decided that the mother's lines would be taken over by the rest of the cast under the ruse that the character remained throughout the production off stage in the kitchen. On the way to the first performance the company rehearsed their plan out loud. As Dick Elsenpeter recalls, "It worked and we finished the week with just dividing the mother's lines." In accounting for its success, fellow performer Don Weage adds,

> Things seem so impossible now, but they weren't. We did them because we had to do them…. And we did what, believe it or not, was a creditable show. It wasn't a destroyed mish-mash. At that point in all our lives we were professionals, thoroughly experienced day in and day out in doing what we did and doing it as well as possible.

While the performance adjustments made in this case approach the heroic, other adaptations seem in hindsight to represent something less ennobling. When an actor experienced a debilitating stomach flu or the leading man showed up intoxicated, circle companies traditionally closed ranks and dealt with such situations as best they could: the show went on. In some instances, this kind of adaptation meant scrapping the play and presenting an entire evening of vaudeville routines. Certainly pride and loyalty motivated such responses but ultimately economics prevailed. Simply put, a performance meant income, while a canceled appearance garnered the company nothing of value—no income and a disgruntled clientele.

Despite the support performers traditionally provided for each other, the physical, mental, and emotional demands of the circle stock system (upon both performers and management alike) were nonetheless considerable indeed. Individuals coped as best they could. Dick Elsenpeter relates that a fine bone china cup and saucer invariably accompanied fellow performer Maude Gentry while touring on circle stock. He states that her reasoning remained simple: "I want to sit and drink tea like a lady." Precisely because circle touring's lifestyle could not by the wildest stretch of the imagination be considered equal to that of "bone china," Gentry's tea ritual helped her to "break some of the confines" that this trouping placed around her and to maintain a healthy attitude.

A handful of veteran performers think that the reservoir of affection and respect between rural audiences and actors may still exist. These troupers even feel that conditions are right for circuit performing to return to middle America in spite of the prevalence of television and motion pictures, and the significant impact of the video recording industry. Rep veteran Dick Wolever provides a representative example of this attitude:

> I think right now aspiring young performers could put a show together, and play the same way as circle stock was played–change their show every week, go back to the same towns every week. I believe they would get a big reception and also a lot of experience. And if it is in their blood, it would be a great experience for young actors and actresses. Highways are better, transportation is no problem anymore, and the shows could be scaled down to where everybody could make money. I think young actors and actresses are passing up a wide open field, because people haven't changed; times may have changed but people haven't changed.

At the same time Wolever acknowledges the burdensome demands that various theater trade unions might place on such a revival in addition to the expenses such touring would entail.

Even though a renaissance of circle stock would undoubtedly provide a valuable training ground for young performers, it would nevertheless largely fail to heed the pleas made during the 1930s and 1940s for the industry to grow and evolve with the times. Rural America is vastly different today from the way it was in the Depression. Country communities can no longer be viewed as isolated villages separated by vast stretches of prairie landscape. Today television satellite disks dot the countryside as frequently as silos. Video rental stores often occupy what were once corner gas stations. Fuel-efficient automobiles and countless miles of highway link the countryside together as they have never done before. For better or worse, circle stock remains largely a product of its own time.

As an institution, it is difficult to estimate the overall impact of circle stock on the dramatic life of this country. Certainly urban theater forms exerted a much greater influence; yet in contrasting relative contributions we must remember that the evidence we have about American theater practice is weighted disproportionately on the very side of highly commercial entertainment forms that dominated the news in the metropolitan papers and trade publications in the past and continue to do so.

Nevertheless, we must confront the question of the lasting importance of circle stock. From a literary and performance standpoint, an honest estimate must be that the industry's legacy to American theater was minimal. On an organizational level, however, circle stock served as an important vehicle in maintaining and strengthening the entire touring rep industry. Although never as popular as the tent shows, circle stock supplied management with the ability to maintain a successful ensemble for an indefinite period of time by providing a bridge through difficult times and situations. In doing so circle stock not only reduced managerial concerns and problems, but raised the performance standards of companies able to draw upon the combined strengths of ensemble.

On a personal level, circle stock provided the means for a multitude of performers to feed both "body and soul" during difficult times, especially the Depression. The ease of establishing and maintaining a circle company allowed countless performers to continue earning a living (albeit a meager one) doing what they yearned to do: perform before appreciative audiences. Yet the elements in the circle format which initially provided this strength eventually led to its destruction. The ease of setup, seen as a lifesaver for many during the struggle of the Depression years, eventually brought about an overabundance of circles, causing quality and public support to deteriorate. Treating circle stock as only a stopgap measure slowly led it to its eventual quiet demise.

Perhaps the greatest impact made by the circle stock industry was not so much theatrical as sociological. For in maintaining consistent performance schedules in rural America through the depths of the Depression, circle stock companies met important needs of both audiences and themselves. From the public's perspective, circle stock met a genuine hunger for entertainment—a need for some levity to lighten the burden of the social and economic troubles of the Great Depression and, shortly following, the Second World War. From the perspective of the circle stock company, one can view the intense desire of professional actors to perform for involved and supportive audiences. In this way the circle stock performance satisfied the needs of both groups. In this setting, the traditional theatrical equation of audience and performers uniting in time and space took on special, memorable meaning and importance.

Notes

Chapter 1

1. Jere Mickel's four-page discussion of circle stock in *Footlights on the Prairie* is the most extensive to be found in print.

Chapter 2

1. *Bill Bruno's Bulletin*, published in Kansas City between 1928 and 1930, and 1935 and 1940, was a popular trade publication for Midwest rep companies. Hereafter it will be referred to in documentation as *BBB*.

2. Richard Mansfield (1854–1907), a controversial American actor noted for performances of the title characters in *Dr. Jekyll and Mr. Hyde*, *Richard III*, *Beau Brummel*, and *Cyrano de Bergerac*, in addition to Dick Dudgeon in *The Devil's Disciple*.

3. *New York Dramatic Mirror*, established in January 1879, will be referred to in the text as *Dramatic Mirror* and in documentation as *Mirror*. For many years edited by Harrison Grey Fiske, the *Mirror* extensively chronicled the early years of circle stock.

4. William A. Brady (1863–1950) maintained a lengthy career in the theater, spanning from 1882 to the Depression era, during which he managed the careers of, among others, Wilton Lackaye, Robert Mantell, Henry E. Dixey, Helen Hayes, and his second wife, Grace George.

5. Contemporary articles and advertising do not make it clear whether Trahern also wrote the music for some of the songs attributed to him. Occasionally both Trahern and Lee Orean Smith (a musical director, composer, and arranger) are jointly credited with a composition.

6. Trahern is credited to have served as the music editor for the *Dramatic Mirror* early in his career (*Suffolk County News*, 7 May 1915, 1).

7. Jessie's sister, Blanche Hall, also a professional actress, made periodic guest appearances with Trahern's company. For many years the leading lady at Oliver Morosco's Burbank Theatre in Los Angeles, the length of her performances there was record setting.

8. *New York Clipper* was published from 1853 until it merged with *Billboard* in the early 1920s. Stock and Repertoire information was dropped from the publica-

tion in January 1920. Hereafter it will be referred to in the text and documentation as *Clipper.*

9. Population information for this chapter is drawn from the *Thirteenth Census of the United States,* 1910, volumes 2 and 3.

10. According to information provided by Trahern in an advertisement, he was approximately 33–34 years of age at the time of his initial circuit, apparently having been born in 1873 or 1874 (*Mirror,* 7 Oct. 1905, 11). Even so, Trahern's tombstone notes 1871.

11. The proposed 12 towns included Babylon, East Hampton, Glen Cove, Greenport, Huntington, Northport, Patchogue, Port Jefferson, Riverhead, Sag Harbor, Sayville, and Southampton (*Mirror,* 31 Aug. 1907, 7).

12. The *Clipper* reports Trahern's southern circuit, early in the 1908 season, as consisting of Sag Harbor, Southampton, Riverhead, Sayville, Bay Shore, and Patchogue (4 Apr., 190).

13. A program from this period lists Trahern's idea of what constituted quality vaudeville: "Good music, bright sparkling twenty-minute playlets, novel musical acts, witty monologue artists, high class dancing, [and] singing really worth listening to…" (Collection of the Author).

14. According to the *Suffolk County News,* the theaters controlled by Trahern at this time through lease and contract, along with those he desired, were "the Lyceum Theatre, Patchogue, the headquarters of the Trahern circuit; the Sayville Opera House, Sayville; the Huntington Opera House, Huntington; the Auditorium, Greenport; the Carleton House, Bay Shore; the Athenaeum, Sag Harbor. He is also interested in booking the following: Athena Hall, Port Jefferson; Agawam Hall, Southampton; Clinton Hall, East Hampton; Library Hall, Mattituck; the Glen Cove Opera House, Glen Cove" (21 Aug. 1908, 7).

15. Schiller's bill for the week of 25–30 October 1909 included "Herman and Rice, comedy acrobats; the Bradfords, singers and dancers; Mrs. Coates and Daughter in a singing act; John Sackell in illustrated songs; Smith and Mathews, singing and dancing comedians; Hubert Wilke and company in *The Anti-Climax,* and motion pictures" (*Mirror,* 13 Nov. 1909, 22).

16. The capacity of theaters under Trahern's control at this time averaged only 600 (*Suffolk County News,* 12 Aug. 1910, 2).

17. By 1913, in addition to Nashville, Trahern boasted of successful stock engagements in San Antonio, Philadelphia, plus Camden and Bayonne, both of New Jersey (*Clipper,* 6 Sept., 3).

18. After leaving Long Island and prior to joining Keith's organization, Trahern spent some of the time managing the Arvine Players in Lancaster, Pennsylvania (*Suffolk County News,* 8 Aug. 1913, 5).

19. Other midwinter tours include ones in December 1914/January 1915 and November/December 1919. Such productions often utilized performers available during holiday recesses from other obligations.

20. In the 1915 circuit, the communities and theaters played remained the same as found in the extensive 1909 listing, except the Bijou was now being played in Huntington and likewise the Star Palace in Patchogue. The communities were (in order of rotation beginning with Monday) Riverhead, Greenport, Huntington, Patchogue, Bay Shore, and Sayville (*Clipper,* 1 May 1915, 23).

21. Of seven communities named in Parker's circuit, three (Riverhead, Bay Shore, and Patchogue) had been consistently part of Trahern's circuits since 1908.

Other stops would include three of the following: Huntington, Greenport, Port Jefferson, or Oyster Bay (*Billboard,* 13 Jan. 1917, 4).

22. The first tour of *Madame X* ran from 31 December 1912 to 7 April 1913; the second tour ran from 30 August 1913 to 13 December 1913 (Latchaw, appendices).

23. Earle did not establish a circle at this time, opening instead a one-night-stand company of *The Rejuvenation of Aunt Mary.*

24. Information on the Theatrical Syndicate and the Shuberts is drawn primarily from Alfred Bernheim's *The Business of the Theatre* (46–74).

25. Southern Illinois is referred to as "Little Egypt" primarily due to the Mississippi and the Ohio Rivers converging at Cairo, Illinois.

Chapter 3

1. For a thorough explanation of diamond dye scenery, see Chapter 5.

2. This is following Mid Tilton and Bill Guthrie ending their business partnership in the well-known Tilton-Guthrie Players. Tilton's Comedians have the distinction of being one of the last companies ever to follow the circle stock format.

3. Throughout Weage's show business career he kept notebooks meticulously detailing his parts and specialties performed with each company, in addition to the cast names of the company and the base town of each circuit.

4. *Bob Feagin's Bulletin* (January 1941 to May 1942): a Midwest theatrical newsletter that succeeded *Bill Bruno's Bulletin.* To avoid confusion with its predecessor, it will be entered in text as *Feagin's Bulletin* and as *BFB* in documentation.

5. In a commonwealth arrangement all members of the troupe shared equally the expenses and profits of the show, an organizational method frequently used by circle companies during the Depression era. For more information on commonwealth ensembles, see Chapter 6.

6. Program found in the Chick Boyes Collection housed at the Otoe County Museum of Memories in Syracuse, Nebraska.

Chapter 4

1. Because these plays were used in varying settings, the general term *rep* will be used when referring to the genre as a whole, with more specific references to circle stock appropriately using its own title. Accordingly, some editorial comments chosen to present the history of circle stock make specific references to other forms of touring, specifically tent rep. It should be understood that such inclusions in a narrative on circle stock are not inappropriate.

2. For an exploration of show-and-dance circles, see Chapter 6.

3. While countless scripts have been lost, many survive. Significant collections are found at the Museum of Repertoire Americana, Mount Pleasant, Iowa; Michigan State University, East Lansing, Michigan; and the Popular Culture Library at Bowling Green State University, Bowling Green, Ohio.

4. Repertoire Research Seminar '87 held 10–12 April 1987 in Mount Pleasant, Iowa; jointly sponsored by the National Society for the Preservation of Tent, Folk, and Repertoire Theatre and the Midwest Old Settlers and Threshers Association.

5. Among various Depression-era play script catalogs available in the MRA Collection, this analysis is based upon ones from: Century Play Company of New York City, Coburn Play Bureau of Kansas City, Harrison & Colegrove of Denver, International Play Company of Carmel-by-the-Sea (California), Producers Play Company of Chicago, and Standard Play Service of Kearney (Nebraska).

6. Limitations in the various facilities used for circle stock performances are explored in detail in Chapter 5.

7. The terms *double* or *doubling* can take on different meanings in relation to the circle stock performance. Here the term refers to the practice of an individual needing to perform more than one role in a production. Elsewhere in this writing, the term is used to describe an individual performing in the play but also presenting vaudeville specialty acts.

8. A "3–2" cast would likely include the male roles of a leading man, heavy, and comic, plus the female roles of a leading woman and an ingenue or character woman.

9. The G-string character was typically portrayed as an eccentric and garrulous old man complete with chin whiskers, similar in some respects to the Yankee character of early nineteenth-century American theater. The most plausible explanation for the G-string name comes from the character's customary portrayal based on a high-pitched voice, said to resemble the "G" string on a violin.

10. Being rather novelty items, such Toby plays were likely reworkings of older scripts updated to a new time and environment. Such a practice was widely used in the waning years of rep.

11. While certainly delicate subject matter, the release of *Toby at Pearl Harbor* followed the attack on Pearl Harbor, available in March 1942. Advance publicity stated, "It has been a military secret, but the truth can be told. Toby was at Pearl Harbor and saved the situation there."

12. It is important to note that the Simpson Agency and the Wayne Agency were also respected as the leading talent placement bureaus for the Midwest rep field.

13. This ad lists the following playwrights represented by the Wayne Exchange: Herschell Weiss, J. Harvey Haas, Al W. Clark, L. Verne Slout, Allen Wishert, John W. Brakebill, Betty Brooks, Don Melrose, Sherman L. Jones, E. A. McNutt, Tommy Ward, and G. A. Harrington.

14. *Those Show Folks* is an unusual play, which, advertising states, "depicts show folks in a different light than usually portrayed on stage and screen. It shows them as the vast majority really are, CLEAN and DECENT. It is the kind of a play that will give your audience a glimpse of SHOW FOLKS as they REALLY are" (*BBB*, 24 Apr. 1930, 9).

15. Russell Kittle's research attributes around 40 original plays and 100 adapted works to the husband-and-wife team of Neil and Caroline Schaffner.

16. Flesner relates that Collier even cut Bob Feagin's *Jailbird*, a "3–2" script (normally considered the smallest practical casting) down to only a "2–2" cast.

17. The latter was surely a less serious problem in circle stock because of the frequency of a company's visits. The potential for such abuse existed to a far greater degree in tent rep because these companies traditionally made only yearly appearances.

18. Standard practice when leasing a play was to receive one complete script and a set of parts. A "part" consisted of individual pages (normally 5 1/2" by 8

1/2"), each page referred to as a "side." Contained within a part were a character's lines, each one normally preceded with only the last three words of its cue line.

19. The 1925 and 1940-41 ledgers are housed at the Otoe County Museum of Memories in Syracuse, Nebraska, while the 1936-37 ledger can be found at the Museum of Repertoire Americana in Mount Pleasant, Iowa.

20. On this occasion, because of a problem with their baggage being incorrectly sent to Olin, Iowa, the previous week, the company actually performed two plays—*Home Folks* and *Papa's Boy*—without an increase in prices.

21. Mickel places the performance of Helvey's "Holland" presentation only under canvas; however, there is little reason to believe that if this same presentation were performed on circle stock it would be any less elaborate.

Chapter 5

1. Clifford Ashby and Suzanne DePauw May in their biography of Sadler report that this circle in 1938 lasted only "eight trips around the wheel" (136). The authors state their information is based on route books connected with the show at that time.

2. Records do not clearly establish that this particular Edgar Jones circle, or the Ted North circuit that follows, was based on either a six- or seven-day format.

3. This figure is probably only one-way mileage, stated in this fashion to make the circle appear more appealing.

4. Weather data records an unparalleled seven-week period of severely cold temperatures in large parts of the Midwest during January and February 1936.

Chapter 6

1. Information concerning entertainment prices is taken from news stories and advertisements appearing in these Nebraska newspapers during the 1920s: the *Alexandria Argus*, the *Carleton Enterprise*, the *Edgar Sun*, the *Harvard Courier*, the *Hebron Journal*, the *Hebron Register-Champion*, the *Sutton News*, and the *Wymore Weekly Arbor State*.

2. Note that prices and salaries quoted throughout this study are not corrected for inflation or deflation.

3. A typewritten 1933 contract between merchants and the L. B. Wesselman Players specifically required "Said tickets to be given away to their customers one ticket with each twenty-five cent purchase or more, but in no event shall said tickets be given away unless said person or persons receiving tickets shall make a purchase of twenty-five cents or more" (MRA Collection).

4. The Bailey F. Alart Orchestra, composed of a cornet, trombone, pianist, bass, and trap drummer, provided the music for these dances in 1915 (*Suffolk County News*, 30 Apr., 8).

5. This testimony is found in the *Gordon-Howard News* (vol. 5, no. 5), an informational newsletter printed by the candy supply company of the same name. Although undated, a handwritten note claims 1931 as the vintage of this scarce artifact.

6. During the Second World War, however, because of the shortage of men, females often were required also to sell candy in rep.

7. For additional discussion of the various forms of circle stock housed in motion picture venues, such as tabloid companies, see Chapter 7.

8. During World War I, Al Trahern learned a similar lesson: "*The War Bride* did not particularly appeal ... perhaps because people have been having too much of the war..." (*Suffolk County News,* 27 Aug. 1915, 4).

Chapter 8

1. For example, *Billboard,* 4 Oct. 1924, 29, and *Bill Bruno's Bulletin,* 12 Nov. 1936, 3.

Works Consulted

Alexandria Argus. Alexandria, Neb. 1924–25.

Allen, Ralph G. "Our Native Theatre: Honky-Tonk, Minstrel Shows, Burlesque." *The American Theatre: A Sum of Its Parts.* New York: Samuel French, 1971.

Alliance Times and Herald. Alliance, Neb. 1940.

Anamosa Eureka. Anamosa, Iowa. 1915.

Andrews, Clarence. Letter to the author, 21 Apr. 1986.

____. "The Trouping Trousdales." *The Iowan* (Summer 1982): 23–27.

Ashby, Clifford, and Suzanne DePauw May. *Trouping Through Texas: Harley Sadler and his Tent Show.* Bowling Green, Ohio: Bowling Green Univ. Popular Press, 1982.

Ashe, Martin. Letter to the author, 11 Mar. 1987.

Bader, Frances Moore. Letter to the author, 23 Feb. 1987.

____. Personal interview, 11 Apr. 1987.

Baldwin, W. O. Letter to the author, 6 June 1986.

Barnouw, Erik. *A Tower in Babel: A History of Broadcasting in the United States to 1933.* New York: Oxford Univ. Press, 1966.

"Barter Theatre Trades Drama for Ham and Eggs." *Life,* 31 July 1939, 54.

BBB. See *Bill Bruno's Bulletin.*

Bell, Charles Harris, III. "An Ohio Repertoire–Tent Show Family: The Kinsey Komedy Kompany and the Madge Kinsey Players, 1881–1951." Ph.D. diss., Bowling Green State Univ., 1978.

Bernheim, Alfred L. *The Business of the Theatre: An Economic History of the American Theatre, 1750–1932.* 1932; New York: Benjamin Blom, 1964.

BFB. See *Bob Feagin's Bulletin.*

Billboard. Cincinnati. 1905–56.

Bill Bruno's Bulletin. Kansas City. 1928–30, 1935–40.

Birdwell, Christine R. "Heroines of American Midwestern Repertoire Theatre Comedy-Dramas." Ph.D. diss., Michigan State Univ., 1984.

Bob Feagin's Bulletin. Topeka, Kans., Jan. 1941–Apr. 1941; Colon, Mich., Apr. 1941–June 1941; Topeka, Kans., July 1941–May 1942.

Bordman, Gerald. *The Oxford Companion to American Theatre.* New York: Oxford Univ. Press, 1984.

Boyes, Chick, ledgers. 1925; 1936-37; 1940-41.

Brady, William A. *Showman.* New York: Dutton, 1936.

Bronner, Edwin. *The Encyclopedia of the American Theatre 1900–1975.* San Diego: A. S. Barnes, 1980.

Brooks, Joanne J. Letters to the author, 8 July 1989, 13 Jan. 1990, 13 June 1990.

Brunk, Mercedes. Letters to the author, 12 June 1985, 16 Feb. 1986, 15 Sept. 1987.

Burchard, Grace. "40 Years in Nebraska Tent Show." *Omaha* (Neb.) *World-Herald,* 11 July 1948, C:14.

Bureau of the Census. *Thirteenth Census of the United States Taken in the Year 1910.* Vols. 2 and 3. Washington, D.C., 1913.

Carleton Enterprise. Carleton, Neb. 1925.

Carter, Nancy B. Letter to the author, 19 Mar. 1986.

Case, Victoria, and Robert Ormond Case. *We Called It Culture: The Story of Chautauqua.* Garden City, N.Y.: Doubleday, 1948.

Chandler, Lester V. *America's Greatest Depression, 1929–1941.* New York: Harper, 1970.

Chapman, John, and Garrison P. Sherwood, eds. *The Best Plays of 1894–1899.* New York: Dodd, 1955.

Choate, Billy. Audiotape to the author, 8 Apr. 1986.

Clark, Al W. "Circles and Tents." *Writer's Digest,* Feb. 1941: 39ff.

Clark, Larry D. "Toby Shows: A Form of American Popular Theatre." Ph.D. diss., Univ. of Illinois, Urbana-Champaign, 1963.

Clipper. See *New York Clipper.*

Codel, Martin, ed. *Radio and Its Future.* 1930; New York: Arno, 1971.

Conner, Patricia S. "Steve Mills and the Twentieth Century American Burlesque Show: A Backstage History and a Perspective." Ph.D. diss., Univ. of Illinois, Urbana-Champaign, 1979.

Connors, Timothy D. "American Vaudeville Managers: Their Organization and Influence." Ph.D. diss., Univ. of Kansas, 1981.

Corrector. See *Sag Harbor Corrector.*

County Review. Riverhead, N.Y. 1929.

Crete News. Crete, Neb. 1925-26.

Csida, Joseph, and June Bundy Csida. *American Entertainment: A Unique History of Popular Show Business.* New York: Watson-Guptill, 1978.

Currie, Constance A. Letters to the author, 25 July 1989, 30 Jan. 1990, 13 June 1990.

Darling, Flo. Letters to the author, 6 Aug. 1985, 15 Sept. 1987.

Depenbrink, Noreen. Letters to the author, 13 Mar. 1987, 15 Sept. 1987.

Deshler Ruster. Deshler, Neb. 1924-25.

DiMeglio, John E. *Vaudeville U.S.A.* Bowling Green, Ohio: Bowling Green Univ. Popular Press, 1973.

Douglas, George H. *The Early Days of Radio Broadcasting.* Jefferson, N.C.: McFarland, 1987.

Dramatic Mirror. See *New York Dramatic Mirror.*

Durham, Weldon B. *American Theatre Companies, 1888–1930.* Westport, Conn.: Greenwood, 1987.

Earley, Steven C. *An Introduction to American Movies.* New York: New American Library, 1979.

East Hampton Star. East Hampton, N.Y. 1900–1912.

Edgar Sun. Edgar, Neb. 1925.

Elsenpeter, Dick. Audiotape to the author, 16 Mar. 1987.

_____. Letters to the author, 1 Mar. 1987, 16 Mar. 1987.

_____. Personal interviews, 20 Jan. 1987, 5 Sept. 1987.

Emory, Barbara Brooks. Letters to the author, 13 Feb. 1987, 28 Sept. 1987.

Equity. New York. 1925–35.

Feagin's Bulletin. See *Bob Feagin's Bulletin.*

Felton, Hazel. Letter to the author, 24 Feb. 1986.

Flesner, Jay Bee. Letter to the author, 17 Sept. 1987.

____. Personal interviews. 11–12 Apr. 1987.

Frick, John W. *New York's First Theatrical Center: The Rialto at Union Square.* Ann Arbor: UMI Research Press, 1985.

Gabriel, Ralph H. *The Evolution of Long Island: A Story of Land and Sea.* New Haven: Yale Univ. Press, 1921.

Garrett, Sally C. Letters to the author, 20 July 1989, 19 July 1990.

Gentry, Maude. Letters to the author, 17 Jan. 1987, 19 Sept. 1987.

Gilbert, Douglas. *American Vaudeville: Its Life and Times.* 1940; New York: Dover, 1963.

Gillette, Don Carle. "The Vast Tent Drama Industry." *New York Times,* 16 Oct. 1927, sec. 9, 2.

Grau, Robert. *The Business Man in the Amusement World.* New York: Broadway, 1910.

Green, Abel, and Joe Laurie, Jr. *Show Biz from Vaude to Video.* 1951; Port Washington, N.Y.: Kennikat, 1972.

Guthrie, Laura. Letters to the author, 19 Jan. 1987, 24 Oct. 1987.

Hanscom, Warren D. *Pioneers in Grease Paint.* Bradenton, Fla.: Collins, n.d.

Harding, Alfred. *The Revolt of the Actors.* New York: Morrow, 1929.

Harrison, Harry P., and Karl Detzer. *Culture Under Canvas: The Story of Tent Chautauqua.* New York: Hastings House, 1958.

Harvard Courier. Harvard, Neb. 1925.

Haverstock, Peggy. Letter to the author, 17 Aug. 1985.

Hebron Journal. Hebron, Neb. 1920–23.

Hebron Register. Hebron, Neb. 1931.

Hebron Register-Champion. Hebron, Neb. 1922–29.

Hedges, R. Alan. "Actors Under Canvas: A Study of the Theatre of the Circuit Chautauqua, 1910–1933." Ph.D. diss., Ohio State Univ., 1976.

Hemingford Ledger. Hemingford, Neb. 1940.

Henderson, Lewis, Jr. Personal interviews, 7 Sept. 1985, 24 May 1986, 6 Sept. 1986, 11 Apr. 1987, 5 Sept. 1987.

Henderson, Mary C. *The City and the Theatre: New York Playhouses from Bowling Green to Times Square.* Clifton, N.J.: James T. White, 1973.

Henderson, William. Letter to the author, 8 Apr. 1986.

Higham, Charles, and Joel Greenberg. *Hollywood in the Forties.* London: A. Zwemmer, 1968.

Hockett, Anna [Henderson]. Personal interviews, 7 Sept. 1985, 24 May 1986, 6 Sept. 1986, 11 Apr. 1987, 5 Sept. 1987.

Holcomb, E. W. "Climatological Data, Illinois Section." *U. S. Department of Agriculture, Weather Bureau* 41.13 (1936): 49.

Hollingsworth, Iris. Letters to the author, 9 July 1985, 15 Sept. 1987.

____. Personal interview, 11 Apr. 1987.

Horner, Charles F. *Strike the Tents: The Story of the Chautauqua.* Philadelphia: Dorrance, 1954.

Hoyt, Harlowe R. *Town Hall Tonight.* Englewood Cliffs, N.J.: Prentice, 1955.

"'Indoor Tent Show' Draws Crowds." *Pantagraph* (Bloomington, Ill.), 30 Nov. 1949, 20.

Kansas City Star. Kansas City, Mo. 1914.

King, Dorothy T. Letters to the author, 10 Mar. 1990, 18 June 1990, 6 Aug. 1990.

Kingdon, Sid. Letter to the author, 3 Mar. 1986.

_____. Personal interview, 5 Sept. 1987.

Kittle, Russell D. "Toby and Susie: The Show-Business Success Story of Neil and Caroline Schaffner 1925–1962." 2 vols. Ph.D. diss., Ohio State Univ., 1969.

Klassen, Robert D. "The Tent-Repertoire Theatre: A Rural American Institution." Ph.D. diss., Michigan State Univ., 1969.

Koch, Dave. Letters to the author, 11 Apr. 1986, 18 Sept. 1987, 30 Oct. 1987.

Kramme, Michael. "Circle Stock." Popular Culture Association. Toronto, Canada, 1 Apr. 1984.

Latchaw, Truly Trousdale. Letters to the author, 17 Feb. 1987, 21 Apr. 1987, 1 Nov. 1987.

_____. Personal interview, 24 Mar. 1986.

_____. "The Trousdale Brothers Theatrical Companies from 1896 to 1915." Master's thesis, Univ. of Minnesota, 1948.

La-They, Robert. Audiotapes to the author, 14 Feb. 1986, 26 June 1986.

_____. Letter to the author, 2 Oct. 1987.

Laurie, Joe, Jr. *Vaudeville: From the Honky-Tonks to the Palace.* New York: Henry Holt, 1953.

Lawrence, John. "Circles Like Tobys and G Strings." *Writer's Digest,* Dec. 1939, 36–40.

Lewin, Jacqueline. Letter to the author, 7 Aug. 1989.

Lewis, Philip C. *Trouping: How the Show Came to Town.* New York: Harper, 1973.

Lippman, Monroe. "The Effect of the Theatrical Syndicate on Theatrical Art in America." *Quarterly Journal of Speech* 26 (1940): 275–82.

Lodge Pole Express. Lodgepole, Neb. 1940–41.

Loney, Glenn, ed. *Musical Theatre in America: Papers and Proceedings of the Conference on the Musical Theatre in America.* Westport, Conn.: Greenwood, 1984.

Long Islander. Huntington, N.Y. 1900–23.

MacDonald, Maree. Letters to the author, 15 Oct. 1987, 17 Nov. 1987.

MacDonald, Peggy [Henderson]. Personal interviews, 6 Sept. 1986, 5 Sept. 1987.

MacKay, Robert B. Letter to the author, 20 Apr. 1987.

MacKay, Robert B., Geoffrey L. Rossano, and Carol A. Traynor, eds. *Between Ocean and Empire: An Illustrated History of Long Island.* Northridge, Calif.: Windsor, 1985.

Madden, Dale, Sr. Letters to the author, 16 Jan. 1987, 21 Sept. 1987.

Magnuson, Landis. "The Development of Theatrical Presentations within the Clarinda [Iowa] Chautauqua Movement, 1897–1932." Master's thesis, Bowling Green State Univ., 1983.

Manley, Seon. *Long Island Discovery: An Adventure into the History, Manners, and Mores of America's Front Porch.* Garden City, N.Y.: Doubleday, 1966.

Mantle, Burns, ed. *The Best Plays of 1919–20.* Boston: Small, Maynard, 1920.

Mantle, Burns, and Garrison P. Sherwood, eds. *The Best Plays of 1899–1909.* Philadelphia: Blakiston, 1944.

_____, eds. *The Best Plays of 1909–1919.* New York: Dodd, 1933.

Marion Sentinel. Marion, Iowa. 1913–15.

Martin, Jerry L. *Henry L. Brunk and Brunk's Comedians: Tent Repertoire Empire of the Southwest.* Bowling Green, Ohio: Bowling Green Univ. Popular Press, 1984.

Matlaw, Myron, ed. *American Popular Entertainment: Papers and Proceedings of the Conference on the History of American Popular Entertainment.* Westport, Conn.: Greenwood, 1979.

McDonald, Robert A. "The Popular Drama of Repertoire, 1880–1914: A Formula Approach." Ph.D. diss., Michigan State Univ., 1978.

McKennon, Joe. Letter to the author, 16 July 1985.

Meltzer, Milton. *Brother, Can You Spare a Dime?* New York: Knopf, 1969.

Mickel, Jere C. *Footlights on the Prairie.* St. Cloud, Minn.: North Star, 1974.

Mirror. See *New York Dramatic Mirror.*

Mitchell County Press. Osage, Iowa. 1913–14, 1917.

Mitchell Index. Mitchell, Neb. 1940.

Monticello Express. Monticello, Iowa. 1914.

Montrose, Monte. Letters to the author, 13 Apr. 1986, 16 Sept. 1987.

Morosco, Helen M., and Leonard Paul Dugger. *The Oracle of Broadway: Life of Oliver Morosco.* Caldwell, Idaho: Caxton, 1944.

Morrison, Theodore. *Chautauqua: A Center for Education, Religion, and the Arts in America.* Chicago: Univ. of Chicago Press, 1974.

MRA Collection. See Museum of Repertoire Americana Collection.

Museum of Repertoire Americana Collection. The National Society for the Preservation of Tent, Folk, and Repertoire Theatre; The Midwest Old Settlers and Threshers Association, Mount Pleasant, Iowa.

Nelson Gazette. Nelson, Neb. 1925.

Neuhaus, Gus. Letter to the author, 30 Jan. 1987.

New York Clipper. New York. 1905–20.

New York Dramatic Mirror. New York. 1905–17.

Nye, Russel. *The Unembarrassed Muse: The Popular Arts in America.* New York: Dial, 1970.

Odell, George C. D. *Annals of the New York Stage.* Vol. 15. 1949; New York: AMS, 1970.

Oleferchik, Waunetta Rosier. Letters to the author, 7 Mar. 1986, 23 Apr. 1986, 29 Apr. 1986, 21 Sept. 1987.

———. Personal interview, 11 Apr. 1987.

Olson, Clarence E. "Toby Entertains at Schools." *St. Louis Post-Dispatch,* 15 Dec. 1963, pictures sec., 17–19.

Orton, Marlene A. Letters to the author, 3 Mar. 1986, 4 June 1986.

Osage News. Osage, Iowa. 1914–15.

Otoe County Museum of Memories Collection. Chick Boyes Papers. Syracuse, Neb.

Poe, Wendell. Letters to the author, 14 Feb. 1987, 20 Oct. 1987.

Poggi, Jack. *Theater in America: The Impact of Economic Forces 1870–1967.* Ithaca, N.Y.: Cornell Univ. Press, 1966.

Port Jefferson Echo. Port Jefferson, N.Y. 1907–18.

Potter Review. Potter, Neb. 1941.

Reformatory Press. Anamosa, Iowa. 1915.

Rigdon, Walter, ed. *The Biographical Encyclopaedia & Who's Who of the American Theatre.* New York: James H. Heineman, 1966.

Roten, Alice [Henderson]. Personal interviews, 6 Sept. 1986, 5 Sept. 1987.

Ruester, Lynn. "It's Town Hall Tonight!" *Champaign-Urbana Courier* (Ill.), 12 Feb. 1950, sec. 3, 33.

Sag Harbor Corrector. Sag Harbor, N.Y. 1900–10.

Schaffner, Caroline. Letters to the author, 4 May 1985, 24 Feb. 1986.

____. Personal interviews, 14–15 Mar. 1986, 8–13 Dec. 1986, 11 Apr. 1987, 5 Sept. 1987.

Schaffner, Neil E., and Vance Johnson. *The Fabulous Toby and Me.* Englewood Cliffs, N.J.: Prentice, 1968.

Schottland, Charles I. *The Social Security Program in the United States.* New York: Appleton, 1963.

Schuller, Billie [Henderson]. Letter to the author, 17 Sept. 1987.

____. Personal interviews, 7 Sept. 1985, 24 May 1986, 6 Sept. 1986, 11 Apr. 1987, 5 Sept. 1987.

Scottsbluff Daily Star-Herald. Scottsbluff, Neb. 1940.

Shindler, Colin. *Hollywood Goes to War: Films and American Society 1939–1952.* London: Routledge and Kegan Paul, 1979.

Slout, William. Letters to the author, 13 June 1985, 14 Sept. 1987, 25 Sept. 1987.

____. Personal interviews, 11–12 Apr. 1987.

____. *Theatre in a Tent: The Development of a Provincial Entertainment.* Bowling Green, Ohio: Bowling Green Univ. Popular Press, 1972.

____. "Traveling Repertoire: From Shakespeare to Sherman." Repertoire Research Seminar, National Society for the Preservation of Tent, Folk, and Repertoire Theatre. Mount Pleasant, Iowa, 11 Apr. 1987.

Smith, Harold. *Eastern Long Island Theatres: 1880–1920.* Riverhead, N.Y.: Council for the Vail-Leavitt Music Hall, n.d.

____. Letters to the author, 15 July 1989, 12 July 1990, 25 Aug. 1990.

____. *The Most Popular Eastern Long Island Plays & Players: 1880–1920.* Riverhead, N.Y.: Council for the Vail-Leavitt Music Hall, 1987.

Smith, Milo L. "The Klaw-Erlanger Bogeyman Myth." *Players Magazine* 44 (Dec./Jan. 1969): 70–75.

Snyder, Frederick E. "American Vaudeville–Theatre in a Package: The Origins of Mass Entertainment." Ph.D. diss., Yale Univ., 1970.

Snyder, Sherwood, III. "The Toby Shows." Ph.D. diss., Univ. of Minnesota, 1966.

Sobel, Bernard. *Burleycue: An Underground History of Burlesque Days.* New York: Farrar & Rinehart, 1931.

____. *A Pictorial History of Burlesque.* New York: Putnam's, 1956.

____. *A Pictorial History of Vaudeville.* New York: Citadel, 1961.

Spitzer, Marian. *The Palace.* New York: Atheneum, 1969.

Suffolk County News. Sayville, N.Y. 1900–39.

Sund, Dot. Letters to the author, 4 Aug. 1985, 1 Feb. 1986, 31 May 1986, 21 July 1986, 15 Sept. 1987.

____. Personal interview, 25 Mar. 1986.

Sund, Jess. Personal interview, 25 Mar. 1986.

Sutton News. Sutton, Neb. 1924–27, 1929–30.

Taylor, Leona. Letter to the author, 2 Mar. 1987.

Telegraph-News. Sidney, Neb. 1940–41.

Toll, Robert C. *The Entertainment Machine: American Show Business in the Twentieth Century.* New York: Oxford Univ. Press, 1982.

____. *On with the Show: The First Century of Show Business in America.* New York: Oxford Univ. Press, 1976.

Toman, Vera. Letter to the author, 19 May 1990.

Tormey, Patricia S. Letters to the author, 16 Aug. 1990, 17 Aug. 1990.

Twyman, Arlone. "What's Become of Toby?" *Omaha World-Herald* (Neb.) (1943?), n.p. (MRA Collection).

U.S. Bureau of the Census. *Historical Statistics of the United States: Colonial Times to 1970.* Part 1. Washington, D.C., 1975: 326, 468.

Variety. New York. 1905–15.

Vinton Review. Vinton, Iowa. 1914–15.

Walther, R. Norton. Audiotape to the author, 19 Feb. 1986.

____. Letter to the author, 10 June 1985.

____. Personal interviews, 11 Apr. 1987, 5 Sept. 1987.

Waverly Democrat. Waverly, Iowa. 1914–15.

Waverly Republican. Waverly, Iowa. 1914.

Weage, Don. Audiotapes to the author, 19 Jan. 1987, 29 Sept. 1987.

____. Letters to the author, 19 Jan. 1987, 27 Feb. 1987.

Weekly Arbor State. Wymore, Neb. 1924–26.

Wells, Justine W. Letter to the author, 13 June 1990.

Wenden, D. J. *The Birth of the Movies.* New York: Dutton, 1974.

Who Was Who in the Theatre: 1912–1976. Vol. 1. Detroit: Gale, 1978.

Williamson, Jackie. Letter to the author, 28 Mar. 1986.

Wilstach, Paul. *Richard Mansfield: The Man and The Actor.* 1908; Freeport, N.Y.: Books for Libraries Press, 1970.

Winsche, Richard A. Letter to the author, 6 Sept. 1989.

Winter, William. *Life and Art of Richard Mansfield, with Selections from His Letters.* 2 vols. 1910; Freeport, N.Y.: Books for Libraries Press, 1970.

Wiziarde, Frank. Audiotape to the author, 26 Jan. 1987.

Wolever, Dick. Audiotape to the author, 15 Apr. 1986.

York Daily News-Times. York, Neb. 1924–26.

Zeidman, Irving. *The American Burlesque Show.* New York: Hawthorn, 1967.

Zellers, Parker. *Tony Pastor: Dean of the Vaudeville Stage.* Ypsilanti: Eastern Michigan Univ. Press, 1971.

Index

247